THE
RED ARMY
IN
WWII

ORDER OF BATTLE
THE
RED ARMY
IN
WWII

DAVID PORTER

amber
BOOKS

First published in 2009 by
Amber Books Ltd
Bradley's Close
74–77 White Lion Street
London N1 9PF
www.amberbooks.co.uk

ISBN: 978-1-906626-52-5

Project Editor: Michael Spilling
Design: Hawes Design
Picture Research: Terry Forshaw

Printed in Dubai

PICTURE CREDITS

Courtesy of the Central Museum of the Armed Forces, Moscow: 116, 123
Corbis: 20 (Bettmann), 52 (Hulton)
Ukrainian State Archive: 6, 24, 64, 88, 122, 164

All artworks Oliver Missing
Except page 74, Art-Tech/Aerospace

All maps Cartographica © Amber Books
Except page 11, Patrick Mulrey © Amber Books

CONTENTS

Pre-War Years: 1939–41

Stalin remarked that the Soviet Union was '…fifty to a hundred years behind the advanced countries' and must narrow 'this distance in ten years'. In what was perhaps a foreboding of World War II, he declared, 'Either we do it or we shall be crushed.'

Dressed in snow camouflage, a Soviet infantry patrol sets out during the Russo-Finnish War, December 1939.

The Red Army was founded on 23 February 1918 to protect Lenin's new government against the rapidly growing threat from the anti-Communist White Armies. Its initial organization was largely the work of Leon Trotsky, People's Commissar for War from 1918 to 1924. His ruthlessness mobilized a force of 5.5 million men, although many of these had very little equipment or training and front-line strength rarely exceeded 580,000. In its early years, the Red Army was engaged in constant fighting against both the White forces in the Civil War (1918–22) and the Polish Army in the Russo-Polish War (1919–21). Despite a humiliating defeat by Poland, victory in the Civil War ensured the survival of the Communist regime, but it had cost the Red Army an estimated one million casualties. The Red Army's desperate need for access to Western military technology was met by a secret annex to the Treaty of Rapallo, signed in 1922, by which the Soviet government authorized the establishment of German military and aviation bases within Russia. These were to be used for research and development (R&D) and training with weapons banned under the terms of the Treaty of Versailles. In return, Germany would allow the Red Army to monitor all research and tests, besides sharing industrial and military technology.

Forging weapons but destroying an army, 1928–39

As Stalin consolidated his power in the late 1920s, he became concerned at Soviet economic and military weakness compared to Western powers. In 1927–28, he began to transform the USSR into an industrial superpower by a series of 'Five Year Plans'. By the early 1930s, major industrial complexes had been completed, all of which were either built specifically for producing military equipment or could easily be switched to war production. The Five Year Plans provided the resources for modernizing the Red Army, an achievement that was largely due to the drive and determination of Mikhail Tukhachevsky, who served as Chief of Staff of the Red Army (1925–28) and as Deputy Commissar for Defence. He attempted to transform the ill-trained conscripts of the Red Army into a professional military force, with particular emphasis on the replacement of cavalry by powerful armoured forces. Such radical views fell foul of traditionalists in the Soviet military establishment and

his ideas were rejected by Stalin, leading to his removal from the Red Army staff.

Despite this official hostility, an experimental mechanized brigade was formed during the summer of 1929, comprising a tank regiment, a motor rifle regiment, an artillery battalion and support units. This demonstrated the potential of such formations and Tukhachevsky was given a chance to put his ideas into practice in 1931, following Stalin's acceptance of the need for modernized armed forces.

During this period, annual tank production figures soared, which allowed the creation of larger armoured formations, the mechanized corps, each of which included two mechanized brigades totalling 430 tanks and 215 armoured cars plus a lorried infantry brigade and support units. These were used to test Tukhachevsky's theories in a series of manoeuvres culminating in the huge 1935 exercises held in the Kiev Military District. Western observers at these manoeuvres were staggered to see the hundreds of AFVs deployed and to witness a mock airborne assault by two battalions of paratroops. They would have been even more amazed had they known that the Soviets had three full airborne brigades and more tank units (and indeed more AFVs) than the rest of the world's armies combined.

Tukhachevsky's very ability proved to be fatal, as Stalin came to see him as a threat to his power, a view that may have been influenced by information planted by German intelligence. Stalin began a series of bloody purges of the Communist party in 1936 and turned his attention to the Red Army the following year. On 9 June 1937, Tukhachevsky and his most prominent supporters were suddenly arrested on treason charges, tried by a special military court on the 11th and shot at dawn the next day. Over the following year or so, the total of those executed or imprisoned rose to three of the five Marshals of the Soviet Union, plus 14 of the 16 army commanders, 60 of 67 corps commanders, 136 of 199 divisional commanders and 221 of 397 brigade commanders. Thousands of more junior officers were also shot or imprisoned, and the terror encompassed defence industry heads and even weapons design teams.

Stalin reintroduced Trotsky's system of dual command, under which each unit had its commissar, a political officer effectively equal in rank to the unit commander and with the authority to countermand his orders. The effect of the Purges was to stifle innovation and professionalism in the Red Army as the survivors were cowed and understandably terrified of the secret police, the NKVD. Many now vacant key posts were filled by incompetents appointed purely because they were politically 'safe'. Although large armoured formations remained, the traditionalists such as Marshal Budenny regained their former influence, ensuring that the cavalry remained a major component of the army.

Khalkin Gol

By the late 1930s, Japan had established control of Manchuria, which it transformed into the puppet state of Manchukuo. This brought it into conflict with the Soviet satellite state of Mongolia as the Japanese claimed that the Khalkin Gol (Khalka River) formed the border between Manchukuo and Mongolia, whilst the Mongolians and Soviets maintained that it ran some 16km (10 miles) east of the river, just east of the village of Nomonhan.

The Kwantung Army formed the main Japanese force in Manchukuo and included some of the best Japanese units. On the other side of the frontier, the Red Army's LVII Special Corps, deployed from the Trans-Baikal Military District, was responsible for the defence of the border between Siberia and Manchuria. Small border skirmishes in May 1939 gradually escalated, leading to the destruction of a regiment of the Kwantung Army's 64th Division at the end of the month. Large-scale Japanese air attacks the following month raised the

KHALKIN GOL: TANK STRENGTHS (JULY 1939)								
Unit	BT-5/7	T-26	T-37	BA-20	FAI	BA-3	BA-6	BA-10
11th Tank Bde	115	10	1	2	39	–	–	–
6th Tank Bde/XX Tank Corps	245	–	–	5	–	–	–	20
7th Armoured Car Bde	–	–	–	20	–	–	31	–
8th Armoured Car Bde	10	–	–	14	9	4	6	22
9th Armoured Car Bde	–	–	–	18	8	–	9	21
5th Rifle Bde	–	–	–	11	5	–	16	15
82nd Rifle Div	–	14	14	2	–	–	–	–
149th Rifle Rgt/36th Rifle Div	–	–	–	10	8	3	–	–
24th Rifle Rgt/36th Rifle Div	–	–	–	–	3	1	–	–
175th Artillery Rgt/36th Rifle Div	–	–	–	2	–	–	–	–
406th Communication Btn	–	–	–	9	8	1	–	2
Other Formations	–	–	–	–	–	–	–	–
Total Number	370	24	15	93	80	9	62	80
Under Repair	75	3	2	5	6	2	8	11

tension as the Kwantung Army prepared an offensive to 'expel the invaders'. This was to be a pincer movement by elements of the 23rd Division and the Yasuoka Detachment to encircle and destroy Soviet and Mongolian forces along the Khalkin Gol. (The Yasuoka Detachment was one of the few sizeable Japanese armoured formations, with almost 100 AFVs.)

Whilst preparations for the offensive were under way, Georgi Zhukov, the most promising general to survive Stalin's Purges, was appointed to command the Soviet forces. He quickly recognized the need for massive transport resources to support the powerful armoured force that would be required to inflict a decisive defeat on the Japanese – initially 1000 fuel tankers and more than 1600 cargo trucks were deployed over the 750km (469-mile) route from his supply bases to the front line, later supplemented by a further 1625 vehicles from European Russia. This logistic support allowed him to

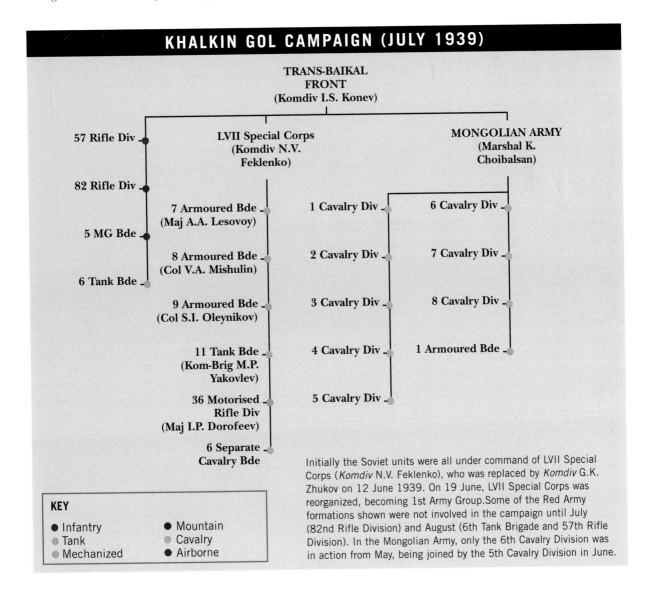

KHALKIN GOL CAMPAIGN (JULY 1939)

TRANS-BAIKAL FRONT
(Komdiv I.S. Konev)

LVII Special Corps
(Komdiv N.V. Feklenko)

MONGOLIAN ARMY
(Marshal K. Choibalsan)

57 Rifle Div

82 Rifle Div

5 MG Bde

6 Tank Bde

7 Armoured Bde
(Maj A.A. Lesovoy)

8 Armoured Bde
(Col V.A. Mishulin)

9 Armoured Bde
(Col S.I. Oleynikov)

11 Tank Bde
(Kom-Brig M.P. Yakovlev)

36 Motorised
Rifle Div
(Maj I.P. Dorofeev)

6 Separate
Cavalry Bde

1 Cavalry Div

2 Cavalry Div

3 Cavalry Div

4 Cavalry Div

5 Cavalry Div

6 Cavalry Div

7 Cavalry Div

8 Cavalry Div

1 Armoured Bde

Initially the Soviet units were all under command of LVII Special Corps (*Komdiv* N.V. Feklenko), who was replaced by *Komdiv* G.K. Zhukov on 12 June 1939. On 19 June, LVII Special Corps was reorganized, becoming 1st Army Group. Some of the Red Army formations shown were not involved in the campaign until July (82nd Rifle Division) and August (6th Tank Brigade and 57th Rifle Division). In the Mongolian Army, only the 6th Cavalry Division was in action from May, being joined by the 5th Cavalry Division in June.

KEY
- ● Infantry
- ● Tank
- ● Mechanized
- ● Mountain
- ● Cavalry
- ● Airborne

assemble a striking force of as many as 550 tanks (mainly T-26s and BT-7s), plus 450 armoured cars.

Zhukov prevails

When the Japanese offensive opened on 2 July, the Yasuoka Detachment lost over half its tanks to Soviet anti-tank guns, whilst perhaps 120 Soviet AFVs were destroyed, many by 37mm (1.5in) anti-tank guns and infantry with Molotov Cocktails. Despite these losses, Zhukov still had overwhelming armoured strength – nearly 500 tanks and 350 armoured cars – to spearhead a devastating counter-offensive launched on 20 August.

Within five days, this achieved a classic double envelopment of the Japanese 23rd Division, which was effectively destroyed by the 31st.

Zhukov had proved himself a capable commander of armoured forces. His victory ended the power of the 'Strike North' group in the Japanese High Command, which sought to expand into Soviet Central Asia and Siberia. Influence shifted to the 'Strike South' group, who favoured gaining control of the natural resources of Southeast Asia and the Pacific islands. In April 1941, the Soviet-Japanese Neutrality Pact removed the lingering threat to Stalin's eastern frontiers.

Invasion of Poland

The fighting in the Far East had barely ended when, on 17 September 1939, Soviet forces invaded Poland, which had been desperately fighting against the German invasion for over two weeks.

The Red Army deployed seven field armies totalling at least 450,000 men with more than 3000 AFVs against Polish forces that were hopelessly outnumbered; yet the Soviets took unnecessary losses in a number of actions through overconfidence and tactical ineptitude. At Grodno on 20 September, the XV Tank Corps attempted a frontal assault on the city with minimal infantry support and was beaten off with the loss of 19 tanks and four armoured cars. On 28 September near Szack, a scratch Polish force comprising elements of the Border Defence Corps and the Independent Operational Group Polesie ambushed the Soviet 52nd Rifle Division and its supporting T-26 brigade, inflicting approximately 2000 casualties and destroying or capturing 40 tanks.

In all, Polish forces may have destroyed as many as 75 Soviet AFVs (a further 429 broke down) whilst Soviet records indicate that the Red Army suffered 996 fatal casualties and a further 2400 wounded. The invaders took a total of over 452,000 prisoners, although many of these are likely to have been police or reservists rather than members of the Polish regular forces. (At least 22,500 of these prisoners, mainly senior officers, were subsequently murdered by the NKVD.)

INVASION OF POLAND: TANK STRENGTHS					
Unit	T-37	T-26	BT	T-28	Armoured cars
BELORUSSIAN FRONT					
XV Tank Corps	–	–	461	–	122
6th Tank Bde	–	–	248	–	–
21st Tank Bde	–	–	29	105	19
22nd Tank Bde	–	219	–	–	3
25th Tank Bde	–	251	–	–	27
29th Tank Bde	–	188	–	–	3
32nd Tank Bde	–	220	–	–	5
UKRAINIAN FRONT					
XXV Tank Corps	–	27	435	–	74
10th Tank Bde	–	10	30	98	19
23rd Tank Bde	–	8	209	–	5
24th Tank Bde	–	8	205	–	28
26th Tank Bde	–	228	–	–	22
36th Tank Bde	–	301	–	–	24
38th Tank Bde	4	141	–	–	4

SOVIET INVASION OF POLAND

September 1939

Soviet resentment at the Red Army's humiliating defeat in the Russo–Polish War and the subsequent loss of territory to Poland was obvious throughout the 1920s and 1930s. In response, the Polish Army concentrated its efforts on fortifying key areas of the eastern borders, such as the Sarny Fortified Area, and the development of *Plan Wschód* (Plan East) to counter any Soviet offensive. The plan was rendered irrelevant by the rapid progress of the German invasion on 1 September 1939, which forced all Polish reserves to be diverted westwards in an attempt to stem the *Wehrmacht*'s advance. This ensured that when the Red Army launched its offensive on 17 September it encountered only isolated defending forces, which were crushed by sheer weight of Soviet numbers.

Many Western military attachés in Moscow were not impressed by the Red Army – reports referred to the 'low standard of intelligence and slovenly appearance of the officers….' In Lvov, the same officers created quite a stir by the way that they rushed to the restaurants and ate their way through enormous meals. The other ranks were often thin from the miserable Red Army rations and equally anxious to gorge themselves on the relatively plentiful Polish food. Despite these episodes, there was little looting or drunkenness since discipline was savagely enforced by shooting the few offenders in front of their units.

Within a matter of a few months, the Red Army's insatiable need for manpower led to conscription being imposed throughout the newly conquered territories.

The thousands of new recruits were allotted to units spread throughout the Leningrad, Bryansk and Kiev military districts and there were never more than 15 Poles per company, but they soon caused disruption. In common with many of their fellow conscripts from the more remote Soviet provinces in Central Asia and the Far East, most could not speak Russian.

Although this worsened the army's already acute language problem, the potential threat to its cohesion was far more acute. The majority of these Poles were devout Catholics who now found themselves in an ostentatiously atheistic force – their religion set them apart from the other conscripts and their more sophisticated backgrounds led them to ask awkward questions. One report warned that they '…not only show unhealthy states of mind, complaining about the severity of discipline and the hardship of serving in the Red Army, but in some places are trying to form separatist groups.' This questioning of authority, coupled with clumsy official attempts to explain the German-Soviet Non-Aggression Pact, led to Communist party posters in many barracks being defaced and provoked some alarming comments from conscripts drawn from the Russian heartland, one of whom

remarked, 'From my point of view, it makes no odds if we have fascist or Soviet power.'

Improvised action

In operational terms, the Soviet armoured and motorized units proved capable of maintaining a rapid rate of advance – 56–64km (35–40 miles) per day by road. A British intelligence report provided a neat summary of the workings of the Red Army of the period:

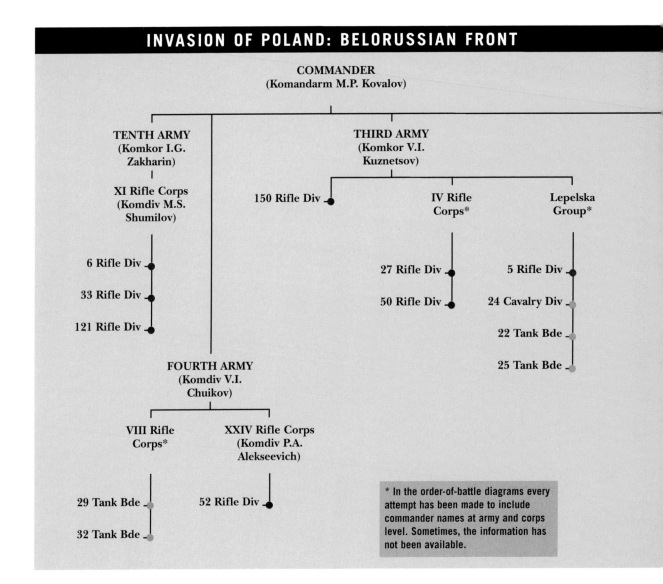

INVASION OF POLAND: BELORUSSIAN FRONT

COMMANDER
(Komandarm M.P. Kovalov)

TENTH ARMY
(Komkor I.G. Zakharin)

XI Rifle Corps
(Komdiv M.S. Shumilov)

6 Rifle Div
33 Rifle Div
121 Rifle Div

THIRD ARMY
(Komkor V.I. Kuznetsov)

150 Rifle Div

IV Rifle Corps*

27 Rifle Div
50 Rifle Div

Lepelska Group*

5 Rifle Div
24 Cavalry Div
22 Tank Bde
25 Tank Bde

FOURTH ARMY
(Komdiv V.I. Chuikov)

VIII Rifle Corps*

XXIV Rifle Corps
(Komdiv P.A. Alekseevich)

29 Tank Bde
32 Tank Bde

52 Rifle Div

* In the order-of-battle diagrams every attempt has been made to include commander names at army and corps level. Sometimes, the information has not been available.

'Russian military administration remains much as it used to be. Train timings are chaotic, motor transport is seldom available at the right time and place, petrol supplies break down and no-one has any clear idea at what time anything is going to arrive. In spite of it all something happens … one is left with the impression that the Russian genius for piecemeal improvisation will always carry them through to a strictly limited extent.' The warning signs were ignored by Stalin and his cronies, who embarked on another round of reorganization. In November 1939, the tank corps (which had replaced the mechanized corps barely a year earlier) were broken up to form motorized divisions of roughly 275 tanks apiece to operate in conjunction with horsed cavalry. Independent tank brigades were to be more closely integrated with infantry and cavalry, and the armoured component of rifle divisions was to be increased from a tank battalion to a tank brigade.

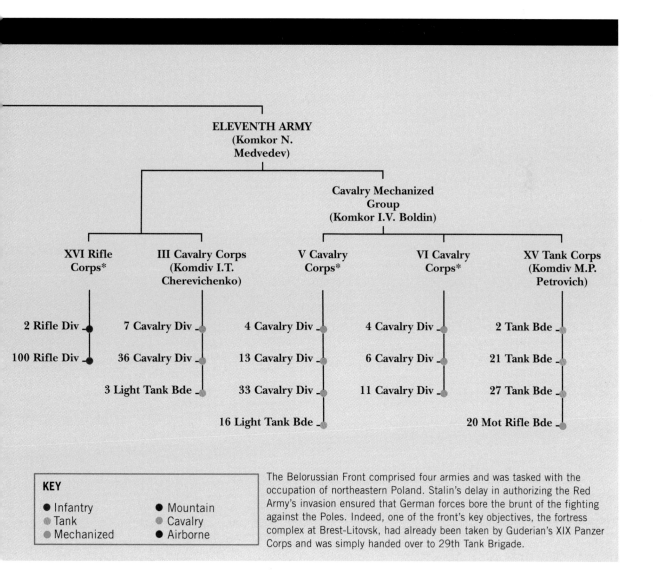

ELEVENTH ARMY
(Komkor N. Medvedev)

Cavalry Mechanized Group
(Komkor I.V. Boldin)

XVI Rifle Corps*

III Cavalry Corps
(Komdiv I.T. Cherevichenko)

V Cavalry Corps*

VI Cavalry Corps*

XV Tank Corps
(Komdiv M.P. Petrovich)

2 Rifle Div

100 Rifle Div

7 Cavalry Div

36 Cavalry Div

3 Light Tank Bde

4 Cavalry Div

13 Cavalry Div

33 Cavalry Div

16 Light Tank Bde

4 Cavalry Div

6 Cavalry Div

11 Cavalry Div

2 Tank Bde

21 Tank Bde

27 Tank Bde

20 Mot Rifle Bde

KEY

- Infantry
- Tank
- Mechanized
- Mountain
- Cavalry
- Airborne

The Belorussian Front comprised four armies and was tasked with the occupation of northeastern Poland. Stalin's delay in authorizing the Red Army's invasion ensured that German forces bore the brunt of the fighting against the Poles. Indeed, one of the front's key objectives, the fortress complex at Brest-Litovsk, had already been taken by Guderian's XIX Panzer Corps and was simply handed over to 29th Tank Brigade.

INVASION OF POLAND: UKRAINIAN FRONT

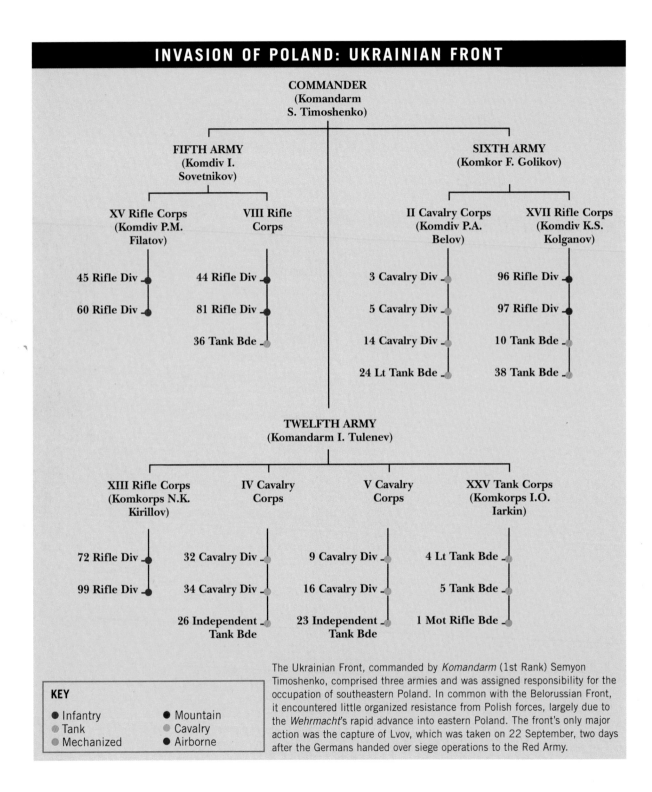

COMMANDER
(Komandarm
S. Timoshenko)

FIFTH ARMY
(Komdiv I.
Sovetnikov)

SIXTH ARMY
(Komkor F. Golikov)

XV Rifle Corps
(Komdiv P.M.
Filatov)

**VIII Rifle
Corps**

II Cavalry Corps
(Komdiv P.A.
Belov)

XVII Rifle Corps
(Komdiv K.S.
Kolganov)

45 Rifle Div

60 Rifle Div

44 Rifle Div

81 Rifle Div

36 Tank Bde

3 Cavalry Div

5 Cavalry Div

14 Cavalry Div

24 Lt Tank Bde

96 Rifle Div

97 Rifle Div

10 Tank Bde

38 Tank Bde

TWELFTH ARMY
(Komandarm I. Tulenev)

XIII Rifle Corps
(Komkorps N.K.
Kirillov)

**IV Cavalry
Corps**

**V Cavalry
Corps**

XXV Tank Corps
(Komkorps I.O.
Iarkin)

72 Rifle Div

99 Rifle Div

32 Cavalry Div

34 Cavalry Div

26 Independent
Tank Bde

9 Cavalry Div

16 Cavalry Div

23 Independent
Tank Bde

4 Lt Tank Bde

5 Tank Bde

1 Mot Rifle Bde

The Ukrainian Front, commanded by *Komandarm* (1st Rank) Semyon Timoshenko, comprised three armies and was assigned responsibility for the occupation of southeastern Poland. In common with the Belorussian Front, it encountered little organized resistance from Polish forces, largely due to the *Wehrmacht*'s rapid advance into eastern Poland. The front's only major action was the capture of Lvov, which was taken on 22 September, two days after the Germans handed over siege operations to the Red Army.

KEY

● Infantry
◐ Tank
● Mechanized
● Mountain
● Cavalry
● Airborne

The Winter War: Finland

The extent of the self-inflicted damage to the combat capability of the Red Army was shown in the bloody fiasco of the Soviet Union's Winter War against Finland, which began on 30 November 1939.

Before being overwhelmed by sheer weight of numbers, the Finns graphically demonstrated the often self-inflicted problems that bedevilled contemporary Soviet warfare. One such problem was the fact that the majority of the Red Army's troops fighting in the Winter War were conscripts from the Ukraine, since Stalin believed that troops from the areas bordering Finland could not be trusted to fight against the Finns. These conscripts with no experience of Arctic winter conditions or training in forest survival skills stood little chance against the Finns, who were experts in winter warfare and knew the land. Even the weather was against them, as the winter of 1939/40 was one of the three worst winters in Finland in the twentieth century.

Karelian setback

In Karelia, the initial Soviet assaults by the Seventh Army against the fortifications of the Mannerheim Line were repulsed with heavy losses, despite the support of the three tank brigades of X Tank Corps and four artillery regiments. At least 180,000 troops, 900 guns and 1400 AFVs were committed against roughly 133,000 Finnish defenders who were woefully short of artillery and armour – the most critical shortage being in anti-tank guns, only 67 of which were available.

In many respects, the Red Army's lavish artillery and armoured support proved to be counter-productive. The tanks and guns were largely road-bound due to the heavily forested terrain over which much of the war was fought. (The tanks and tracked artillery tractors tore up road surfaces, creating a mass of frozen ruts that made them virtually impassable for supply vehicles.)

Even the Soviet infantry had dire problems in attempting cross-country movement, as very few units had skis. The hapless Soviet conscripts stumbling through the deep snow were easy targets for Finnish ski patrols, which made repeated 'hit and run' attacks,

inflicting heavy casualties with their Suomi submachine guns. Their demoralized and frustrated targets could not even return fire effectively, as Red Army policy was that submachine guns were 'a pure police weapon' and too inaccurate for general issue to the infantry. Even at night there was no respite for the Soviet troops, as their camp fires attracted Finnish snipers who picked off the exhausted, freezing men silhouetted against the flames.

Incompetent leadership

Staggering incompetence on the part of many Red Army officers and commissars helped even the odds – at one stage, camouflage was condemned as a sign of cowardice and units formed up for mass assaults in the open, in

HEAVY TANK BRIGADE (NOVEMBER 1939)				
Unit	Personnel	BA-20	BT	T-28
Brigade HQ	–	–	–	2
HQ Company	130	5	–	–
HQ Protection Platoon	33	–	–	–
Reconnaissance Company	70	10	6	–
3 x Tank Battalions, each				
Battalion HQ	84	–	–	–
Signal Platoon	23	2	3	–
Reconnaissance Platoon	9	3	–	–
3 x Tank Companies, each	73	–	–	10
Anti-Air MG Platoon	30	–	–	–
Chemical Company	90	–	–	–
Pioneer Company	200	–	–	–
Motor Transport Battalion	200	–	–	–
Maintenance Battalion	200	–	–	–
Reserve Tank Company	100	–	–	–
Medical Company	60	–	–	–
Other Trains Elements	200	–	–	–

full view of Finnish machine guns and artillery observers, who were able to inflict horrendous casualties. There were reports of Soviet artillery opening fire without orders 'to help the infantry keep its spirits up' and causing mass panic amongst the very infantry that they were supposedly supporting.

The system of dual command was proving to be a disaster in a war against a professional army. One Soviet report quoted a typical incident where 'Some ten men stood around and monitored the actions of the battalion commander and … his subordinates. There was someone from the divisional headquarters, two or three

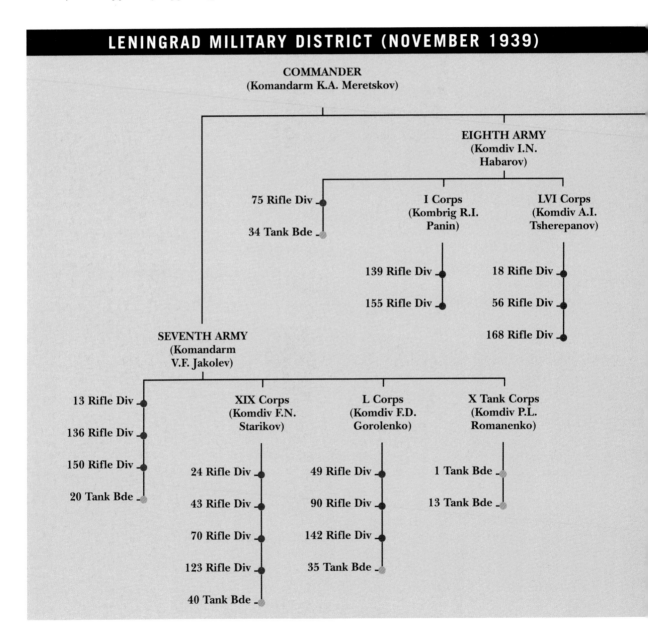

LENINGRAD MILITARY DISTRICT (NOVEMBER 1939)

COMMANDER
(Komandarm K.A. Meretskov)

EIGHTH ARMY
(Komdiv I.N. Habarov)

75 Rifle Div

34 Tank Bde

I Corps
(Kombrig R.I. Panin)

139 Rifle Div

155 Rifle Div

LVI Corps
(Komdiv A.I. Tsherepanov)

18 Rifle Div

56 Rifle Div

168 Rifle Div

SEVENTH ARMY
(Komandarm V.F. Jakolev)

13 Rifle Div

136 Rifle Div

150 Rifle Div

20 Tank Bde

XIX Corps
(Komdiv F.N. Starikov)

24 Rifle Div

43 Rifle Div

70 Rifle Div

123 Rifle Div

40 Tank Bde

L Corps
(Komdiv F.D. Gorolenko)

49 Rifle Div

90 Rifle Div

142 Rifle Div

35 Tank Bde

X Tank Corps
(Komdiv P.L. Romanenko)

1 Tank Bde

13 Tank Bde

from the corps headquarters, someone from the army's political directorate, a man from the army's newspaper – a dozen besides the battalion commander. I remember … the battalion commander stepped aside and said to me: "I don't know what to do, shall I quit and let them run things themselves?"'

The Red Army's tanks were frequently committed to assaults without adequate reconnaissance and with abysmal levels of artillery and infantry support. These failings made them horribly vulnerable to well-camouflaged Finnish anti-tank guns and infantry anti-tank teams, which scored numerous 'kills' with Molotov

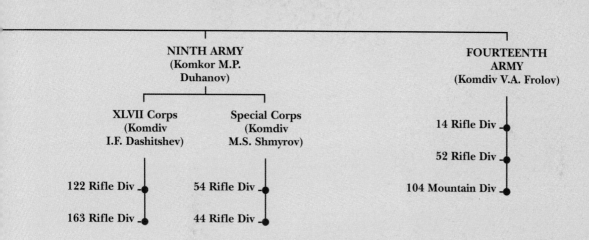

NINTH ARMY
(Komkor M.P. Duhanov)

XLVII Corps
(Komdiv I.F. Dashitshev)

Special Corps
(Komdiv M.S. Shmyrov)

FOURTEENTH ARMY
(Komdiv V.A. Frolov)

122 Rifle Div

163 Rifle Div

54 Rifle Div

44 Rifle Div

14 Rifle Div

52 Rifle Div

104 Mountain Div

Planning for the invasion of Finland was carried out by *Komandarm* (2nd Rank) Kirill Meretskov after Stalin had rejected a more cautious plan drawn up by *Komandarm* (1st Rank) Boris Shaposhnikov, the Chief of the General Staff. Meretskov's plan was based on the assumption that the Finns would not put up much serious resistance and could in any event be overwhelmed by sheer weight of numbers.

Seventh Army was the most powerful of the four Soviet armies and was tasked with breaking through the defences of the Mannerheim Line in the Karelian Isthmus. Eighth Army was to move through Ladoga-Karelia, swinging around the northern shore of the lake before advancing southwestwards to trap the defenders of the Mannerheim Line.

Ninth Army deployed further north, facing the thinly defended central sectors of the Finnish frontier. Its objective was to advance through central Finland to Oulu on the Gulf of Bothnia, cutting the country in two. Fourteenth Army's three divisions deployed to the west of Murmansk were tasked with the capture of Petsamo and the occupation of northern Finland to prevent the entry of foreign aid via Norway or Sweden.

KEY

- Infantry
- Tank
- Mechanized
- Mountain
- Cavalry
- Airborne

November 1939 – March 1940

By late 1939, the Red Army had apparently demonstrated its capabilities by its victory at Khalkin Gol and the swift occupation of eastern Poland. These successes made Stalin feel confident enough to move against Finland when the Finnish government rejected his demands to:

• Cede a strip of territory in the Karelian Isthmus, which would move the border 25km (16 miles) back from Leningrad.

• Grant the USSR a 30-year lease of the Hanko Peninsula and the right to construct a naval base there.

Amazingly, the tiny Finnish forces not only beat off the initial massive Soviet offensive launched on 30 November 1939 but maintained a highly effective defence for over three months. Although Finland was finally forced to make extensive territorial concessions to the Soviet Union, its fierce resistance ensured that it retained its independence.

THE WINTER WAR

The Winter War
November 1939–March 1940

- Soviet attacks
- Finnish attacks
- Finnish reinforcements
- Soviet positions
- Finnish positions
- Pre-1940 border
- Extent of coastal ice cover December 1939

0   100 km
0   100 miles

LIGHT TANK BATTALION (JANUARY 1940)

By the standards of 1939–40, the T-26 was a good light tank, but in common with other Soviet AFVs it was largely road-bound by the densely forested terrain over which much of the Winter War was fought. Whilst the type was well armed, it was vulnerable to Finnish mines and anti-tank guns. (Anti-tank rifle teams also scored numerous kills by making skilful use of cover to take close-range shots against its thin side and rear armour.)

Battalion HQ (3 x T-26)

Reconnaissance Platoon (1 x T-37 plus 1 x AC)

1 Tank Company (17 x T-26)

2 Tank Company (17 x T-26)

3 Tank Company (17 x T-26)

MIKHAIL NIKOLAYEVICH TUKHACHEVSKY (1893–1937)

Born into an aristocratic family at Alexandrovskoye near Smolensk, Tukhachevsky was commissioned as a lieutenant in the Semyenovsky Guards in 1914, seeing service in World War I.

• Tukhachevsky joined the Red Army in 1918 and showed exceptional ability, being promoted to command both the Eighth and Ninth Armies in 1919.

• From 1925–28, he was Red Army Chief of Staff, before becoming commander of Leningrad Military District. In 1931 he became Deputy Commissar for War and Head of the Red Army's Technical & Armament Division and was instrumental in modernizing the Red Army.

• Promoted to the newly created rank of Marshal of the Soviet Union in 1935, he wrote the '1936 Field Service Regulations', which emphasized the importance of armoured warfare, airborne forces and close air support. Tukhachevsky was arrested in Stalin's Purges of the Red Army, tortured, subjected to a 'show trial' and shot on 12 June 1937.

LIGHT TANK BRIGADE (NOVEMBER 1939)				
Unit	Personnel	AC	T-37	BT or T-26
Brigade HQ	–	–	–	–
Signal Company	130	5	–	–
HQ Protection Ptn	33	–	–	–
Reconnaissance Btn				
Battalion HQ	13	–	–	–
Signal Platoon	18	–	–	–
Motorized Rifle Coy	44	–	–	–
Armoured Car Coy	55	16	–	–
Light Tank Coy	40	–	16	–
Battalion Trains	43	–	–	–
3 x Tank Btns, each				
Battalion HQ	14	–	–	3
Signal Platoon	24	–	–	–
Reconnaissance Ptn	10	1	1	–
3 x Tank Coys, each	53	–	–	17
Battalion Trains	60	–	–	–
Motorized Rifle Btn				
Battalion HQ	19	–	–	–
Signal Platoon	32	–	–	–
3 x Rifle Coys, each	160	–	–	–
Anti-Tank Platoon	31	–	–	–
Anti-Air MG Ptn	19	–	–	–
Battalion Trains	78	–	–	–
Anti-Air MG Ptn	30	–	–	–
Chemical Company	90	–	–	–
Pioneer Company	280	–	–	–
Motor Transport Btn	200	–	–	–
Maintenance Btn	200	–	–	–
Reserve Tank Coy	100	–	–	8
Medical Coy	60	–	–	–
Other Trains Elements	200	–	–	–

Cocktail incendiaries and demolition charges. (Whilst most anti-tank guns opened fire at ranges of 400–600m/437–656 yards, an unofficial record was set by a 37mm/1.5in Bofors gun of the 7th Anti-Tank Detachment, which destroyed a T-37 on the ice of Lake Ladoga at a range of 1700 metres/1859 yards.)

It seems likely that as many as 6000 Soviet AFVs were deployed against Finland during the three-and-a-half months of the war and that losses from all causes may have exceeded 3500 vehicles. (Finnish forces had

BATTLE OF SUOMUSSALMI

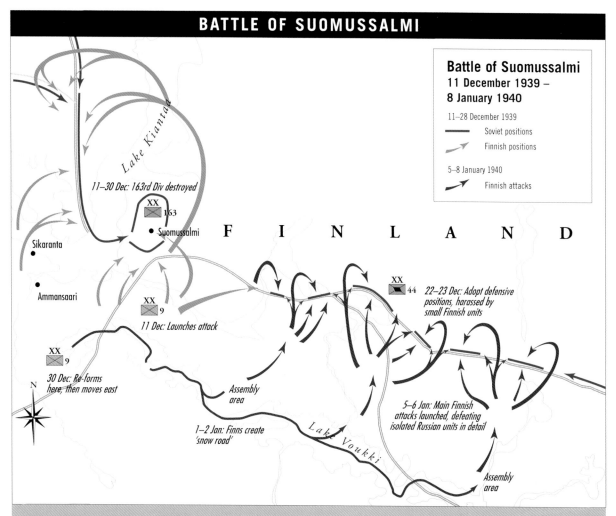

Battle of Suomussalmi
11 December 1939 –
8 January 1940

11–28 December 1939

Soviet positions

Finnish positions

5–8 January 1940

Finnish attacks

Lake Kiantaa

11–30 Dec: 163rd Div destroyed

XX 163

• Suomussalmi

F I N L A N D

• Sikaranta

• Ammansaari

XX 9

11 Dec: Launches attack

XX 9

30 Dec: Re-forms here, then moves east

N

Assembly area

1–2 Jan: Finns create 'snow road'

Lake Voukki

XX 44

22–23 Dec: Adopt defensive positions, harassed by small Finnish units

5–6 Jan: Main Finnish attacks launched, defeating isolated Russian units in detail

Assembly area

11 December 1940 – 6 January 1941

Suomussalmi was the Finnish Army's 'classic victory' of the Winter War. Between 11 December 1939 and 6 January 1940, grossly outnumbered elements of the Finnish 9th Division halted the advance of the Red Army's 163rd Rifle Division at the village of Suomussalmi before encircling the Soviet formation, which was finally destroyed on 31 December. Whilst isolating and destroying the 163rd Rifle Division, the Finns managed to block rescue attempts by the 44th Rifle Division. On the night of 1/2 January, Finnish troops launched their first attack on the 44th, which was strung out along over 32km (20 miles) of road. This first attack cut the road, and over the next few days further attacks broke the 44th into seven isolated detachments, which the Finns dubbed *mottis* – piles of firewood. On 6 January, the remnants of the 44th were finally authorized to withdraw – barely 700 men escaped. At a cost of 900 dead and 1770 wounded, the Finns had inflicted 27,500 fatal casualties on the Soviet forces, besides taking 1600 prisoners.

captured or destroyed roughly 1600 of these, besides inflicting an estimated 250,000 casualties.) By the time of the armistice on 13 March 1940, the Finns had suffered 25,000 dead, 55,000 wounded and 450,000 rendered homeless, a terrible price for a country of barely four million people.

Facing reality, 1940–41

Even Stalin was finally forced to face reality in the aftermath of the German victory in France, and the mechanized corps began to be re-formed from June 1940 onwards. By the time of the German invasion, no less than 30 had been raised.

Although frantic efforts were made, these corps were far from being effective combat units when they were thrown into action a year later, despite the massive numbers of AFVs then available, which may be estimated as follows:

- 400 T-27 tankettes
- 2722 T-37/T-38/T-40 amphibious light tanks
- 400 T-18 light tanks
- 11,000 T-26 light tanks
- 6000 BT fast tanks

- 500 T-28 medium tanks
- 967 T-34 medium tanks
- 40 T-35 heavy tanks
- 508 KV heavy tanks

The situation was even worse than the totals would suggest, as there were far too few modern vehicles – 3000 more KVs and almost 11,000 more T-34s should have been available. Equally seriously, the emphasis on producing new tanks rather than spare parts led to

SOVIET GROUND FORCES (MAY 1940)	
Unit	Number
HEADQUARTERS	
Rifle Corps	52
Cavalry Corps	5
INFANTRY	
Rifle Divisions (inc Mountain & Motorized)	161
Rifle Brigades	3
CAVALRY	
Cavalry Divisions	24
Cavalry Brigades	2
ARMOUR	
Armoured Car Brigades	3
Tank Brigades	38
Separate Tank Regiments	6
Separate Armoured Car and Motorcycle Battalions	3
AIRBORNE	
Airborne Brigades	6
ARTILLERY	
Separate Artillery Regiments	106
Separate Artillery Battalions	12

SOVIET MILITARY DISTRICTS	
Abbreviation	District
BOVO	Belorussian Special Military District
ZapOVO	Western Special Military District
KOVO	Kiev Special Military District
ArkhVO	Arkhangel'sk Military District
ZabVO	Trans-Baikal Military District
ZakVO	Trans-Caucasian Military District
KalVO	Kalinin Military District
LVO	Leningrad Military District
MVO	Moscow Military District
OdVO	Odessa Military District
OrVO	Orel Military District
PribVO	Baltic Military District (redesignated PribOVO – Baltic Special Military District – from 17 August 1940)
PriVO	Volga Military District
SAVO	Central Asian Military District
SibVO	Siberian Military District
SKVO	North Caucasian Military District
UrVO	Ural Military District
KhVO	Kharkov Military District

appalling rates of serviceability; it seems likely that only 27 per cent of Soviet tanks were fully operational at the time of the German invasion.

Reorganization

Infantry divisions had been subjected to three reorganizations in the two years immediately before the German invasion (in September 1939, June 1940 and April 1941). Whilst each progressively improved the divisions' firepower, the resulting formations fared badly in combat in the summer of 1941. This was due to several factors: inexperienced officers who had been hastily promoted to replace those shot or imprisoned during the Purges; poor communications – radio shortages meant that very few divisions had anything like their full entitlement; and the fact that most divisions were also bedevilled by shortages of other vital equipment, such as motor transport.

INFANTRY BATTALION, PERSONNEL (APRIL 1941)				
Unit	Officers	Political Officers	NCOs	Other Ranks
Battalion Headquarters	4	–	–	1
Signal Platoon	1	–	8	24
3 x Rifle Companies, each				
Company Headquarters	1	1	1	4
Medical Section	–	–	1	4
3 x Rifle Platoons, each				
Platoon Headquarters	1	–	1	1
4 x Rifle Squads, each	–	–	1	10
Mortar Squad	–	–	1	3
Machine Gun Platoon				
Platoon Headquarters	1	–	–	1
2 x MG Squads, each	–	–	1	4
Machine Gun Company				
Company Headquarters	1	1	2	4
3 x MG Platoons, each				
Platoon Headquarters	1	–	–	–
4 x MG Squads, each	–	–	1	6
Mortar Company				
Company Headquarters	1	1	1	4
3 x Mortar Ptns, each	1	–	2	12
Anti–Tank Platoon	1	–	2	15
Supply Platoon	1	–	3	29
Medical Platoon	1	–	3	4

INFANTRY REGIMENT, PERSONNEL (APRIL 1941)				
Unit	Officers	Political Officers	NCOs	Other Ranks
Regimental HQ and Staff	15	3	2	2
Supply Department	7	–	2	6
Headquarters Platoon	1	–	4	23
Mounted Recon Platoon				
Platoon Headquarters	1	–	1	–
3 x Mounted Squads, each	–	–	1	9
Infantry Recon Platoon				
Platoon Headquarters	1	–	1	2
4 x Rifle Squads, each	–	–	1	11
Signal Company				
Company Headquarters	1	1	4	18
Radio Platoon	1	–	3	6
1st Tele & Optical Ptn	1	–	3	22
2nd Tele & Optical Ptn	1	–	3	13
Anti-Air Machine Gun Coy				
Company Headquarters	1	1	1	–
Light AAMG Platoon	1	–	6	24
Heavy AAMG Platoon	1	–	3	12
Pioneer Company				
Company Headquarters	2	1	1	1
2 x Pioneer Ptns, each	1	–	6	35
Equipment Squad	–	–	1	3
Chemical Platoon	1	–	3	16
3 x Infantry Battalions	(see table opposite)			
Regimental Gun Battery				
Battery Headquarters				
Command Section	2	1	2	1
Scout Squad	–	–	1	6
Signal Section	–	–	4	12
2 x Gun Platoons, each	1	–	2	21
Ammunition Platoon	1	–	3	21
Trains Group	–	–	2	9
Anti-Tank Battery				
Battery Headquarters	1	1	1	2
3 x AT Platoons, each	1	–	2	14
Heavy Mortar Battery				
Battery Headquarters	1	1	1	8
2 x Mortar Platoons, each	1	–	2	18
Transportation Company	107			
Medical Company	55			
Veterinary Hospital	12			
Workshops	34			

Defending the Motherland: 1941–42

At the beginning of 1941, the Red Army was frantically attempting to repair the damage caused by Stalin's purges, but it was soon to be fighting for its very survival against the most professional military forces in the world.

Cooks from a Red Army field kitchen ladle out a hot meal to troops near Kharkov in the winter of 1941/42.

The German-Soviet Non-Aggression Pact of August 1939 shocked governments across the world, who could not imagine such fierce enemies making a lasting treaty. Indeed, from the beginning, both Stalin and Hitler were trying to twist its provisions for their own advantage.

In less than a year, Stalin seized a great arc of territory to protect his western frontiers, including eastern Poland (September 1939), eastern Finland (March 1940), the Rumanian provinces of Northern Bukovina and Bessarabia (June 1940) and the Baltic countries of Lithuania, Latvia and Estonia (July 1940).

The strategic background

These annexations greatly strengthened the Soviet strategic position – in terms of defence, they provided a valuable buffer zone protecting the industrial and agricultural resources of Belorussia and the Ukraine. However, they also brought Soviet forces within easy striking distance of potential targets essential for the German war effort – the annexation of the Rumanian provinces was especially serious because it posed a direct threat to the vital Ploesti oilfields.

Hitler had, at least temporarily, removed any threat of a war on two fronts and was able to concentrate his forces for the campaigns in Norway and France, but he was understandably concerned by Stalin's moves. Perhaps significantly, it was in July 1940 that Hitler ordered the first studies for the invasion of the Soviet Union which finally evolved into Operation Barbarossa, intended to be launched by a total of 152 divisions on 15 May 1941.

TANK STRENGTHS (JUNE 1941)		
Type	Requirement	Actual
KV Heavy Tanks	3528	508
T-34 Medium Tanks	11,760	967
T-28 Tanks (obsolete)	–	500
BT Light Tanks	7840	6000
T-26 Light Tanks	5880	11,000
T-37/38/40 Scout Tanks	476	4222
Total Tanks	29,484	23,197
Armoured Cars	7448	4819

SOVIET GROUND FORCES (22 JUNE 1941)	
Unit Type	Number
HEADQUARTERS	
Fronts	4
Armies	27
Rifle Corps	62
Cavalry Corps	4
Mechanized Corps	29
INFANTRY	
Rifle Divisions (inc Mountain & Motorized)	198
Rifle Brigades	5
Separate Rifle Regiments	1
Fortified Regions	57
CAVALRY	
Cavalry Divisions	13
MECHANIZED	
Tank Divisions	61
Motorized Divisions	31
Motorcycle Regiments	29
Armoured Train Battalions	8
Armoured Car Brigades	1
Separate Tank Battalions	1
AIRBORNE	
Airborne Brigades	16
ARTILLERY	
Separate Artillery Regiments	169
Anti-Tank Brigades	10
Separate Anti-Aircraft Regiments	2
Separate Artillery Battalions	12
Separate Anti–Aircraft Battalions	45
PVO STRANYI	
PVO Stranyi Corps HQ	3
PVO Stranyi Division HQ	2
PVO Stranyi Brigade HQ	9
PVO Stranyi Corps Region HQ	0
PVO Stranyi Division Region HQ	0
PVO Stranyi Brigade Region HQ	40

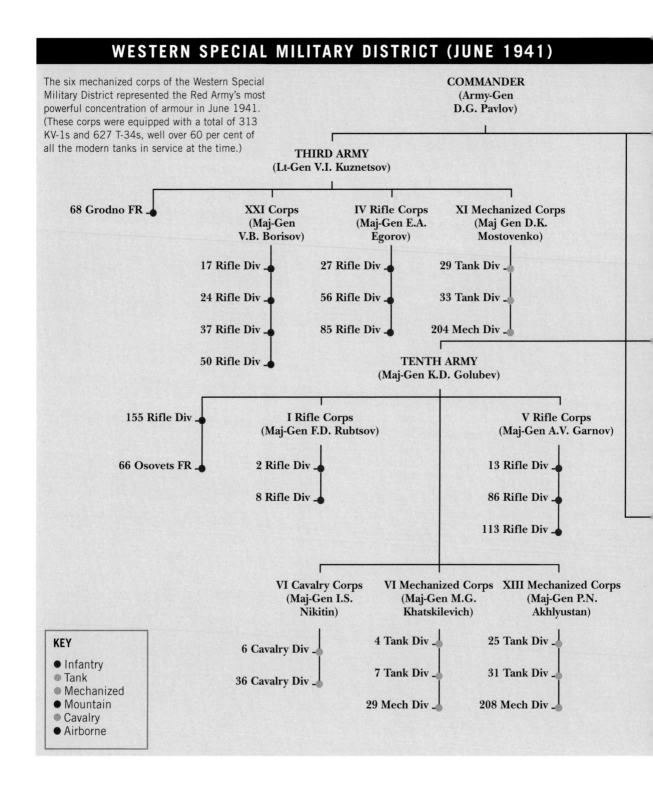

WESTERN SPECIAL MILITARY DISTRICT (JUNE 1941)

The six mechanized corps of the Western Special Military District represented the Red Army's most powerful concentration of armour in June 1941. (These corps were equipped with a total of 313 KV-1s and 627 T-34s, well over 60 per cent of all the modern tanks in service at the time.)

COMMANDER
(Army-Gen D.G. Pavlov)

THIRD ARMY
(Lt-Gen V.I. Kuznetsov)

68 Grodno FR

XXI Corps
(Maj-Gen V.B. Borisov)

- 17 Rifle Div
- 24 Rifle Div
- 37 Rifle Div
- 50 Rifle Div

IV Rifle Corps
(Maj-Gen E.A. Egorov)

- 27 Rifle Div
- 56 Rifle Div
- 85 Rifle Div

XI Mechanized Corps
(Maj Gen D.K. Mostovenko)

- 29 Tank Div
- 33 Tank Div
- 204 Mech Div

TENTH ARMY
(Maj-Gen K.D. Golubev)

155 Rifle Div

66 Osovets FR

I Rifle Corps
(Maj-Gen F.D. Rubtsov)

- 2 Rifle Div
- 8 Rifle Div

V Rifle Corps
(Maj-Gen A.V. Garnov)

- 13 Rifle Div
- 86 Rifle Div
- 113 Rifle Div

VI Cavalry Corps
(Maj-Gen I.S. Nikitin)

- 6 Cavalry Div
- 36 Cavalry Div

VI Mechanized Corps
(Maj-Gen M.G. Khatskilevich)

- 4 Tank Div
- 7 Tank Div
- 29 Mech Div

XIII Mechanized Corps
(Maj-Gen P.N. Akhlyustan)

- 25 Tank Div
- 31 Tank Div
- 208 Mech Div

KEY
- ● Infantry
- ● Tank
- ● Mechanized
- ● Mountain
- ● Cavalry
- ● Airborne

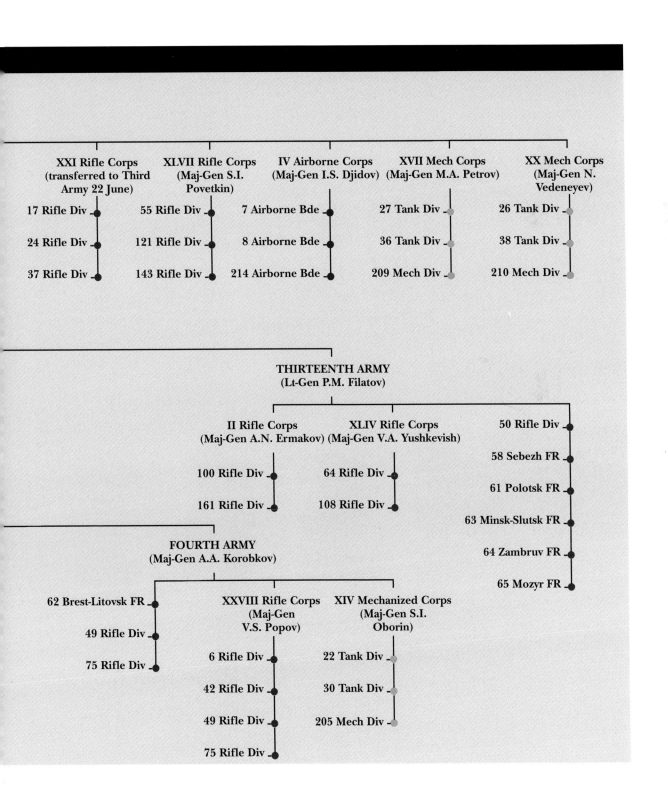

XXI Rifle Corps
(transferred to Third
Army 22 June)

17 Rifle Div

24 Rifle Div

37 Rifle Div

XLVII Rifle Corps
(Maj-Gen S.I.
Povetkin)

55 Rifle Div

121 Rifle Div

143 Rifle Div

IV Airborne Corps
(Maj-Gen I.S. Djidov)

7 Airborne Bde

8 Airborne Bde

214 Airborne Bde

XVII Mech Corps
(Maj-Gen M.A. Petrov)

27 Tank Div

36 Tank Div

209 Mech Div

XX Mech Corps
(Maj-Gen N.
Vedeneyev)

26 Tank Div

38 Tank Div

210 Mech Div

THIRTEENTH ARMY
(Lt-Gen P.M. Filatov)

II Rifle Corps
(Maj-Gen A.N. Ermakov)

XLIV Rifle Corps
(Maj-Gen V.A. Yushkevish)

50 Rifle Div

100 Rifle Div

64 Rifle Div

58 Sebezh FR

161 Rifle Div

108 Rifle Div

61 Polotsk FR

63 Minsk-Slutsk FR

64 Zambruv FR

65 Mozyr FR

FOURTH ARMY
(Maj-Gen A.A. Korobkov)

62 Brest-Litovsk FR

49 Rifle Div

75 Rifle Div

XXVIII Rifle Corps
(Maj-Gen
V.S. Popov)

6 Rifle Div

42 Rifle Div

49 Rifle Div

75 Rifle Div

XIV Mechanized Corps
(Maj-Gen S.I.
Oborin)

22 Tank Div

30 Tank Div

205 Mech Div

Unit	Arm Car	T-26	T-34	T-40	KV	37mm AA	122mm How	152mm How	Flame Thrower	50mm Mort	82mm Mort	76mm Inf Gun	45mm AT	AAMG	MG	LMG
Divisional HQ	–	–	–	–	–	–	–	–	–	–	–	–	–	–	–	–
Signal Battalion	–	–	–	–	–	–	–	–	–	–	–	–	–	–	–	–
Recon Battalion	15	–	–	17	–	–	–	–	–	3	–	–	–	–	–	12
2 x Tank Rgt, each	13	–	1	–	–	–	–	–	–	–	–	–	–	3	–	–
Heavy Tank Btn	3	–	–	–	31	–	–	–	–	–	–	–	–	–	–	–
2 x Med Btns, each	3	–	52	–	–	–	–	–	–	–	–	–	–	–	–	–
Flamethrower Btn	3	10	–	–	–	–	–	–	27	–	–	–	–	–	–	–
Motor Infantry Rgt	10	–	–	–	–	–	–	–	–	27	6	4	6	6	18	108
Artillery Regiment	–	–	–	–	1	–	12	12	–	–	–	–	–	3	–	12
Anti-Aircraft Btn	–	–	–	–	–	12	–	–	–	–	–	–	–	–	–	–
Pioneer Battalion	–	–	–	–	–	–	–	–	–	–	–	–	–	–	–	–

TANK DIVISION EQUIPMENT (JUNE 1941)

LIGHT TANK COMPANY (JUNE 1941)

The T-40 was the last Soviet amphibious light tank to see action during the war. It was a sophisticated design, but like all inherently amphibious AFVs it was bulky to ensure adequate buoyancy when afloat. Weight was also restricted for the same reason, limiting armour to a maximum of 14mm (0.55in) and armament to a 12.7mm (0.5in) HMG plus a co-axial 7.62mm (0.3in) MG. T-40-equipped light tank companies were potentially useful reconnaissance units, but their effectiveness in this role was reduced by a shortage of radios and poor crew training.

Company (17 x T-40)

The key roles of the three main German army groups were finalized:

- Army Group North, under Field Marshal Wilhelm von Leeb, was to advance from East Prussia through the Baltic states and join with the Finns to take Leningrad.

- The initial operations of Field Marshal Fedor von Bock's Army Group Centre from its concentration areas around the Polish capital, Warsaw, were intended to clear the traditional invasion route to Moscow as far as Smolensk before swinging north to help the attack on Leningrad. After the Soviet Union's

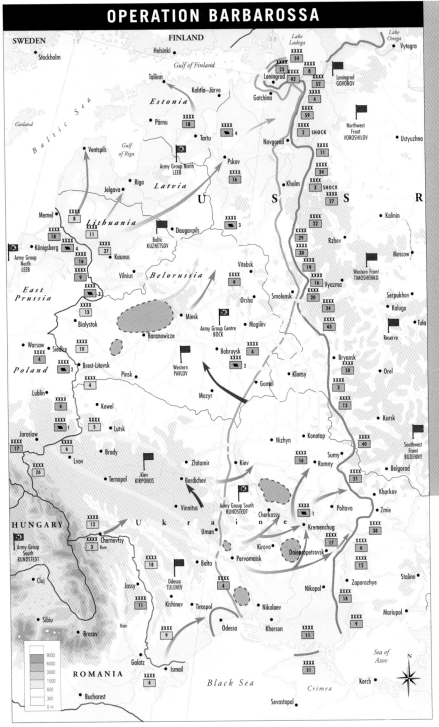

OPERATION BARBAROSSA

22 June – early October 1941

The German plan involved three army groups (North, South and Centre), with the bulk of the forces concentrated in Army Groups North and Centre. Army Group Centre, which contained around half the German armour, was to shatter Soviet forces in Belorussia before turning to assist Army Group North in the drive on Leningrad. Army Group South, meanwhile, was to deal with Soviet forces in the Ukraine. At 3.05 a.m. on 22 June, Army Group North began the drive to Leningrad. By the evening of the first day, the leading Panzers were 60km (37 miles) into Lithuania. By the end of the second day, only the wrecks of 140 Soviet tanks lay between the Panzer divisions and Pskov. But the *Panzergruppe*'s infantry could not keep up. The terrain encountered on the Soviet side of the border was so marshy and impenetrable that even the motorized infantry were reduced to the pace of the marching columns.

Operation Barbarossa
22 June – early October 1941

German attack

Soviet positions, 22 June

Soviet units encircled

Soviet counterattacks

German front line, end of August

German front line, early October

Soviet positions, early October

TANK BRIGADE PERSONNEL (AUGUST 1941)					
Unit	Officers	Political Officers	Warrant Officers	NCOs	Other Ranks
Brigade HQ	11	7	15	9	12
HQ Company					
Company HQ	1	1	3	4	4
Armoured Car Ptn	1	–	–	2	11
Traffic Control Ptn	1	–	–	3	20
Signal Platoon	1	–	–	8	34
Pioneer Platoon	1	–	–	4	32
Chemical Platoon	1	–	–	2	17
Supply & Trans Ptn	–	–	1	3	20
Reconnaissance Coy					
Company HQ	1	1	2	4	7
Heavy Arm Car Ptn	1	–	–	6	13
Light Arm Car Ptn	1	–	–	4	10
Motorcycle Rifle Ptn	1	–	–	4	44
Tank Regiment					
Regimental HQ	6	4	12	5	1
HQ Company	3	1	–	6	25
Med/Hvy Tank Btn	18	4	7	94	14
2 x Lt Tnk Btns, each	15	5	5	53	2
Rgtl Trains Coy	3	1	10	25	91
Medical Company	–	–	3	3	10
Infantry Battalion					
Battalion HQ	6	3	8	1	4
HQ Platoon	1	–	–	4	19
3 x Rifle Coy, each	3	1	–	10	100
Tank Destroyer Coy	4	1	–	8	51
Mortar Company	4	1	–	11	54
Anti-Tank Coy	5	1	–	9	48
Trans & Trains Coy	3	1	3	19	61
Medical Platoon	–	–	2	2	3
Anti-Aircraft Btn					
Battalion HQ	3	3	1	2	–
HQ Platoon	–	–	–	2	7
AAMG Platoon	1	–	–	3	24
2 x AA Battery, each	3	1	–	6	39
Trains Group	–	–	3	9	18
Maintenance Coy	2	1	10	23	55
Motor Transport Coy	4	1	8	11	50
Medical Platoon	–	–	8	4	16

rich agricultural lands of the Ukraine and clearing the Black Sea coast.

The overall objective was to trap and destroy the bulk of the Red Army in a series of encirclements in western Russia before finally securing a line from Arkhangel'sk to Astrakhan. The invasion's chances of success depended on the 19 Panzer divisions concentrated in four *Panzergruppen,* which also incorporated the 14 motorized divisions.

Dispositions

These were to form the cutting edge of the German offensive and had the daunting task of cutting through the massive forces that the Red Army could deploy in European Russia, which totalled perhaps 170 divisions, including up to 60 tank divisions and at least 13 motorized divisions.

Most of these units were deployed close to the frontier, and the accepted explanation for this has been Stalin's obsession with securing his newly conquered territories. German wartime claims that they invaded to pre-empt a Soviet attack have almost always been dismissed as crude propaganda, but this view has been challenged as new material has emerged from Soviet archives. One of the most significant of these documents is the plan formulated by Zhukov in May 1941 within a few months of his appointment as Chief of the Soviet General Staff. The introduction to the draft plan stated:

'In view of the fact that Germany at present keeps its army fully mobilized with its rear services deployed, it has the capacity of deploying ahead of us and striking a sudden blow. To prevent this I consider it important not to leave the operational initiative to the German command in any circumstances, but to anticipate the enemy and attack the German army at the moment when it is in the process of deploying and before it has time to organize its front and the coordination of its various arms.'

This proposed a pre-emptive strike by 152 Red Army divisions (with 76 tank divisions and 44 mechanized divisions) against the Axis forces assembling in German-occupied Poland. Whilst this may have been no more than a contingency plan, it is at least possible that Stalin really was intending to make just such an attack.

second city had been taken, the advance on Moscow would be resumed.

• Army Group South, under the command of Field Marshal Gerd von Rundstedt and including Rumanian and Hungarian divisions, was tasked with taking the

Certainly the first months of 1941 saw frantic activity as 500,000 Red Army reservists were mobilized in March, followed by a further 300,000 a few days later. In the same month, Stalin ordered the formation of a total of 20 new mechanized corps and 106 new air regiments, only a small fraction of which were combat-ready at the time of the German invasion. (This lack of combat-readiness does not necessarily rule out the possibility that Stalin was planning a pre-emptive attack – in the

aftermath of the Purges it is possible that no one dared to tell him about the true state of these formations.)

The opening moves

The German offensive achieved almost complete surprise when it opened on 22 June 1941. The *Panzergruppen* quickly broke through the Soviet lines; *Generaloberst* Erich Hoepner's *Panzergruppe* IV destroyed the Soviet III and XII Mechanized Corps before driving

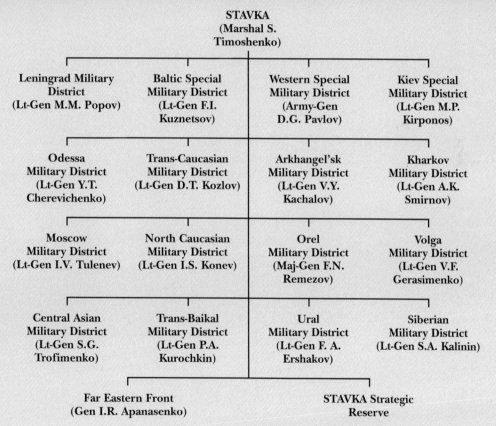

RED ARMY ORGANIZATION (JUNE 1941)

STAVKA
(Marshal S. Timoshenko)

| Leningrad Military District (Lt-Gen M.M. Popov) | Baltic Special Military District (Lt-Gen F.I. Kuznetsov) | Western Special Military District (Army-Gen D.G. Pavlov) | Kiev Special Military District (Lt-Gen M.P. Kirponos) |

| Odessa Military District (Lt-Gen Y.T. Cherevichenko) | Trans-Caucasian Military District (Lt-Gen D.T. Kozlov) | Arkhangel'sk Military District (Lt-Gen V.Y. Kachalov) | Kharkov Military District (Lt-Gen A.K. Smirnov) |

| Moscow Military District (Lt-Gen I.V. Tulenev) | North Caucasian Military District (Lt-Gen I.S. Konev) | Orel Military District (Maj-Gen F.N. Remezov) | Volga Military District (Lt-Gen V.F. Gerasimenko) |

| Central Asian Military District (Lt-Gen S.G. Trofimenko) | Trans-Baikal Military District (Lt-Gen P.A. Kurochkin) | Ural Military District (Lt-Gen F. A. Ershakov) | Siberian Military District (Lt-Gen S.A. Kalinin) |

Far Eastern Front (Gen I.R. Apanasenko)   STAVKA Strategic Reserve

This diagram illustrates the situation in the first days of the German invasion as *Stavka* (GHQ) was formed and the 'front-line' Military Districts began conversion to operational Fronts. (The Far Eastern Front had been formed in 1938 to counter the Japanese threat to Mongolia.) The manning levels of the various Military Districts varied greatly – whilst those along the borders were generally well up to strength, the units assigned to interior MDs were often little more than administrative and training cadres.

SOUTHWEST FRONT (JUNE 1941) (1)

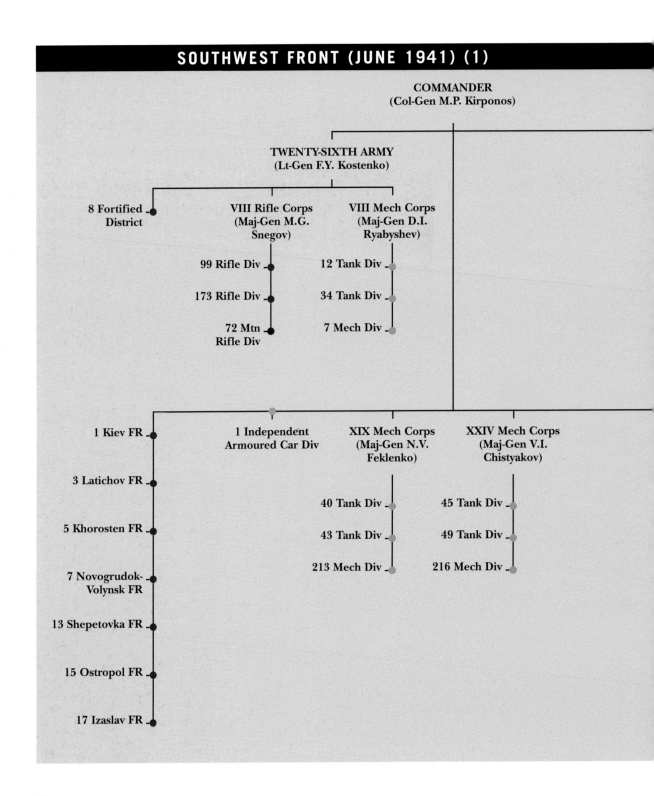

COMMANDER
(Col-Gen M.P. Kirponos)

TWENTY-SIXTH ARMY
(Lt-Gen F.Y. Kostenko)

8 Fortified
District

VIII Rifle Corps
(Maj-Gen M.G.
Snegov)

VIII Mech Corps
(Maj-Gen D.I.
Ryabyshev)

99 Rifle Div

173 Rifle Div

72 Mtn
Rifle Div

12 Tank Div

34 Tank Div

7 Mech Div

1 Kiev FR

3 Latichov FR

5 Khorosten FR

7 Novogrudok-
Volynsk FR

13 Shepetovka FR

15 Ostropol FR

17 Izaslav FR

1 Independent
Armoured Car Div

XIX Mech Corps
(Maj-Gen N.V.
Feklenko)

XXIV Mech Corps
(Maj-Gen V.I.
Chistyakov)

40 Tank Div

43 Tank Div

213 Mech Div

45 Tank Div

49 Tank Div

216 Mech Div

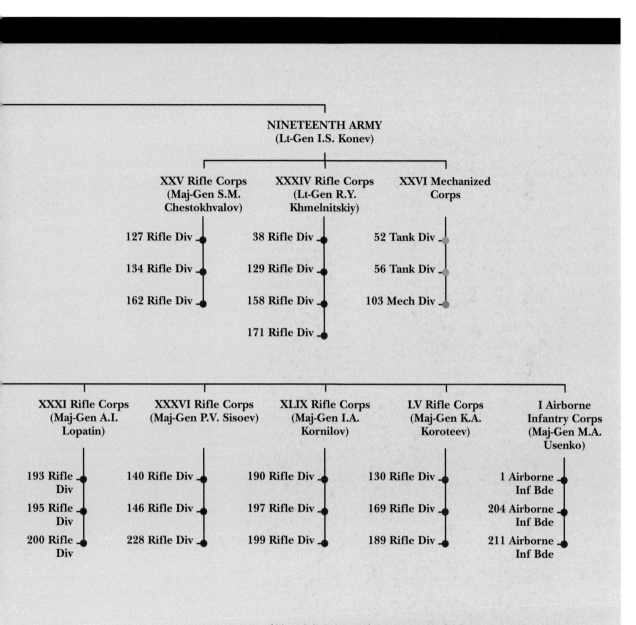

NINETEENTH ARMY
(Lt-Gen I.S. Konev)

XXV Rifle Corps
(Maj-Gen S.M. Chestokhvalov)

XXXIV Rifle Corps
(Lt-Gen R.Y. Khmelnitskiy)

XXVI Mechanized Corps

127 Rifle Div

134 Rifle Div

162 Rifle Div

38 Rifle Div

129 Rifle Div

158 Rifle Div

171 Rifle Div

52 Tank Div

56 Tank Div

103 Mech Div

XXXI Rifle Corps
(Maj-Gen A.I. Lopatin)

XXXVI Rifle Corps
(Maj-Gen P.V. Sisoev)

XLIX Rifle Corps
(Maj-Gen I.A. Kornilov)

LV Rifle Corps
(Maj-Gen K.A. Koroteev)

I Airborne Infantry Corps
(Maj-Gen M.A. Usenko)

193 Rifle Div

195 Rifle Div

200 Rifle Div

140 Rifle Div

146 Rifle Div

228 Rifle Div

190 Rifle Div

197 Rifle Div

199 Rifle Div

130 Rifle Div

169 Rifle Div

189 Rifle Div

1 Airborne Inf Bde

204 Airborne Inf Bde

211 Airborne Inf Bde

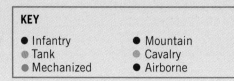

KEY

- Infantry
- Tank
- Mechanized
- Mountain
- Cavalry
- Airborne

Although it was one of the most powerful Fronts at the time of the German invasion, the Southwest Front's strength was rapidly eroded – its mechanized corps attempted to destroy Kleist's *Panzergruppe* I in a concentrated counterattack at Brody-Dubno (25–30 June) but were heavily defeated and destroyed as effective combat formations. The Front suffered further major losses at the Battle of Uman (15 July – 8 August), in which the Sixth and Twelfth Armies were surrounded and destroyed, suffering over 200,000 casualties.

SOUTHWEST FRONT (JUNE 1941) (2)

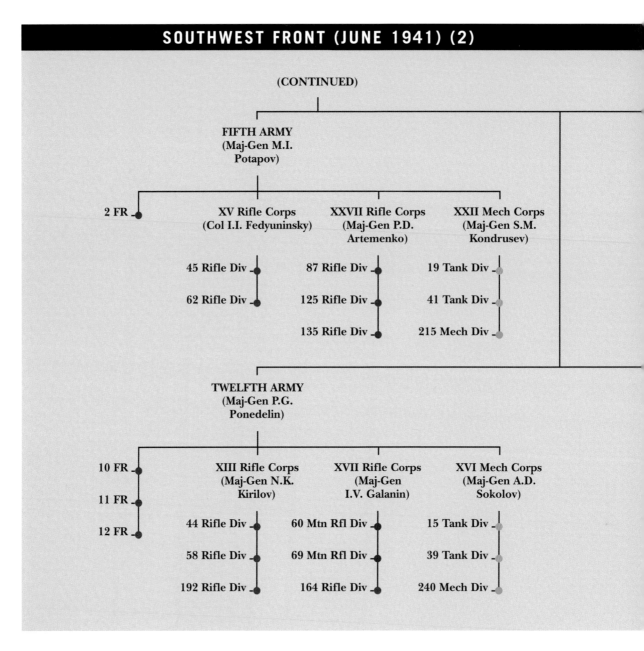

(CONTINUED)

FIFTH ARMY
(Maj-Gen M.I.
Potapov)

2 FR

XV Rifle Corps
(Col I.I. Fedyuninsky)

XXVII Rifle Corps
(Maj-Gen P.D.
Artemenko)

XXII Mech Corps
(Maj-Gen S.M.
Kondrusev)

45 Rifle Div

62 Rifle Div

87 Rifle Div

125 Rifle Div

135 Rifle Div

19 Tank Div

41 Tank Div

215 Mech Div

TWELFTH ARMY
(Maj-Gen P.G.
Ponedelin)

10 FR

11 FR

12 FR

XIII Rifle Corps
(Maj-Gen N.K.
Kirilov)

XVII Rifle Corps
(Maj-Gen
I.V. Galanin)

XVI Mech Corps
(Maj-Gen A.D.
Sokolov)

44 Rifle Div

58 Rifle Div

192 Rifle Div

60 Mtn Rfl Div

69 Mtn Rfl Div

164 Rifle Div

15 Tank Div

39 Tank Div

240 Mech Div

through the Baltic states as the spearhead of Army Group North's advance on Leningrad, which was besieged by 8 September. *Panzergruppen* II (*Generaloberst* Heinz Guderian) and III (*Generaloberst* Hermann Hoth), leading Army Group Centre's advance, pulled off a spectacular encirclement east of Minsk which trapped about 30 Soviet divisions (including six mechanized corps) barely a week after the invasion began.

These units were destroyed by the following German infantry divisions over the next three weeks whilst Guderian and Hoth raced on to trap a further 21 Red Army divisions around Smolensk in mid-July. Far away to

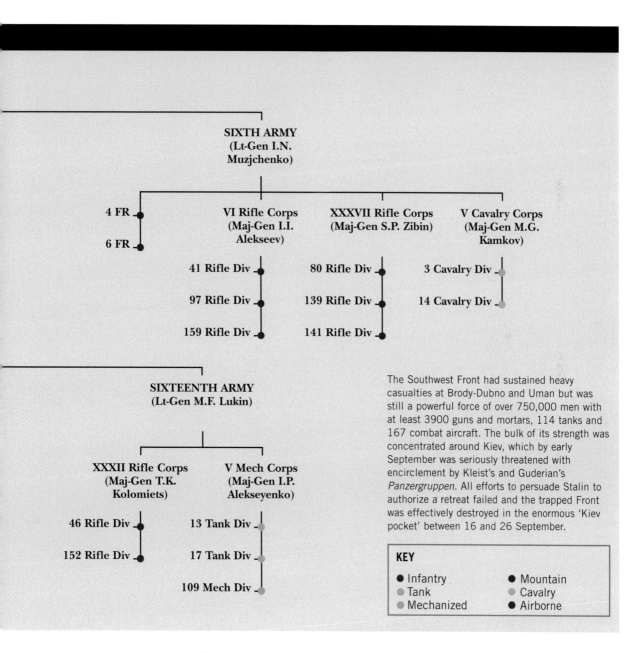

SIXTH ARMY
(Lt-Gen I.N.
Muzjchenko)

4 FR

6 FR

VI Rifle Corps
(Maj-Gen I.I.
Alekseev)

XXXVII Rifle Corps
(Maj-Gen S.P. Zibin)

V Cavalry Corps
(Maj-Gen M.G.
Kamkov)

41 Rifle Div

97 Rifle Div

159 Rifle Div

80 Rifle Div

139 Rifle Div

141 Rifle Div

3 Cavalry Div

14 Cavalry Div

SIXTEENTH ARMY
(Lt-Gen M.F. Lukin)

XXXII Rifle Corps
(Maj-Gen T.K.
Kolomiets)

V Mech Corps
(Maj-Gen I.P.
Alekseyenko)

46 Rifle Div

152 Rifle Div

13 Tank Div

17 Tank Div

109 Mech Div

The Southwest Front had sustained heavy casualties at Brody-Dubno and Uman but was still a powerful force of over 750,000 men with at least 3900 guns and mortars, 114 tanks and 167 combat aircraft. The bulk of its strength was concentrated around Kiev, which by early September was seriously threatened with encirclement by Kleist's and Guderian's *Panzergruppen*. All efforts to persuade Stalin to authorize a retreat failed and the trapped Front was effectively destroyed in the enormous 'Kiev pocket' between 16 and 26 September.

KEY

● Infantry
● Tank
● Mechanized

● Mountain
● Cavalry
● Airborne

the south, *Generaloberst* Ewald von Kleist's *Panzergruppe* I, attached to Army Group South, thrust deep into the Ukraine, advancing to within 20km (12.5 miles) of the Ukrainian capital, Kiev, by 11 July after decimating counterattacks by the five mechanized corps of the Kiev Special Military District.

Evidence of the Red Army's ineptitude was to be seen everywhere during the first months of the German offensive. Just as had happened in World War I, poorly trained Russian radio operators used simple codes that were easily broken by German monitoring stations. (It was not uncommon for German commanders to receive

CAVALRY DIVISION (JULY 1941)								
Unit	Officers	Political Officers	Warrant Officers	NCOs	Other Ranks	Riding Horses	Draft Horses	Trucks
Divisional HQ	12	8	15	12	66	100	3	4
Signal Squadron	6	1	–	10	80	96	20	4
3 x Cavalry Regiments, each	40	10	17	113	760	842	180	8
Horse Artillery Battalion	31	9	11	118	464	444	290	6
Artillery Ammunition Column	4	1	4	11	123	28	84	25
Tank Squadron	4	1	1	9	19	–	–	3
Pioneer Squadron	4	1	–	15	70	60	10	–
Chemical Squadron	3	1	3	12	45	36	10	7
Rations Supply Column	3	1	3	7	57	–	–	30
Medical Squadron	–	1	22	5	24	–	–	16

intercepted Red Army orders before situation reports from their own troops.) Sometimes desperate Soviet signals officers resorted to sending messages in clear – as one lieutenant remarked, 'What else are we supposed to do when they want everything sent without delay?'

Contrasting command structures

The most glaring contrasts between the two sides lay in their basic methods of operation – German forces were supremely professional, working on the basis of *Auftragstaktik*, which today has been widely adopted by the world's leading armies under the title of 'Mission Command'. Detailed written orders were largely abolished and replaced by general directives – for example, a unit might be told to take a village, in which case the unit commander was free to use whatever tactics were appropriate in the circumstances and was expected to take full advantage of any unexpected opportunities that arose.

On the other side of the front line, Soviet commanders simply did not know what to do in the absence of detailed orders – one of the most telling episodes on the first day of the invasion was the German interception of a mass of frantic signals from Soviet units to their HQs, all plaintively asking the same question: 'We're being fired on – what shall we do?'

By mid-July, Russian losses were staggering, totalling perhaps 5700 AFVs, 4500 guns and 610,000 prisoners,

whilst the Soviet Air Force had been virtually wiped out, losing almost 6000 aircraft. Complete German air superiority allowed the *Luftwaffe* to mount unopposed reconnaissance and bombing sorties, which disrupted many of the Soviet counterattacks before they got under way. Those counterattacks that survived the air raids were usually badly mishandled, often being launched using armour without any proper infantry or artillery support. In most cases, Soviet armour was shot to pieces by the German anti-tank units screening the flanks of the advance, and the remnants mopped up by the Panzers.

The technical balance

On the technical level, the majority of Soviet AFVs were far outclassed by their German counterparts – very few Red Army vehicles had radios, which reinforced their tendency to stick rigidly to detailed orders regardless of rapidly changing battlefield conditions, whereas the radio-fitted Panzers could rapidly concentrate to defeat the clumsy counterattacks. (Hapless Red Army tank crews soon found that the signal flags on which they were supposed to rely were almost impossible to read accurately under combat conditions.)

Moreover, the thinly armoured BTs and T-26s which formed such a high proportion of the total Soviet tank strength at the beginning of the campaign were vulnerable to almost all German tank and anti-tank guns at normal battle ranges. In contrast, the Soviet 45mm

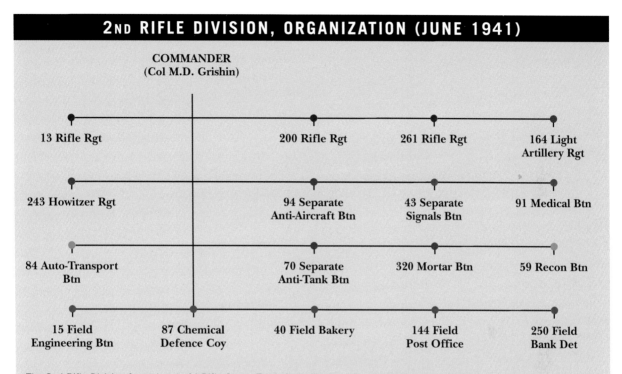

2ND RIFLE DIVISION, ORGANIZATION (JUNE 1941)

COMMANDER
(Col M.D. Grishin)

13 Rifle Rgt	200 Rifle Rgt	261 Rifle Rgt	164 Light Artillery Rgt
243 Howitzer Rgt	94 Separate Anti-Aircraft Btn	43 Separate Signals Btn	91 Medical Btn
84 Auto-Transport Btn	70 Separate Anti-Tank Btn	320 Mortar Btn	59 Recon Btn
15 Field Engineering Btn	87 Chemical Defence Coy	40 Field Bakery	144 Field Post Office	250 Field Bank Det

The 2nd Rifle Division formed part of I Rifle Corps, Tenth Army (Western Special Military District). The elaborate divisional structure shown here, with its powerful integral artillery support totalling 16 x 76mm (3in) guns, 32 x 122mm (4.8in) howitzers and 12 x 152mm (6in) howitzers, proved too complex for the inexperienced Soviet commanders. (The smaller and simpler rifle divisions that evolved in 1941–42 were also a reflection of the enormous losses of manpower and equipment during this time.)

(1.8in), in both its anti-tank and tank gun versions, could penetrate the up-armoured Panzer IIIH/J and Panzer IVE/F only at point-blank range. These Panzers' three-man turrets allowed the commander to concentrate on command, giving the vehicles a distinct edge in tank-versus-tank actions with most Red Army AFVs, which had two-man turrets in which the commander also had to act as gunner or loader.

2ND RIFLE DIVISION, SERVICE RECORD

Date	Action
22 Jun 1941	Went into action 15km (9.4 miles) north of Osovets fortress at 1100.
23–26 Jun 1941	Defence of the line of River Bobr.
26 Jun 1941	Division isolated and forced to retreat – most heavy equipment abandoned.
28 Jun–04 Jul 1941	Division effectively destroyed.

RIFLE DIVISION, PERSONNEL (JUNE 1941)

Unit	Officers	Warrant & Political Officers	NCOs	Other Ranks
Divisional HQ	26	49	14	37
Signal Battalion	17	15	47	184
Recon Company	4	1	15	101
3 x Inf Rgt, each	107	51	365	2172
Artillery Regiment	57	36	141	729
Anti-Aircraft Btn	16	13	42	172
Pioneer Battalion	17	14	70	316
Chemical Platoon	1	–	4	33
Motor Trans Coy	4	8	24	83
Medical Battalion	2	31	32	165
Bakery	–	4	12	144
Other Services	–	5	4	14

The loss of Belorussia

On paper, General Dmitry Pavlov's Western Front was a match for Army Group Centre as it had 700,000 men, over 2000 tanks (including 383 T-34s and KVs) plus 1900 aircraft – but events were to turn out very differently.

Army Group Centre's initial offensive into Belorussia achieved almost complete surprise. Its progress was greatly assisted by *Luftflotte* II's 1000 or so aircraft, which effectively destroyed the VVS (Red Air Force) units

assigned to the Western Front within a matter of days. Elements of the garrison of the border fortress of Brest-Litovsk, which included fanatical NKVD units, held out for almost a month, but most of the Front's formations were swept away by the speed of the German advance.

Pavlov's initial reaction was to order an immediate counterattack by Tenth Army, which was concentrated around Bialystok – this predictably failed and simply ensured that Tenth Army would be the first major Soviet

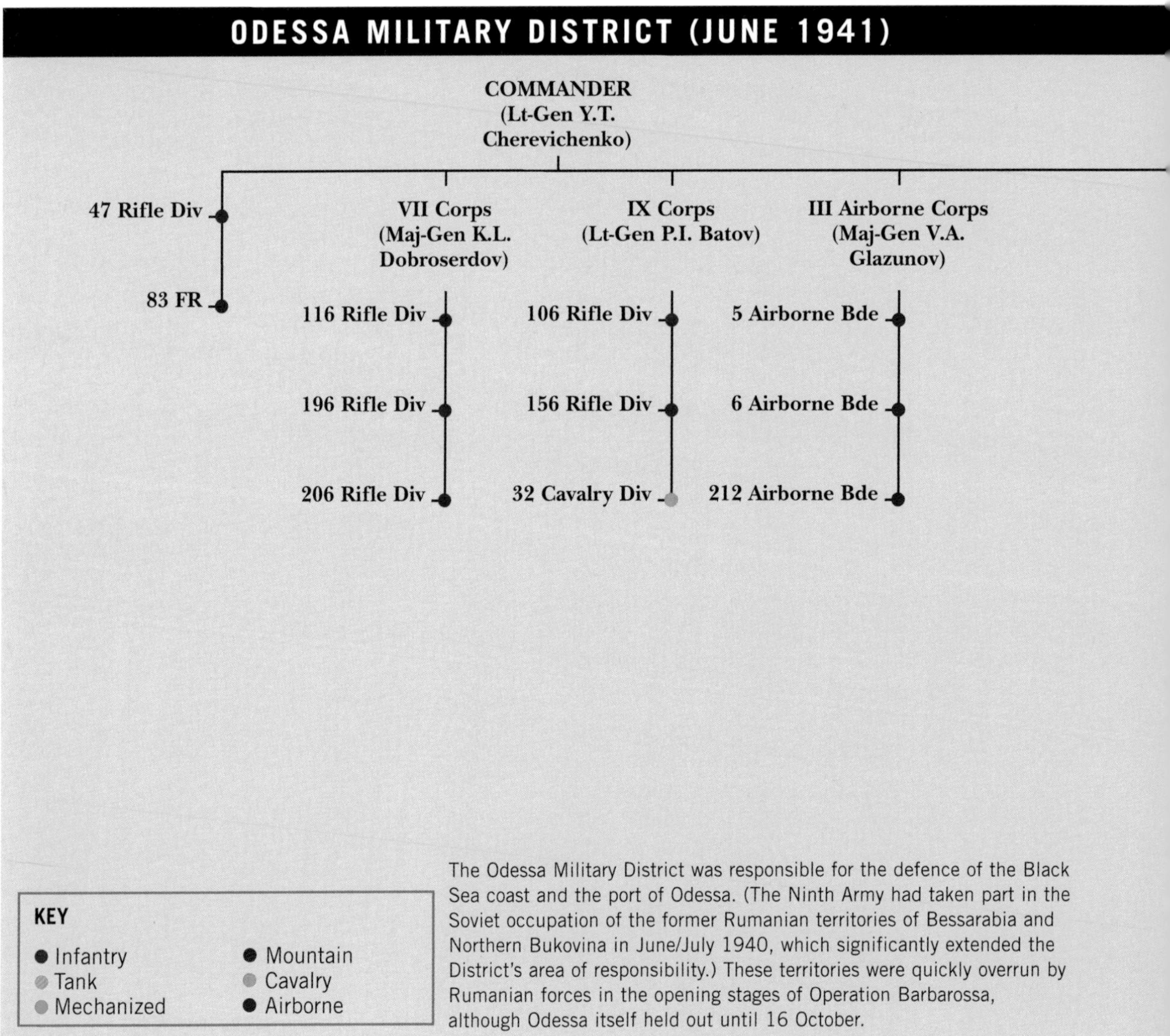

ODESSA MILITARY DISTRICT (JUNE 1941)

COMMANDER
(Lt-Gen Y.T. Cherevichenko)

47 Rifle Div	VII Corps (Maj-Gen K.L. Dobroserdov)	IX Corps (Lt-Gen P.I. Batov)	III Airborne Corps (Maj-Gen V.A. Glazunov)
83 FR	116 Rifle Div	106 Rifle Div	5 Airborne Bde
	196 Rifle Div	156 Rifle Div	6 Airborne Bde
	206 Rifle Div	32 Cavalry Div	212 Airborne Bde

KEY

- Infantry
- Tank
- Mechanized
- Mountain
- Cavalry
- Airborne

The Odessa Military District was responsible for the defence of the Black Sea coast and the port of Odessa. (The Ninth Army had taken part in the Soviet occupation of the former Rumanian territories of Bessarabia and Northern Bukovina in June/July 1940, which significantly extended the District's area of responsibility.) These territories were quickly overrun by Rumanian forces in the opening stages of Operation Barbarossa, although Odessa itself held out until 16 October.

formation to be encircled and destroyed when the German Third and Fourth Armies sealed off the Bialystok pocket on 25 June. A further counterattack by VI and XI Mechanized Corps plus VI Cavalry Corps was ordered against the flank of *Panzergruppe* III, which was making rapid progress towards Vilnius. The operation was harried by constant air attacks and finally collapsed when the Soviet forces hit a strong German anti-tank screen supported by infantry.

On 28 June, *Panzergruppen* II and III linked up east of Minsk, the Belorussian capital, which was captured 24 hours later. In six days, they had advanced over 320km (200 miles), covering a third of the distance to Moscow. It was undoubtedly a spectacular achievement – when the remnants of the Soviet Third, Fourth, Tenth and Thirteenth Armies finally surrendered, the Red Army had lost roughly 420,000 men (including 290,000 prisoners) plus 2500 tanks and 1500 guns. However, the

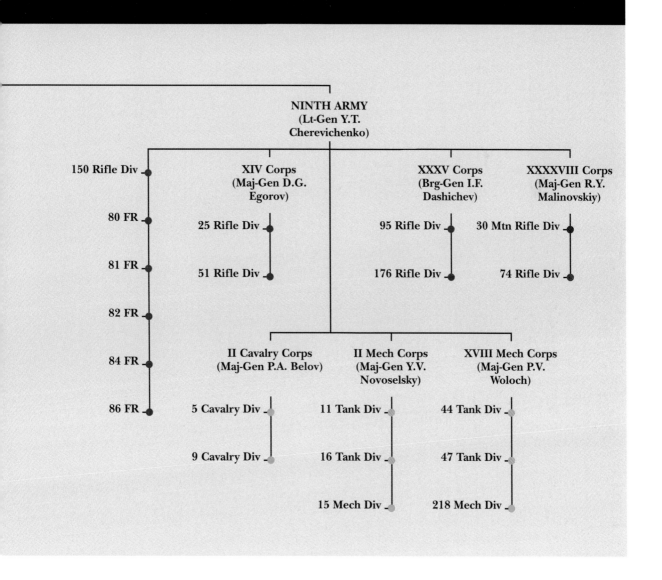

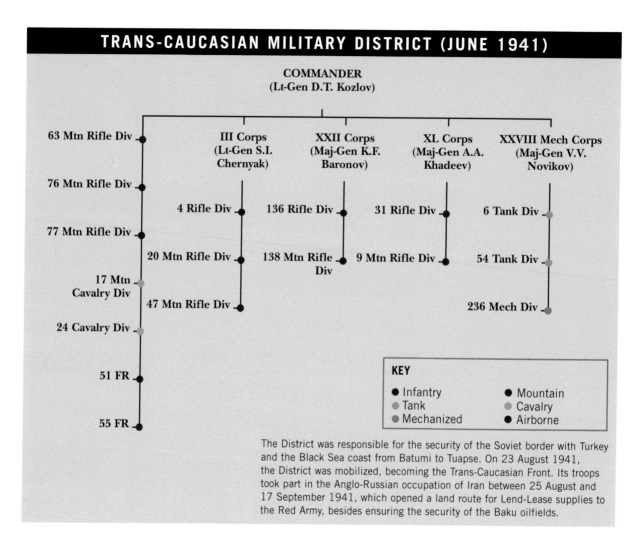

TRANS-CAUCASIAN MILITARY DISTRICT (JUNE 1941)

COMMANDER
(Lt-Gen D.T. Kozlov)

63 Mtn Rifle Div	III Corps (Lt-Gen S.I. Chernyak)	XXII Corps (Maj-Gen K.F. Baronov)	XL Corps (Maj-Gen A.A. Khadeev)	XXVIII Mech Corps (Maj-Gen V.V. Novikov)
76 Mtn Rifle Div	4 Rifle Div	136 Rifle Div	31 Rifle Div	6 Tank Div
77 Mtn Rifle Div	20 Mtn Rifle Div	138 Mtn Rifle Div	9 Mtn Rifle Div	54 Tank Div
17 Mtn Cavalry Div	47 Mtn Rifle Div			236 Mech Div
24 Cavalry Div				
51 FR				
55 FR				

KEY

- ● Infantry
- ● Tank
- ● Mechanized
- ● Mountain
- ● Cavalry
- ● Airborne

The District was responsible for the security of the Soviet border with Turkey and the Black Sea coast from Batumi to Tuapse. On 23 August 1941, the District was mobilized, becoming the Trans-Caucasian Front. Its troops took part in the Anglo-Russian occupation of Iran between 25 August and 17 September 1941, which opened a land route for Lend-Lease supplies to the Red Army, besides ensuring the security of the Baku oilfields.

Panzers had far outrun their supporting infantry divisions, which were essential for effectively sealing the pocket, and a large number of Soviet troops (possibly as many as 250,000) were able to break out after abandoning their heavy equipment. Nonetheless, it seemed as though the road to Moscow was now open.

The loss of the Ukraine

These same victories led to Hitler's increasing interference in all aspects of operations, with devastating consequences for Germany's chances of victory. Despite Army Group South's success at Uman in early August, where 20 Russian divisions were surrounded and

destroyed, he ordered the suspension of the advance on Moscow so that Guderian's *Panzergruppe* II was freed to turn south to help complete the conquest of the Ukraine. Kleist's *Panzergruppe* I was ordered to strike northeastwards to link up with Guderian and encircle Kiev. These moves caught the Soviets entirely by surprise and their frantic efforts to reinforce Kiev only increased the losses when the city's defenders (four Soviet armies, totalling nearly 50 divisions) were finally surrounded on 16 September.

Over the next two weeks, they were subjected to constant air and ground attacks before the final collapse of Kiev, where the Germans took 665,000 prisoners,

NORTH CAUCASIAN MILITARY DISTRICT (JUNE 1941)

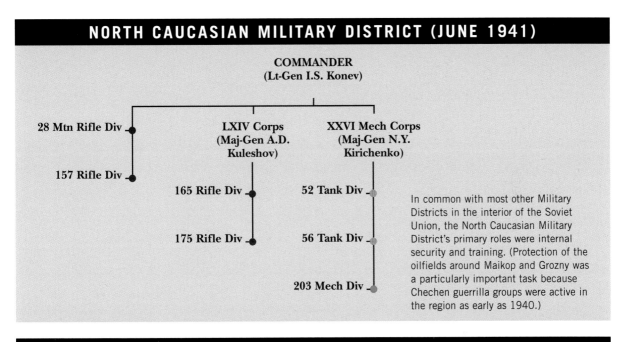

COMMANDER
(Lt-Gen I.S. Konev)

28 Mtn Rifle Div

157 Rifle Div

LXIV Corps
(Maj-Gen A.D.
Kuleshov)

165 Rifle Div

175 Rifle Div

XXVI Mech Corps
(Maj-Gen N.Y.
Kirichenko)

52 Tank Div

56 Tank Div

203 Mech Div

In common with most other Military Districts in the interior of the Soviet Union, the North Caucasian Military District's primary roles were internal security and training. (Protection of the oilfields around Maikop and Grozny was a particularly important task because Chechen guerrilla groups were active in the region as early as 1940.)

OREL MILITARY DISTRICT (JUNE 1941)

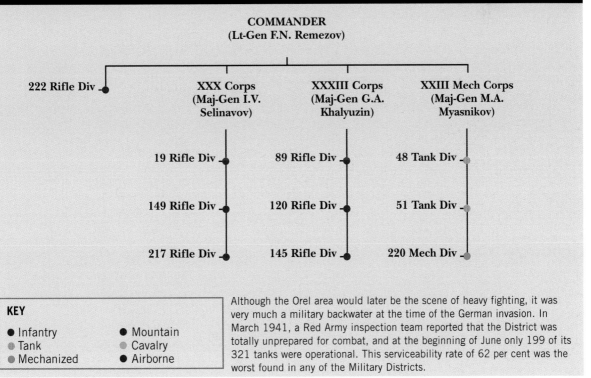

COMMANDER
(Lt-Gen F.N. Remezov)

222 Rifle Div

XXX Corps
(Maj-Gen I.V.
Selinavov)

19 Rifle Div

149 Rifle Div

217 Rifle Div

XXXIII Corps
(Maj-Gen G.A.
Khalyuzin)

89 Rifle Div

120 Rifle Div

145 Rifle Div

XXIII Mech Corps
(Maj-Gen M.A.
Myasnikov)

48 Tank Div

51 Tank Div

220 Mech Div

KEY

- Infantry
- Tank
- Mechanized
- Mountain
- Cavalry
- Airborne

Although the Orel area would later be the scene of heavy fighting, it was very much a military backwater at the time of the German invasion. In March 1941, a Red Army inspection team reported that the District was totally unprepared for combat, and at the beginning of June only 199 of its 321 tanks were operational. This serviceability rate of 62 per cent was the worst found in any of the Military Districts.

880 AFVs and 3700 guns. Barely 15,000 men escaped from the Kiev pocket.

Germany at the Black Sea

As a result of this victory, Army Group South was able to complete the occupation of the Black Sea coast as far east as the Crimea and the Sea of Azov. The Axis advance into the Crimea was aided by Soviet Colonel-General Fyodor Kuznetsov's insistence on deploying his Fifty-First Independent Army in accordance with pre-war plans to defend the area.

These plans had been drawn up to counter amphibious landings rather than to withstand a land assault – less than 25 per cent of Kuznetsov's force was assigned to defend the Isthmus of Perekop linking the Crimea to the mainland. Stalin then intervened, ordering Fifty-First Independent Army to launch its own offensive to pre-empt the inevitable German attack. Predictably, Kuznetsov's hastily organized attack failed and the heavy losses sustained seriously jeopardized the defence of the Crimea.

Desperate defence

The initial Axis assault on the Perekop defences was launched on 24 September by *General der Infanterie* Erich von Manstein's Eleventh Army, but was repelled after five days of heavy fighting. A second attempt on 18 October finally broke through the fortified zone, despite the arrival of Soviet forces evacuated from Odessa just before the city fell to Rumanian forces. The operation was now largely a matter of pursuit – by 16 November, virtually the whole of the Crimea, except for the port city of Sevastopol on the southwest tip of the peninsula, was under Axis occupation.

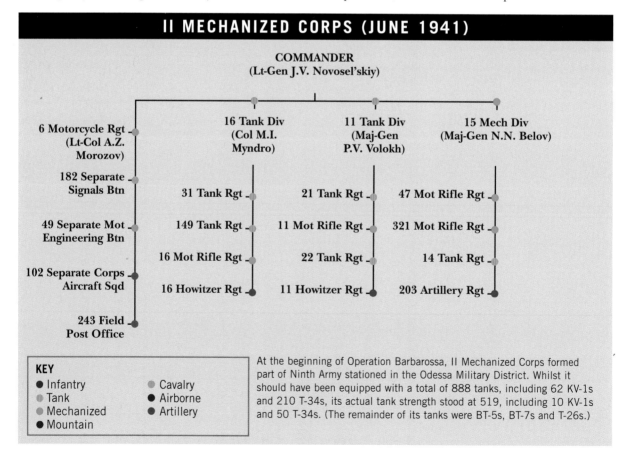

II MECHANIZED CORPS (JUNE 1941)

COMMANDER
(Lt-Gen J.V. Novosel'skiy)

6 Motorcycle Rgt
(Lt-Col A.Z. Morozov)

182 Separate
Signals Btn

49 Separate Mot
Engineering Btn

102 Separate Corps
Aircraft Sqd

243 Field
Post Office

16 Tank Div
(Col M.I. Myndro)

31 Tank Rgt

149 Tank Rgt

16 Mot Rifle Rgt

16 Howitzer Rgt

11 Tank Div
(Maj-Gen P.V. Volokh)

21 Tank Rgt

11 Mot Rifle Rgt

22 Tank Rgt

11 Howitzer Rgt

15 Mech Div
(Maj-Gen N.N. Belov)

47 Mot Rifle Rgt

321 Mot Rifle Rgt

14 Tank Rgt

203 Artillery Rgt

KEY
- Infantry
- Tank
- Mechanized
- Mountain
- Cavalry
- Airborne
- Artillery

At the beginning of Operation Barbarossa, II Mechanized Corps formed part of Ninth Army stationed in the Odessa Military District. Whilst it should have been equipped with a total of 888 tanks, including 62 KV-1s and 210 T-34s, its actual tank strength stood at 519, including 10 KV-1s and 50 T-34s. (The remainder of its tanks were BT-5s, BT-7s and T-26s.)

The Northern Front

Stalin had taken over the Baltic states – Lithuania, Latvia and Estonia – in July 1940, in order to secure an outer defensive zone for Leningrad. That zone was overrun in two months and on 1 September Army Group North's artillery opened fire on Leningrad.

The picture of Panzer superiority was marred only by the relatively few encounters with T-34s and KVs, both of which were formidable opponents. The T-34's sloped armour was almost invulnerable to all German AFV weapons – apart from the 50mm (2in) L/60 gun mounted on a few Panzer IIIs – except at point-blank range, whilst the KV could be effectively countered only by 88mm (3.5in) Flak guns or medium artillery.

The KV had the greatest psychological impact, as even single vehicles could impose significant delays on the German advance. On 23–24 June, a single KV-2 of III Mechanized Corps cut the supply route to 6th Panzer

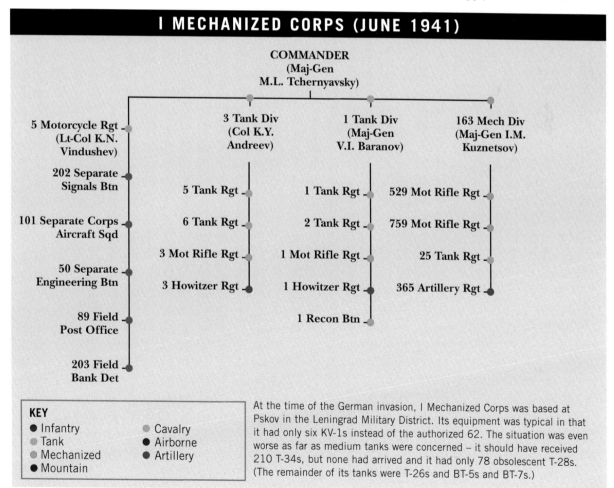

I MECHANIZED CORPS (JUNE 1941)

COMMANDER
(Maj-Gen
M.L. Tchernyavsky)

5 Motorcycle Rgt
(Lt-Col K.N.
Vindushev)

202 Separate
Signals Btn

101 Separate Corps
Aircraft Sqd

50 Separate
Engineering Btn

89 Field
Post Office

203 Field
Bank Det

3 Tank Div
(Col K.Y.
Andreev)

5 Tank Rgt

6 Tank Rgt

3 Mot Rifle Rgt

3 Howitzer Rgt

1 Tank Div
(Maj-Gen
V.I. Baranov)

1 Tank Rgt

2 Tank Rgt

1 Mot Rifle Rgt

1 Howitzer Rgt

1 Recon Btn

163 Mech Div
(Maj-Gen I.M.
Kuznetsov)

529 Mot Rifle Rgt

759 Mot Rifle Rgt

25 Tank Rgt

365 Artillery Rgt

KEY
- Infantry
- Tank
- Mechanized
- Mountain
- Cavalry
- Airborne
- Artillery

At the time of the German invasion, I Mechanized Corps was based at Pskov in the Leningrad Military District. Its equipment was typical in that it had only six KV-1s instead of the authorized 62. The situation was even worse as far as medium tanks were concerned – it should have received 210 T-34s, but none had arrived and it had only 78 obsolescent T-28s. (The remainder of its tanks were T-26s and BT-5s and BT-7s.)

Division's bridgeheads across the Dubissa River in Lithuania for over 24 hours. It proved invulnerable to fire from German tanks and was only destroyed by an '88' brought up to close range whilst a Panzer platoon acted as a decoy. In another incident, the leading elements of 8th Panzer Division were badly mauled on 14 August by five well-camouflaged KV-1s dug in at Krasnogvardeysk near Leningrad. The Soviet

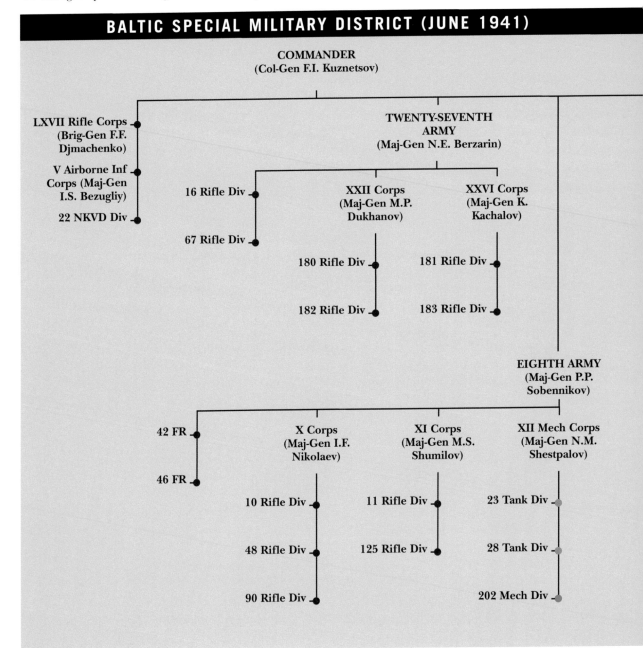

BALTIC SPECIAL MILITARY DISTRICT (JUNE 1941)

COMMANDER
(Col-Gen F.I. Kuznetsov)

LXVII Rifle Corps
(Brig-Gen F.F. Djmachenko)

V Airborne Inf Corps (Maj-Gen I.S. Bezugliy)

22 NKVD Div

16 Rifle Div

67 Rifle Div

TWENTY-SEVENTH ARMY
(Maj-Gen N.E. Berzarin)

XXII Corps
(Maj-Gen M.P. Dukhanov)

180 Rifle Div

182 Rifle Div

XXVI Corps
(Maj-Gen K. Kachalov)

181 Rifle Div

183 Rifle Div

EIGHTH ARMY
(Maj-Gen P.P. Sobennikov)

42 FR

46 FR

X Corps
(Maj-Gen I.F. Nikolaev)

10 Rifle Div

48 Rifle Div

90 Rifle Div

XI Corps
(Maj-Gen M.S. Shumilov)

11 Rifle Div

125 Rifle Div

XII Mech Corps
(Maj-Gen N.M. Shestpalov)

23 Tank Div

28 Tank Div

202 Mech Div

commander, Lieutenant Zinoviy Kolobanov, had selected the position to cover the region's only road as it crossed a swamp. Each KV-1 was loaded with extra ammunition and Kolobanov issued instructions that the other tanks should hold fire until ordered, to conceal the strength of the detachment. As 8th Panzer Division's vanguard approached, Kolobanov's KV knocked out the lead tank with its first shot. The Germans assumed an anti-tank

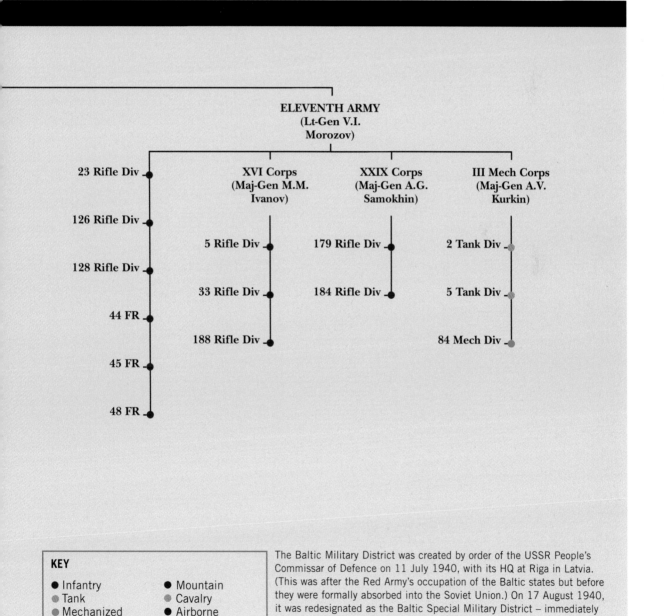

ELEVENTH ARMY
(Lt-Gen V.I.
Morozov)

23 Rifle Div

126 Rifle Div

128 Rifle Div

44 FR

45 FR

48 FR

XVI Corps
(Maj-Gen M.M.
Ivanov)

5 Rifle Div

33 Rifle Div

188 Rifle Div

XXIX Corps
(Maj-Gen A.G.
Samokhin)

179 Rifle Div

184 Rifle Div

III Mech Corps
(Maj-Gen A.V.
Kurkin)

2 Tank Div

5 Tank Div

84 Mech Div

KEY

- Infantry
- Tank
- Mechanized
- Mountain
- Cavalry
- Airborne

The Baltic Military District was created by order of the USSR People's Commissar of Defence on 11 July 1940, with its HQ at Riga in Latvia. (This was after the Red Army's occupation of the Baltic states but before they were formally absorbed into the Soviet Union.) On 17 August 1940, it was redesignated as the Baltic Special Military District – immediately after the German invasion it became the Northwest Front.

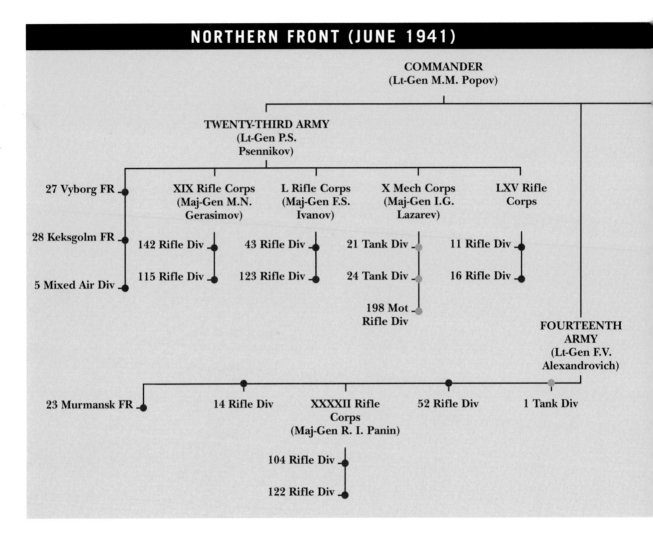

NORTHERN FRONT (JUNE 1941)

COMMANDER
(Lt-Gen M.M. Popov)

TWENTY-THIRD ARMY
(Lt-Gen P.S. Psennikov)

27 Vyborg FR

XIX Rifle Corps
(Maj-Gen M.N. Gerasimov)

L Rifle Corps
(Maj-Gen F.S. Ivanov)

X Mech Corps
(Maj-Gen I.G. Lazarev)

LXV Rifle Corps

28 Keksgolm FR

142 Rifle Div

43 Rifle Div

21 Tank Div

11 Rifle Div

115 Rifle Div

123 Rifle Div

24 Tank Div

16 Rifle Div

5 Mixed Air Div

198 Mot Rifle Div

FOURTEENTH ARMY
(Lt-Gen F.V. Alexandrovich)

23 Murmansk FR

14 Rifle Div

XXXXII Rifle Corps
(Maj-Gen R. I. Panin)

52 Rifle Div

1 Tank Div

104 Rifle Div

122 Rifle Div

mine was responsible and halted the column, giving Kolobanov the chance to destroy the second tank. Only then did the Germans realize that they were under attack, but they failed to find the source and began firing blindly. At this point, Kolobanov knocked out the rear tank, trapping the entire column. Kolobanov's tank was subjected to heavy fire, but German tanks moving off the road bogged down in the swampy ground and became easy targets. A total of 22 German tanks plus two towed artillery pieces fell victim to Kolobanov's KV before it ran out of ammunition. He then called up another KV-1, and 21 more German tanks were destroyed before the half-hour battle ended. After the

battle, Kolobanov's crew counted 135 hits on their tank, none of which had penetrated the KV-1's armour.

Even the short (L/30.5) 76.2mm (3in) gun of the early T-34s and KV-1s could deal with contemporary Panzer IIIs and IVs but was soon replaced by a 76.2mm (3in) L/41.2 with improved armour-piercing capability. All the skill and courage of such small Soviet armoured detachments could do little more than harass Army Group North's advance. By mid-July, the Northwest Front had sustained 75,000 casualties, besides losing 2500 AFVs, 3600 guns and at least 1000 aircraft. In little more than 10 weeks, Lithuania, Latvia and Estonia were overrun and German artillery was shelling Leningrad.

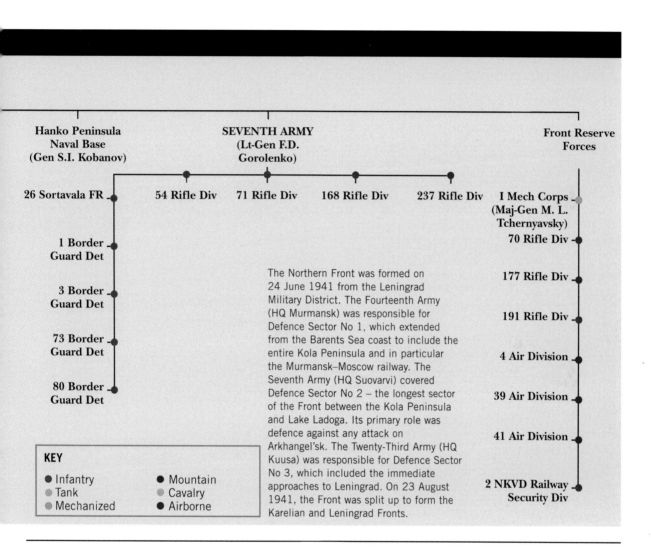

Hanko Peninsula Naval Base (Gen S.I. Kobanov)

SEVENTH ARMY (Lt-Gen F.D. Gorolenko)

Front Reserve Forces

26 Sortavala FR

54 Rifle Div   71 Rifle Div   168 Rifle Div   237 Rifle Div

I Mech Corps (Maj-Gen M. L. Tchernyavsky)

1 Border Guard Det

70 Rifle Div

3 Border Guard Det

177 Rifle Div

73 Border Guard Det

191 Rifle Div

80 Border Guard Det

4 Air Division

39 Air Division

41 Air Division

2 NKVD Railway Security Div

The Northern Front was formed on 24 June 1941 from the Leningrad Military District. The Fourteenth Army (HQ Murmansk) was responsible for Defence Sector No 1, which extended from the Barents Sea coast to include the entire Kola Peninsula and in particular the Murmansk–Moscow railway. The Seventh Army (HQ Suovarvi) covered Defence Sector No 2 – the longest sector of the Front between the Kola Peninsula and Lake Ladoga. Its primary role was defence against any attack on Arkhangel'sk. The Twenty-Third Army (HQ Kuusa) was responsible for Defence Sector No 3, which included the immediate approaches to Leningrad. On 23 August 1941, the Front was split up to form the Karelian and Leningrad Fronts.

KEY

- Infantry
- Tank
- Mechanized
- Mountain
- Cavalry
- Airborne

Siege of Leningrad

As Army Group North's artillery began shelling Leningrad on 1 September, it seemed as though there was little prospect of the city holding out for very long. However, against all probability, the siege was to drag on until the end of January 1944.

Whilst the Germans closed in on Leningrad from the south, Finnish forces were advancing across Karelia. These moves threatened to overwhelm the Leningrad Front, which was starting to suffer severe supply problems. The 250,000 defenders were supported by the 338 guns of the Baltic Fleet and its shore batteries (including the 305mm/12in guns of the battleships *Marat* and *Oktyabrskaya Revolutsia*), for which elaborate

MOUNTAIN INFANTRY DIVISION, PERSONNEL (AUG 1941)					
Unit	Officers	Political Officers	Warrant Officers	NCOs	Other Ranks
Divisional HQ	80			18	72
Signal Battalion					
Btn HQ & Coy	10	4	6	19	76
Radio Company	4	1	–	9	26
Wire/Optical Coy	7	1	–	17	109
Battalion Trains	–	–	5	13	35
Mounted Recon Sqd	7	1	3	21	158
4 x Mtn Inf Rgts	79	16	37	266	1588
Mtn Artillery Rgt					
Rgtl HQ & Trains	14	5	25	43	2
2 x Art Btns, each	22	3	3	69	395
Supply Column	3	1	1	11	99
Howitzer Regiment					
Rgtl HQ & Trains	17	5	26	33	113
2 x How Btns, each	12	1	3	33	213
Supply Column	4	1	–	11	69
Anti-Tank Battery	6	1	4	18	88
Anti-Aircraft Btn					
Btn HQ & Trains	5	3	10	26	40
2 x AA Batts, each	5	1	–	10	54
AAMG Coy	5	1	–	15	70
Ammunition Ptn	1	–	–	2	3
Pioneer Battalion					
Btn HQ & Trains	4	3	8	14	31
Signal Platoon	1	–	–	5	7
Technical Platoon	1	–	1	4	26
2 x Pion Coys, each	4	1	–	15	98
Machinery Coy	4	1	–	14	73
Special Platoon	1	–	1	2	20
Division Services					
Motor Trans Coy	4	1	4	17	64
Ammo Supply Btn	11	5	9	50	221
Medical Battalion	2	3	45	51	192
Bakery			9	16	119
NKVD Rifle Platoon			1	3	32
Maint Workshop			8	18	20
Other Trains			20	11	40

CADET RIFLE BRIGADE, PERSONNEL (OCT 1941)					
Unit	Officers	Political Officers	Warrant Officers	NCOs	Other Ranks
Brigade HQ	20	10	21	21	59
Signal Battalion	14	3	5	28	96
Reconnaissance Coy	4	1	–	9	37
3 x Inf Btns, each	32	8	9	93	620
Mortar Battalion	19	6	6	109	232
Heavy Mortar Btn	11	3	4	26	103
Artillery Battalion	23	6	8	66	254
Anti-Tank Battalion	15	4	4	37	97
Anti-Tank Rifle Coy	6	1	1	38	96
Sub MG Company	5	1	–	20	72
Pioneer Company	5	1	2	18	94
Motor Transport Coy	5	1	7	20	60
Medical Company	–	1	17	10	35

fire plans were prepared, as indicated by the following extracts of an order from Marshal Kliment Voroshilov:

'Since the current naval assets, employed in the defence of Leningrad and Kronstadt, are not sufficiently co-ordinated, and in order to employ all available resources of the Red Banner Baltic Fleet directly for the defence of the city, I hereby order:

1. Concerning naval vessels.
… All armoured vessels and a proportion of the available destroyers should be used to reinforce the artillery positions defending the Leningrad Fortified Area; the following must be therefore deployed:
Battleships: "Marat" and "Oktyabrskaya Revolutsia"
Cruisers: "Kirov", "Maxim Gorky" and "Petropavlovsk"
Destroyers: "Opytnyj", "Strogij" and "Strojnyj"
If necessary, the artillery defence of Leningrad will be reinforced by additional destroyers and gunboats …

3. Organisation of the naval artillery command.
All naval guns, railway artillery and stationary artillery (except that transferred to the Red Army), will be brought together under the command of the chief artillery officer of Leningrad naval defence, who will be responsible for the formation, training and supply of the artillery batteries and for the organisation of communication networks between batteries, naval vessels, Fortified Areas and Red Army units. The artillery commanders of the Fortified Areas shall have the right to call for artillery support and to allocate the targets …'

5. …Henceforth all future excess manpower resources of the Fleet should be employed for:

a) Reinforcement of the 5 naval infantry brigades.

b) Formation of special assault marine battalions for rifle divisions.'

By 10 September, the situation in Leningrad was so critical that Stalin sent Zhukov to take over command from Marshal Voroshilov, who himself had only been in post for a matter of days. In typical fashion, Zhukov ordered a series of counterattacks and imposed ferocious discipline.

On 17 September, he issued an order for the defence of the southern sector of the city, which included the warning that '…all commanders, political workers and soldiers who abandon the indicated line without a written order from the Front or Army Military Council will be shot immediately.'

Fortunately for the defenders of Leningrad, the Finnish forces were ordered not to advance beyond Finland's 1939 borders, but they remained a potent threat, drawing off forces that could have been deployed against Army Group North. However, Zhukov's energetic defence allowed the front line around the city to be stabilized and gave time for its arms factories to re-equip the garrison.

In the 83 days (10 July–30 September) of what was officially the 'Leningrad Strategic Defence Operation', Soviet casualties had been horrendous – the Red Army's 517,000 men had suffered over 214,000 'irrecoverable losses' (dead or prisoners) plus at least 130,000 sick and wounded.

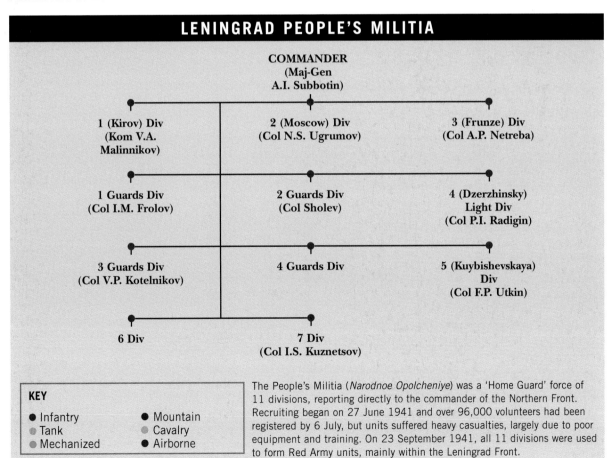

LENINGRAD PEOPLE'S MILITIA

COMMANDER
(Maj-Gen A.I. Subbotin)

1 (Kirov) Div (Kom V.A. Malinnikov)

2 (Moscow) Div (Col N.S. Ugrumov)

3 (Frunze) Div (Col A.P. Netreba)

1 Guards Div (Col I.M. Frolov)

2 Guards Div (Col Sholev)

4 (Dzerzhinsky) Light Div (Col P.I. Radigin)

3 Guards Div (Col V.P. Kotelnikov)

4 Guards Div

5 (Kuybishevskaya) Div (Col F.P. Utkin)

6 Div

7 Div (Col I.S. Kuznetsov)

KEY
- Infantry
- Tank
- Mechanized
- Mountain
- Cavalry
- Airborne

The People's Militia (*Narodnoe Opolcheniye*) was a 'Home Guard' force of 11 divisions, reporting directly to the commander of the Northern Front. Recruiting began on 27 June 1941 and over 96,000 volunteers had been registered by 6 July, but units suffered heavy casualties, largely due to poor equipment and training. On 23 September 1941, all 11 divisions were used to form Red Army units, mainly within the Leningrad Front.

SIEGE OF LENINGRAD

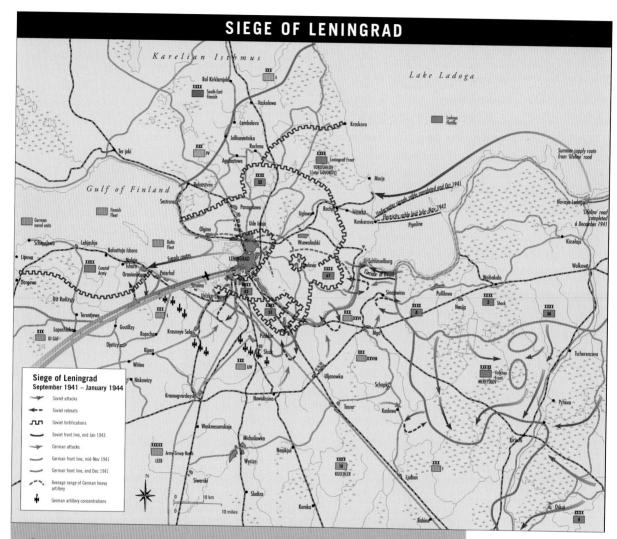

Siege of Leningrad
September 1941 – January 1944

- ➤ Soviet attacks
- ◄ Soviet retreats
- ⌐⌐ Soviet fortifications
- ━ Soviet front line, end Jan 1943
- ➤ German attacks
- ━ German front line, mid-Nov 1941
- ━ German front line, end Dec 1941
- ⌐⌐ Average range of German heavy artillery
- ✚ German artillery concentrations

September 1941 – January 1944

Leningrad was protected by substantial fortifications – from the first days of the war, almost 1 million of its 3.4 million inhabitants were put to work on the construction of field defences. By September 1941, these comprised:

- 190km (119 miles) of timber barricades
- 635km (397 miles) of wire entanglements
- 700km (438 miles) of anti-tank ditches
- 5000 earth-and-timber emplacements and reinforced concrete weapons emplacements
- 2500km (1563 miles) of trenches.

Despite constant artillery and air bombardment, Leningrad's arms factories continued production. Between July and December 1941, they produced over 1100 AFVs, 10,000 mortars and 3 million shells – significant quantities of mortars and ammunition were even flown out for the defence of Moscow.

Movement of Soviet Industry

The Axis advance rapidly threatened the tank and armaments factories that were concentrated around Kharkov and Leningrad. Fortunately for the Red Army, pre-war industrialization of the Urals and Central Asia had provided a measure of reserve capacity well beyond the reach of the invading German forces.

The trains that brought troops to the front were used to evacuate key factories to safe areas such as the Urals, Siberia and Kazakhstan, far from the front lines. Such evacuations often had to be carried out at breakneck speed – the Zaporozhstal' steelworks in the Ukraine was stripped bare in 19 days (19 August–5 September),

during which time 16,000 railway wagons were loaded with vital machinery, including the especially valuable rolling-mill equipment.

The massive evacuation programme put some 300 armaments factories temporarily out of production, but draconian measures quickly restored output.

TANK BATTALION (DECEMBER 1941)

The massive losses suffered by the Red Army during 1941 forced a steady reduction in the size of its armoured formations. By December 1941, they had shrunk to small tank brigades, each comprising two of the illustrated tank battalions and a small motorized infantry battalion. Whilst these small formations were much easier to control than the earlier tank divisions, the dire shortage of tank radio equipment robbed them of much of their potential tactical flexibility.

Light Tank Company (8 x T-60)

Medium Tank Company (10 x T-34)

Heavy Tank Company (5 x KV-1)

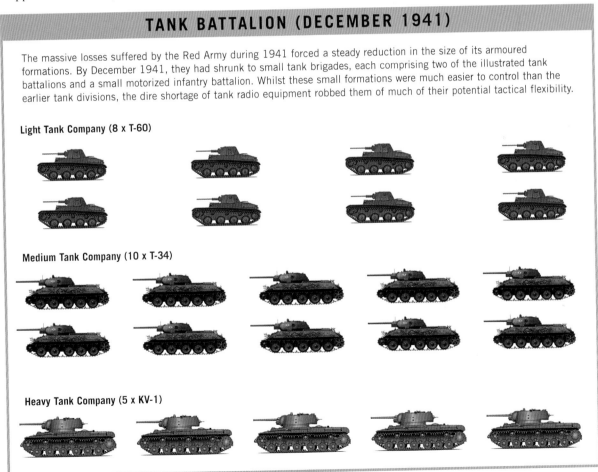

SEMYON MIKHAILOVICH BUDENNY (1883–1973)

Born into a peasant family, Budenny was conscripted into the army, serving in the Russo–Japanese War and World War I. He joined the Bolsheviks in 1918 and rose to command the First Cavalry Army, striking up a friendship with Stalin, one of its commissars.

• In 1935, Budenny was promoted to become one of the first five Marshals of the Soviet Union, two years later being appointed commander of the Moscow Military District.

• On 23 June 1941, he became a member of *Stavka*. The following month he was appointed Commander-in-Chief, Southwest Strategic Direction, responsible for the operations of the Southwest and Southern Fronts, but in September was replaced by Timoshenko and transferred to command the Reserve Front.

• From April to May 1942, Budenny was Commander-in-Chief, North Caucasian Strategic Direction, before taking up his final operational role as Commander, North Caucasian Front. In 1943, he was appointed to the largely honorary post of Commander-in-Chief, Soviet cavalry.

Lavrenti Beria, head of the NKVD, was appointed to the State Defence Committee (GKO) with responsibility for armaments production, and ruthlessly used the millions of prisoners in the Gulag as slave labour.

R&D

In addition to running the Gulag, the NKVD played a key role in Soviet scientific and arms development. Many researchers and engineers who had been convicted for political crimes were held in privileged prisons (which were much more comfortable than the Gulag and colloquially known as *sharashkas*), where they continued their work under close NKVD supervision. After their release, some went on to become world leaders in science and technology, notably the aircraft designer Andrei Tupolev. (Incidentally, the very ruthlessness of the NKVD's supervision of war industries was in some respects counter-productive. Factory managers were all too often set totally unrealistic productivity targets, which led to widespread faking of production statistics, a practice that was to remain endemic throughout the Soviet era.)

Disaster at Kiev

Operation Barbarossa's most demanding tasks were assigned to Field Marshal Gerd von Rundstedt's Army Group South. He had only Kleist's *Panzergruppe* I to provide the armoured punch for a motley collection of forces, including ill-equipped Rumanian, Hungarian and Italian formations.

These faced General M.P. Kirponos' Southwest Front, the best-equipped Soviet Front, which included:

• IV Mechanized Corps – 979 AFVs (including 460 T-34s and KVs)
• VIII Mechanized Corps – 899 AFVs (including 170 T-34s and KVs)
• IX Mechanized Corps – 316 AFVs (all of them older models)
• XV Mechanized Corps – 749 AFVs (including 133 T-34s and KVs)
• XVI Mechanized Corps – 478 AFVs
• XIX Mechanized Corps – 453 AFVs
• XXII Mechanized Corps – 712 AFVs (including 31 KV-2s)
• XXIV Mechanized Corps – 222 AFVs.

SOVIET INDUSTRY

Dispersion of Soviet Industry

——	1941 boundary of USSR
——	German front line 1941–42
-·-·-	Strategic railways
——	Added railways 1941–45
▨	Unoccupied USSR
▨	Under Allied control or influence
▨	Neutral

667 factories to Urals

322 factories to Siberia

308 factories to Central Asia

226 factories to Caucasus

Dispersion of Soviet industry

That the Soviets ultimately achieved victory owed much to the ability of Stalin's war industries to outperform their German counterparts, despite the crippling effect of the mass evacuation of factories from western Russia in the autumn of 1941. An estimated 10–12 million workers were moved. The Soviet performance was even more remarkable considering the loss of natural resources in the territories overrun by Axis forces – coal production dropped from over 151 million tonnes (149 million tons) in 1941 to 75.5 million tonnes (74 million tons) in 1942, whilst steel output fell from 17.9 million tonnes (17.6 million tons) to 8.1 million tonnes (7.9 million tons). Despite the difficulties, between 1941 and 1942, Soviet tank production rose from 6274 to 24,639, dwarfing the German increase from 3256 to 4278 in the same period. This achievement was largely due to the concentration on designs such as the T-34, which were simple but highly effective and suited to mass production in often primitive conditions – as Stalin commented, 'Quantity has a quality of its own.'

The initial Soviet response to the German invasion was to activate the Zhukov pre-emptive strike plan. All eight mechanized corps were to destroy *Panzergruppe* I before launching an offensive across the frontier into German-occupied Poland to seize Lublin. Unfortunately for Kirponos, some of his forces had to cover 400km (250 miles) to intercept Kleist, a recipe for disaster given *Luftwaffe* air superiority. Even worse, most of the mechanized corps were far from being fully trained and equipped formations. At the time, the future Marshal Konstantin Rokossovsky commanded IX Mechanized Corps. In his memoirs, he recalled:

'Up to the beginning of the war our corps was up to half of its establishment for personnel, but had not received basic equipment: tanks and motor transport. Here, the stocks were no more than 30% of the authorised strength ... Put simply, the corps was unready for military operation as a mechanised unit in any form. There was no way that the Kiev Special Military District ... headquarters and the General Staff didn't know this.'

Kirponos initially planned to halt *Panzergruppe* I with flank attacks by six mechanized corps – a total of 3700 tanks. The concentration of the corps was chaotic and air attacks and breakdowns took a steady toll long before they encountered Kleist's Panzers. The Soviet formations were committed to action piecemeal and suffered accordingly. On 26 June, the counterattack finally was

made in the Brody-Dubno area. Elements of VIII, IX, XV and XIX Mechanized Corps were sent against Kleist's flanks, with the aim of cutting the *Panzergruppe* in two. Although 16th Panzer Division took significant casualties and the *Panzergruppe*'s advance was delayed for several days, by the beginning of July all four mechanized corps had been comprehensively defeated. Southwest Front had sustained over 173,000 casualties, besides losing an estimated 4381 tanks and 1218 aircraft.

As Army Group Centre's advance approached Smolensk in mid-July, Hitler became increasingly concerned at the potential threat posed by the still substantial Soviet forces to the south. By late August, he was convinced that Army Group South needed substantial reinforcement to eliminate this threat and ordered Guderian's *Panzergruppe* II into the Ukraine. Guderian made rapid progress, linking up with Kleist on 16 September and trapping the Southwest Front in the vast Kiev pocket, which finally surrendered 10 days later.

The Battle for Moscow

Victory at Kiev removed the potential Soviet threat to Army Group Centre's right flank and opened the way for a renewed drive on Moscow.

As it became clear that the Kiev pocket was doomed, Hitler ordered that Leningrad was not to be stormed but blockaded and starved into surrender in order to free resources for a renewed attack on Moscow. To give

the new offensive a reasonable chance of success before it became bogged down by the autumn rains, both Army Group North and Army Group South had to be stripped of most of their Panzer units. Guderian's command was redesignated Second Panzer Army and launched the

WESTERN FRONT, AFV STRENGTH (1 OCTOBER 1941)						
Unit	KV	T-34	BT	T-26	T-37	Total
107th MRD	3	23	1	92	6	125
101st MRD	3	9	5	52	–	69
126th Tank Bde	1	–	19	41	–	61
127th Tank Bde	5	–	14	37	–	56
128th Tank Bde	7	1	39	14	–	61
143rd Tank Bde	–	9	–	44	–	53
147th Tank Bde	–	9	23	18	–	50
Total	19	51	101	298	6	475

BRYANSK FRONT, AFV STRENGTH (27 SEPT 1941)						
Unit	KV	T-34	BT	T-26	T-40	T-50	Total
108th Tank Div	3	17	1	–	20	–	41
42nd Tank Bde	7	22	–	–	32	–	61
121st Tank Bde	6	18	–	46	–	–	70
141st Tank Bde	6	10	22	–	–	–	38
150th Tank Bde	–	12	–	–	–	8	20
113th Separate Tank Btn	–	4	–	11	–	–	15
Total	22	83	23	57	52	8	245

drive on Moscow (codenamed Operation Typhoon) on 30 September whilst the other two *Panzergruppen* began their attacks two days later.

Both sides were now feeling the effects of three months of fierce combat – the Red Army's massive losses had forced the disbandment of the mechanized corps as early as mid-July, and in August most of the surviving armour was concentrated in tank brigades, each with a nominal strength of 93 tanks in a single tank regiment plus a motor rifle battalion. The tank regiment had a heavy company of KVs, a company of T-34s and a third company equipped with whichever light tanks were available. By September, combat casualties had forced a reduction in the paper strength of these units to 67 tanks, although very few had even that many.

German impetus

On the other side of the lines, the Panzer divisions were in better shape, but their tanks and other vehicles were in need of major overhauls after covering thousands of kilometres across country or over appalling dirt roads. The infantry divisions (which had virtually no motor vehicles) were exhausted by the epic marches needed to keep up with the rapidly advancing Panzers, but all were buoyed up by the sheer scale of their victories and the thought that Moscow was now within reach.

The *Panzergruppen* quickly broke through the Soviet lines and by 9 October had pulled off two more major encirclements, one between Smolensk and Vyazma and the other around Bryansk. These netted a total of 657,000 prisoners, 1241 AFVs plus 5396 guns, and effectively opened the road to Moscow. As early as 6 October, a new factor began to help the Red Army's defence of the capital, when the first snows fell. At first, these melted rapidly, turning the roads to thick, clinging mud that slowed the momentum of the German advance and increased the already alarming rate of breakdowns. (Hard-pressed *Luftwaffe* transport units were diverted to drop tow ropes to supply columns floundering along mud-clogged roads.)

Despite this, by 14 October Hoth's *Panzergruppe* IV had captured Kalinin, cutting the Moscow–Leningrad highway and the main north–south railway. This sparked off a temporary panic in the capital, and it was lucky for Stalin that the German airborne forces were unable to

DEFENCE OF MOSCOW, AFV UNITS (16 OCTOBER 1941)				
Unit	KV	T-34	T-26/BT/T-40	Total
TWENTY-NINTH ARMY				
Separate Mot Rifle Bde	–	12	20	32
THIRTIETH ARMY				
8th Tank Bde	–	29	32	61
21st Tank Bde	–	29	32	61
SIXTEENTH ARMY				
22nd Tank Bde	–	29	32	61
4th Tank Bde	3	7	23	33
FIFTH ARMY				
18th Tank Bde	3	11	15	29
19th Tank Bde	–	12	12	24
20th Tank Bde	–	29	32	61
THIRTY-THIRD ARMY				
17th Tank Bde	–	20	16	36
151st Mot Rifle Bde	–	12	20	32
FORTY-THIRD ARMY				
9th Tank Bde	–	18	33	51
152nd Mot Rifle Bde	–	12	20	32
FIFTIETH ARMY				
108th Tank Bde	3	7	23	33
TWENTY-SIXTH ARMY				
11th Tank Bde	4	12	10	26
Total	13	239	320	572

exploit the situation after their heavy losses in the assault on Crete. By mid-November, sharp frosts had frozen the thick mud and restored the Panzers' mobility, which allowed a renewed drive on Moscow.

Typhoon fails

During the next two weeks, the Germans came tantalizingly close to taking the city – *Panzergruppen* III and IV swung north of Moscow, breaching the Volga Canal defence line on 28 November, whilst away to the south, Guderian's Second Panzer Army had taken Stalinogorsk and cut the capital's main railway link with the south. By 4 December, leading German units were within 45km (28 miles) of Moscow when plummeting

WESTERN FRONT/BRYANSK FRONT (OCTOBER 1941)

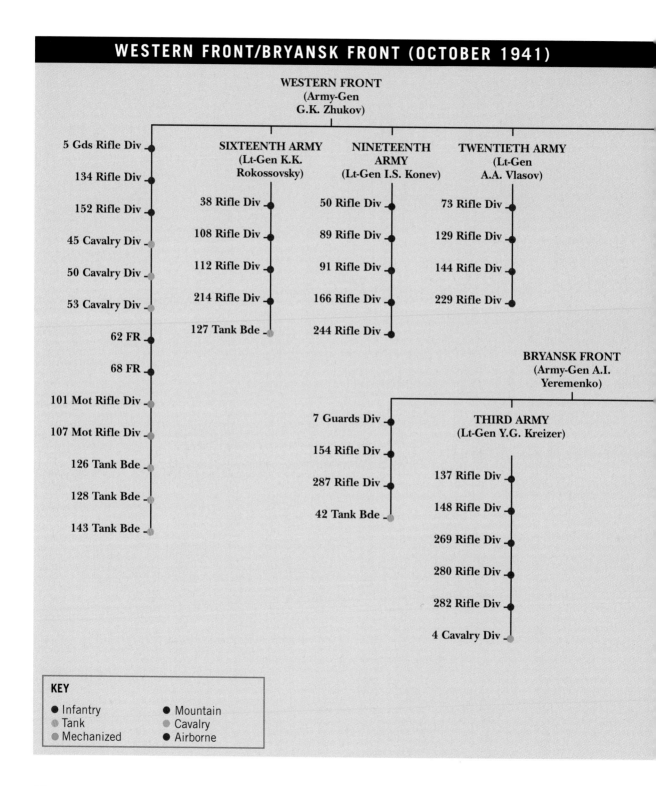

WESTERN FRONT
(Army-Gen
G.K. Zhukov)

5 Gds Rifle Div

134 Rifle Div

152 Rifle Div

45 Cavalry Div

50 Cavalry Div

53 Cavalry Div

62 FR

68 FR

101 Mot Rifle Div

107 Mot Rifle Div

126 Tank Bde

128 Tank Bde

143 Tank Bde

SIXTEENTH ARMY
(Lt-Gen K.K.
Rokossovsky)

38 Rifle Div

108 Rifle Div

112 Rifle Div

214 Rifle Div

127 Tank Bde

**NINETEENTH
ARMY**
(Lt-Gen I.S. Konev)

50 Rifle Div

89 Rifle Div

91 Rifle Div

166 Rifle Div

244 Rifle Div

TWENTIETH ARMY
(Lt-Gen
A.A. Vlasov)

73 Rifle Div

129 Rifle Div

144 Rifle Div

229 Rifle Div

BRYANSK FRONT
(Army-Gen A.I.
Yeremenko)

7 Guards Div

154 Rifle Div

287 Rifle Div

42 Tank Bde

THIRD ARMY
(Lt-Gen Y.G. Kreizer)

137 Rifle Div

148 Rifle Div

269 Rifle Div

280 Rifle Div

282 Rifle Div

4 Cavalry Div

KEY

- Infantry
- Tank
- Mechanized
- Mountain
- Cavalry
- Airborne

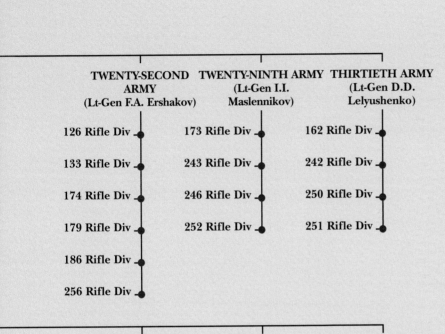

TWENTY-SECOND ARMY
(Lt-Gen F.A. Ershakov)

126 Rifle Div

133 Rifle Div

174 Rifle Div

179 Rifle Div

186 Rifle Div

256 Rifle Div

TWENTY-NINTH ARMY
(Lt-Gen I.I. Maslennikov)

173 Rifle Div

243 Rifle Div

246 Rifle Div

252 Rifle Div

THIRTIETH ARMY
(Lt-Gen D.D. Lelyushenko)

162 Rifle Div

242 Rifle Div

250 Rifle Div

251 Rifle Div

The Western Front had borne much of the effort of contesting the advance of Army Group Centre since the opening of Operation Barbarossa. By late September 1941, it had suffered heavy casualties and lost most of its armoured formations. The Front suffered a further disaster on 7 October, when *Panzergruppen* III and IV linked up to form the Vyazma pocket, trapping the Sixteenth, Nineteenth and Twentieth Armies.

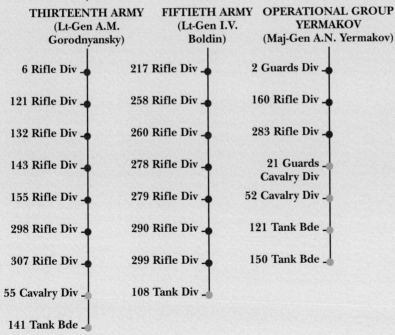

THIRTEENTH ARMY
(Lt-Gen A.M. Gorodnyansky)

6 Rifle Div

121 Rifle Div

132 Rifle Div

143 Rifle Div

155 Rifle Div

298 Rifle Div

307 Rifle Div

55 Cavalry Div

141 Tank Bde

FIFTIETH ARMY
(Lt-Gen I.V. Boldin)

217 Rifle Div

258 Rifle Div

260 Rifle Div

278 Rifle Div

279 Rifle Div

290 Rifle Div

299 Rifle Div

108 Tank Div

OPERATIONAL GROUP YERMAKOV
(Maj-Gen A.N. Yermakov)

2 Guards Div

160 Rifle Div

283 Rifle Div

21 Guards Cavalry Div

52 Cavalry Div

121 Tank Bde

150 Tank Bde

The Bryansk Front was formed in August 1941, initially with the Thirteenth and Fiftieth Armies, totalling 16 rifle divisions, three cavalry divisions and one tank division, many of which had suffered heavy losses in earlier fighting. Although it steadily received reinforcements, these were often battered formations with limited combat value. Urged on by Stalin, the Front launched a series of costly and unsuccessful counterattacks against the left flank of *Panzergruppe* II as it moved to seal off the Kiev pocket in September. As a result, the Front was seriously weakened – Third and Fiftieth Armies were barely able to fight their way clear of Bryansk when Guderian's Panzers took the city and the Front HQ on 6 October. (Yeremenko and his key staff officers were only just able to escape in time.)

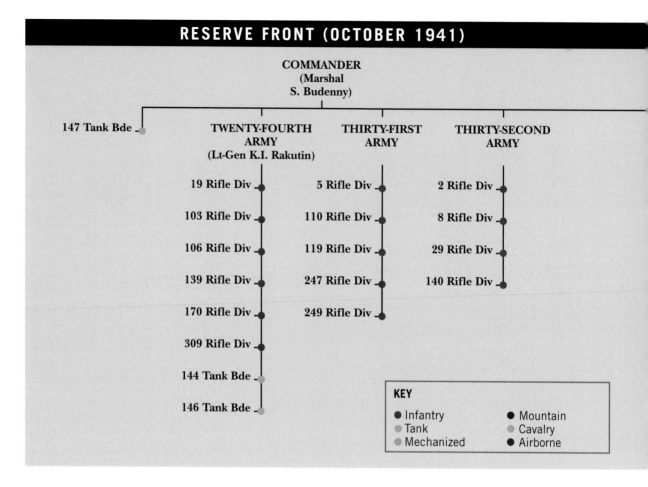

RESERVE FRONT (OCTOBER 1941)

COMMANDER
(Marshal
S. Budenny)

147 Tank Bde

TWENTY-FOURTH ARMY
(Lt-Gen K.I. Rakutin)

THIRTY-FIRST ARMY

THIRTY-SECOND ARMY

TWENTY-FOURTH ARMY	THIRTY-FIRST ARMY	THIRTY-SECOND ARMY
19 Rifle Div	5 Rifle Div	2 Rifle Div
103 Rifle Div	110 Rifle Div	8 Rifle Div
106 Rifle Div	119 Rifle Div	29 Rifle Div
139 Rifle Div	247 Rifle Div	140 Rifle Div
170 Rifle Div	249 Rifle Div	
309 Rifle Div		
144 Tank Bde		
146 Tank Bde		

KEY

- Infantry
- Tank
- Mechanized
- Mountain
- Cavalry
- Airborne

temperatures finally brought the advance to a halt. It was so cold that guns could not be fired because oiled parts froze solid and fires had to be lit under vehicles at night to prevent their engines freezing. Very few German units had proper winter clothing, and cases of severe frostbite soared, rapidly exceeding the number of battlefield casualties.

Soviets fare better

Red Army equipment was far less severely affected by the intense cold and deep snow – the T-34 was fitted with a compressed-air starting system that could operate even in the temperatures of -28°C (-18°F) which were not uncommon that winter. The wide tracks of the KV-1 and T-34 resulted in low ground pressure, which allowed them to operate far more easily in deep snow than

German AFVs, which had narrower tracks and exerted higher ground pressure.

The overall losses on both sides were staggering and will probably never be known for certain, but the German casualties may well have totalled 800,000 men plus 2300 AFVs. These figures were dwarfed by the enormous Soviet losses, which included roughly three million prisoners, 20,000 AFVs and 25,000 guns.

Operation Barbarossa had only just failed, but that failure had a major impact on the course of the entire war, for Germany was now trapped into fighting a war on several fronts. The situation was worsened by Hitler, who on hearing of the Japanese attack on Pearl Harbor chose to declare war on the United States, adding its enormous potential strength to his existing enemies. It was going to be a long war.

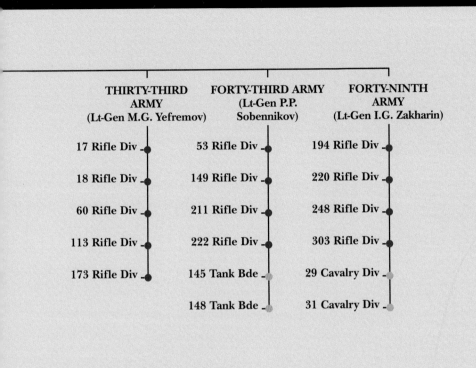

THIRTY-THIRD ARMY (Lt-Gen M.G. Yefremov)	FORTY-THIRD ARMY (Lt-Gen P.P. Sobennikov)	FORTY-NINTH ARMY (Lt-Gen I.G. Zakharin)
17 Rifle Div	53 Rifle Div	194 Rifle Div
18 Rifle Div	149 Rifle Div	220 Rifle Div
60 Rifle Div	211 Rifle Div	248 Rifle Div
113 Rifle Div	222 Rifle Div	303 Rifle Div
173 Rifle Div	145 Tank Bde	29 Cavalry Div
	148 Tank Bde	31 Cavalry Div

The Reserve Front was formed in July 1941 under Zhukov's command to receive and organize the reserve armies assembling behind the Western Front. Budenny took over command in September, only to lose Twenty-Fourth Army and elements of Thirty-Second Army in the Vyazma pocket on 7 October. Later that month, the Front was disbanded and its surviving units absorbed into the Western Front.

From Soviet General Staff to *Stavka*

The first RKKA (Red Army) Staff was formed in 1921 to administer the peacetime army as it shrank from the 5.5 million-strong force of the Russo–Polish War to barely 530,000 men by the mid-1920s. The staff expanded on an ad hoc basis, taking on responsibility for defence policy, administration and training, but lacked any clearly defined structure until Mikhail Frunze was appointed as Chief of Staff by Order No 78 of 1 April 1924.

Frunze's drive and determination ensured that the RKKA Staff was properly organized for the first time, and in January 1925, he was also appointed as Chairman of the Revolutionary Military Council, effectively the commander-in-chief of all Soviet forces. Stalin regarded him as a dangerous rival and it is highly likely that he

engineered Frunze's death in a botched stomach operation on 31 October 1925.

On 22 September 1935, the RKKA Staff was retitled the General Staff, and the professionalism of the Tsarist Imperial General Staff was allowed to revive. The vicious Purges of the late 1930s destroyed many of the most enthusiastic proponents of modernization in the Red Army, including Marshal Tukhachevsky, who was executed in 1937, and brought to the fore a dangerously large number of incompetent 'party hacks', whose sole qualification was unquestioning loyalty to Stalin. Among these was Marshal Kulik, who was appointed head of the Red Army's Main Artillery Directorate, and the sinister Lev Mekhlis, who became the chief of the PURKKA, the Political Administration of the Red Army. Fortunately, some able individuals managed to survive, including the sophisticated Boris Shaposhnikov, an ex-Tsarist colonel who surprisingly managed to hold the post of Chief of the General Staff from 1937 to 1940.

The German invasion led to the establishment on 23 June 1941 of a Soviet version of the Tsarist *Stavka* (Imperial GHQ). The new *Stavka*, officially the headquarters of the Main Command of the Armed Forces of the Union of SSRs (*Stavka Glavnogo Komandovaniya*), was authorized by a top secret decree signed by Stalin in his capacity as both the head of government and the leader of the Communist Party of the Soviet Union. The decree appointed the Defence Commissar (Minister), Marshal Timoshenko, as *Stavka*'s president. The official membership comprised:

• Stalin
• General Zhukov (Chief of the General Staff)
• Marshal Voroshilov
• Marshal Budenny (Deputy Defence Commissar)
• Admiral Nikolay Kuznetsov (Commissar of the Navy)
• Vyacheslav Molotov (Commissar of Foreign Affairs)

The decree also established a group of 'permanent councillors' at *Stavka*, comprising Marshal Kulik, Marshal Shaposhnikov, General Meretskov, Lieutenant-General Zhigarev (Chief of the Air Force Main Directorate), Lieutenant-General Nikolai Vatutin

(Chief of the General Staff's Operational Directorate), General Nikolai Voronov (Head of Main Air Defence Directorate), Beria (Commissar General of State Security), Mekhlis (head of PURKKA) and the 'political councillors' Mikoyan, Kaganovich, Voznesensky, Zhdanov and Malenkov.

Stavka virtually never met as a committee and its members were most frequently used by Stalin to report on key areas of the battlefront. On 10 July 1941, *Stavka*'s full title was changed to *Stavka* of the Supreme Command (*Stavka Verkhovnogo Komandovaniya*). The same day, Stalin created three new commands, the 'Strategic Directions' (*Strategicheskiye Napravleniya*), which were each directly responsible to *Stavka* for control of several fronts plus their associated air and naval forces. Voroshilov was appointed to command the Northwest Strategic Direction, comprising the Northern and Northwest Fronts plus the Baltic Fleet. Timoshenko headed the Western Strategic Direction, whilst Budenny commanded the Southwest Strategic Direction, which included the Southwest and Southern Fronts together with the Black Sea Fleet. (In practice, Stalin and *Stavka* retained close control of the Fronts; the Strategic Directions had little real power and were all abolished in less than a year.) On 8 August 1941, *Stavka*'s full title was altered yet again, becoming *Stavka* of the Supreme Main Command (*Stavka Verkhovnogo Glavnokomandovaniya*).

WESTERN FRONT, AFV TOTALS (NOVEMBER 1941)			
Unit	KV/T-34	T-26/BT/T-40	Total
THIRTIETH ARMY			
58th Tank Div	–	198	198
107th Mot Rifle Div	2	11	13
21st Tank Bde	5	15	20
8th Tank Bde	–	23	23
SIXTEENTH ARMY			
1st Guards Tank Bde	19	20	39
27th Tank Bde	11	10	21
28th Tank Bde	5	10	15
23rd Tank Bde	11	20	31
33rd Tank Bde	–	34	34
Total	53	341	394

September–December 1941

In early October, Hitler finally decided to concentrate all efforts on capturing Moscow before the onset of winter. Initially all went well for the new offensive, which trapped seven Soviet armies in encirclements at Bryansk and Vyazma. The total losses suffered by the Western, Bryansk and Reserve Fronts in these battles amounted to 64 rifle divisions, 11 tank brigades and 50 artillery regiments. As the extent of the disaster became apparent, frantic efforts were made for the defence of Moscow. By mid-October, the German advance sparked off a temporary panic in the capital as government departments were evacuated. However, Stalin himself stayed in the Kremlin and ensured that the NKVD restored order in their usual ruthless fashion. Although Army Group Centre fought its way to within 27km (17 miles) of the Kremlin by early December, fierce Soviet resistance and appalling winter weather prevented any further advance.

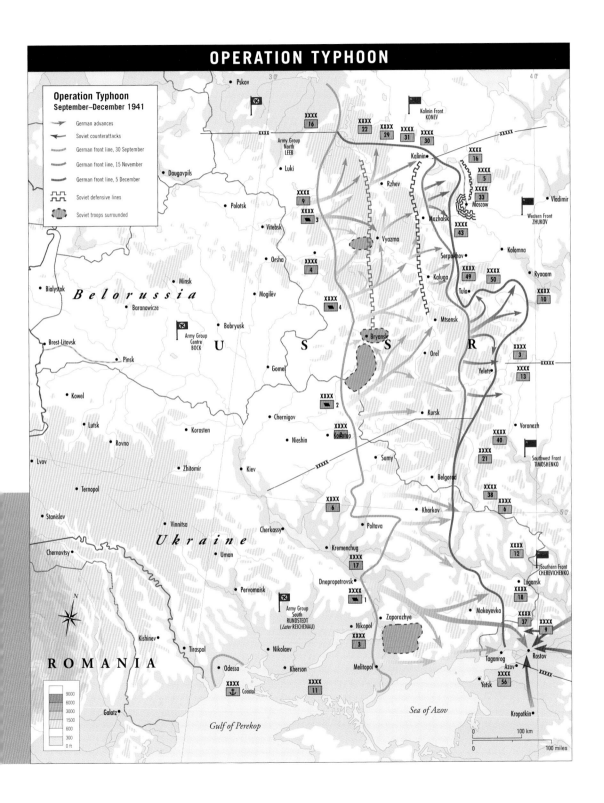

OPERATION TYPHOON

Operation Typhoon
September–December 1941

- German advances
- Soviet counterattacks
- German front line, 30 September
- German front line, 15 November
- German front line, 5 December
- Soviet defensive lines
- Soviet troops surrounded

FATE OF SOVIET TANK DIVISIONS (1941–42)					
Division	Commander	Tank Regiment	Assigned	Destruction	Site of Destruction
1 TD	Maj-Gen V.I. Baranov	1, 2	Independent	24 April 42	–
2 TD	Maj-Gen E.N. Solyankin	3, 4	III Mech Corps	12 July 41	Minsk
3 TD	Col K.Y. Andreev	5, 6	I Mech Corps	7 Dec 41	–
4 TD	Maj-Gen A.G. Potaturchev	7, 8	VI Mech Corps	4 July 41	Bialystok
5 TD	Col F.F. Fedorov	9, 10	III Mech Corps	27 June 41	Olita
6 TD	Col V.M. Alekseev	11, 12	XXVIII Mech Corps	24 July 41	–
7 TD	Maj-Gen S.V. Borzilov	13, 14	VI Mech Corps	17 July 41	Disna
8 TD	Col P.S. Fotchenkov	15, 16	IV Mech Corps	24 Sept 41	–
9 TD	Col V.G. Burkov	17, 18	XXVII Mech Corps	–	–
10 TD	Maj-Gen S.Y. Ogurtsov	19, 20	XV Mech Corps	23 Sept 41	–
11 TD	Col G.I. Kuzmin	21, 22	II Mech Corps	8 Sept 41	South Russia
12 TD	Maj-Gen T.A. Mishanin	23, 24	VIII Mech Corps	13 Sept 41	Dnepropetrovsk
13 TD	Col F.U. Grachev	25, 26	V Mech Corps	4 Aug 41	Smolensk
14 TD	Col I.D. Vasil'ev	27, 28	VII Mech Corps	5 Oct 41	–
15 TD	Col V.I. Polozkov	29, 30	XVI Mech Corps	8 Aug 41	Uman
16 TD	Col M.I. Myndro	31, 149	II Mech Corps	8 Aug 41	Uman
17 TD	Col I.P. Korchagin	33, 34	V Mech Corps	4 Aug 41	Smolensk
18 TD	Maj-Gen F.T. Remizov	35, 36	VII Mech Corps	20 Oct 41	Viazma
19 TD	Maj-Gen K.A. Semenchenko	37, 38	XXII Mech Corps	24 Sept 41	Kiev
20 TD	Col M.E. Katukov	39, 40	IX Mech Corps	29 Sept 41	Kiev
21 TD	Col L.V. Bunin	41, 42	X Mech Corps	4 April 42	–
22 TD	Maj-Gen V.P. Puganov	43, 44	XIV Mech Corps	5 July 41	Slutsk
23 TD	Col T.S. Orlenko	45, 144	XII Mech Corps	28 Sept 41	–
24 TD	Col M.I. Chesnokov	48, 49	X Mech Corps	9 Sept 41	Luga
25 TD	Col N.M. Nikiforov	50, 113	XIII Mech Corps	28 June 41	Bialystok
26 TD	Maj-Gen V.T. Obukhov	51, 52	XX Mech Corps	14 July 41	–
27 TD	Col A.O. Akhmanov	54, 140	XVII Mech Corps	–	–
28 TD	Col I.D. Chernyakhovskiy	55, 56	XII Mech Corps	3 Jan 42	–
29 TD	Col N.P. Studnev	57, 59	XI Mech Corps	6 July 41	Minsk
30 TD	Col S.I. Bogdanov	60, 61	XIV Mech Corps	3 July 41	–
31 TD	Col S.A. Kalikhovich	46, 148	XIII Mech Corps	5 July 41	Bialystok
32 TD	Col E.G. Pushkin	63, 64	IV Mech Corps	17 July 41	Volodorka
33 TD	Col M.F. Panov	65, 66	XI Mech Corps	–	–
34 TD	Col I.V. Vasil'ev	67, 68	VIII Mech Corps	30 June 41	Dubno
35 TD	Maj-Gen N.A. Novikov	69, 70	IX Mech Corps	24 Sept 41	Kiev
36 TD	Col S.Z. Miroshnikov	71, 72	XVII Mech Corps	–	–

FATE OF SOVIET TANK DIVISIONS (1941–42)					
Division	**Commander**	**Tank Regiment**	**Assigned**	**Destruction**	**Site of Destruction**
37 TD	Col F.G. Anikushkin	73, 74	XV Mech Corps	17 July 41	–
38 TD	Col S.I. Kapustin	75, 76	XX Mech Corps	15 July 41	–
39 TD	Col N.V. Starkov	77, 78	XVI Mech Corps	6 Aug 41	–
40 TD	Col M.V. Shirobokov	79, 80	XIX Mech Corps	29 Sept 41	Kiev
41 TD	Col P.P. Pavlov	82, 81	XXII Mech Corps	24 Sept 41	Kiev
42 TD	Col N.I. Voeikov	83, 84	XXI Mech Corps	18 Aug 41	–
43 TD	Col I.G. Tsibin	85, 86	XIX Mech Corps	29 Sept 41	Kiev
44 TD	Col V.P. Krimov	87, 88	XVIII Mech Corps	–	–
45 TD	Col M.D. Solomatin	89, 90	XXIV Mech Corps	8 Aug 41	Uman
46 TD	Col V.A. Koptsov	91, 92	XXI Mech Corps	2 Aug 41	Chola
47 TD	Col G.S. Rodin	93, 94	XVIII Mech Corps	24 Sept 41	Kiev
48 TD	Col D.Y. Yakovlev	95, 96	XXIII Mech Corps	26 Aug 41	Velikiye Luki
49 TD	Col K.F. Shvetsov	97, 98	XXIV Mech Corps	8 Aug 41	Uman
50 TD	Col B.S. Bakhorov	99, 100	XXV Mech Corps	7 Sept 41	–
51 TD	Col P.G. Chernov	101, 102	XXIII Mech Corps	13 Aug 41	–
52 TD	Col G.M. Mikhailov	104, 105	XXVI Mech Corps	–	–
53 TD	Col A.S. Beloglazov	106, 107	XXVII Mech Corps	–	–
54 TD	Col M.D. Sinenko	108, 109	XXVIII Mech Corps	–	–
55 TD	Col V.M. Badanov	110, 111	XXV Mech Corps	29 July 41	–
56 TD	Col I.D. Illarionov	112, 113	XXVI Mech Corps	–	–
57 TD	Col V.A. Mishulin	114, 115	Independent	4 Aug 41	–
58 TD	Maj-Gen A.A. Kotlyarov	116, 117	XXX Mech Corps	2 Dec 41	–
59 TD	Col S.P. Chernoba	118, 119	Independent	–	–
60 TD	Maj-Gen A.F. Popov	120, 121	XXX Mech Corps	10 Feb 42	–
61 TD	Col B.M. Skvortsov	141, 142	Independent	1946	disbanded, Far East
69 TD	–	–	Independent	20 Oct 41	Viazma
101 TD	–	202	Independent	20 Oct 41	Viazma
102 TD	–	204	Independent	20 Oct 41	Viazma
104 TD	–	208, 209	Independent	16 Aug 41	disbanded
105 TD	–	210, 211	Independent	4 Sept 41	disbanded
107 TD	–	–	Independent	20 Oct 41	Viazma
108 TD	–	216, 217	Independent	29 Nov 41	disbanded
109 TD	–	218, 219	Independent	1 Sept 41	disbanded
110 TD	–	220, 221	Independent	12 Sept 41	North Russia
111 TD	–	–	Independent	1946	disbanded, Far East
112 TD	–	–	Independent	6 Nov 42	disbanded

From Moscow to Stalingrad: 1942

The successful defence of Moscow bought time to rebuild the Red Army after the disasters of the opening stages of Operation Barbarossa, but its recovery was to be a long, hard process.

A T-34 Model 1941 photographed during the defence of Moscow in the winter of 1941/42. At the time, Field Marshal von Kleist described it as 'The finest tank in the world'.

On 3 July 1941, Stalin first called for partisan warfare against occupying forces, proclaiming that 'Conditions must be unbearable for the enemy and his collaborators; they must be pursued and annihilated wherever they are ...'

The partisan war

In July 1941, the rapidly deteriorating military situation led Stalin to authorize the formation of partisan groups in Soviet territory occupied by Axis forces. This was a measure of desperation, as he was highly suspicious of such autonomous armed groups and had used the Purges to destroy the pre-war partisan cadres.

The first irregular units were largely formed from Red Army stragglers and units cut off by the German advance, commanded by a mixture of regular and NKVD officers or local Communist party officials. A few were active from the first days of the German invasion, but were often short-lived groups since many regions (notably the Baltic states and the Ukraine) initially welcomed Axis forces as liberators. In these areas, many of the first ill-equipped and poorly organized partisan bands were quickly destroyed, but enough survived to form cadres for future expansion.

NKVD units

A further source of personnel were the destroyer battalions formed under NKVD command to combat spies and saboteurs behind Soviet lines – as their operating areas were overrun by German forces, they re-formed as partisan groups. In the Ukraine, a total of 118,000 'volunteers' formed 651 destroyer battalions between July and September 1941. These units were issued with a total of 96,000 rifles, 1150 submachine guns and 27 heavy machine guns by the NKVD, Border Guards and the Kiev Special Military District.

Gradually, a support organization evolved – at first, some of the support owed more to political dogma than the realities of guerrilla warfare. One of the early training publications was Lenin's 1906 article 'Partisan Warfare', which praised terrorism as a weapon in the class struggle. A Partisan's Oath was also drafted: every recruit had to swear to '...work a terrible, merciless and unrelenting revenge upon the enemy ... Blood for blood! Death for death!'

SOVIET GROUND FORCES (JANUARY 1942)	
Unit Type	Number
HEADQUARTERS	
Fronts	12
Armies	58
Rifle Corps	6
Cavalry Corps	7
Tank Corps	–
Mechanized Corps	–
INFANTRY	
Rifle Divisions (inc Mountain & Motorized)	389
Rifle Brigades	159
Ski Brigades	1
Tank Destroyer Brigades	–
Separate Rifle Regiments	13
Fortified Regions	19
Ski Battalions	85
CAVALRY	
Cavalry Divisions	82
Cavalry Brigades	–
Separate Cavalry Regiments	7
MECHANIZED	
Tank Divisions	7
Motorized Divisions	–
Armoured Car Brigades	1
Tank Brigades	76
Assault Gun Brigades	–
Mechanized Brigades	1
Motor Rifle Brigades	2
Motorcycle Brigades	–
Separate Tank Regiments	1
Separate Assault Gun Regiments	–
Motorcycle Regiments	7
Separate Tank Battalions	100
Separate Aerosan Battalions	18
Special Motorized Battalions	–
Armoured Train Battalions	40
Separate Arm Car & Motorcycle Battalions	2

SOVIET GROUND FORCE (JANUARY 1942)	
Unit Type	Number
AIRBORNE	
Airborne Brigades	36
ARTILLERY	
Separate Artillery Brigades	–
Separate Anti-Aircraft Brigades	1
Separate Mortar Brigades	1
Separate Artillery Regiments	158
Separate Anti-Tank Regiments	57
Separate Rocket Regiments	8
Separate Anti-Aircraft Regiments	2
Separate Artillery Battalions	28
Separate Anti-Aircraft Battalions	108
Separate Rocket Battalions	73
Separate Mortar Battalions	15
PVO STRANYI	
PVO Stranyi Corps HQ	2
PVO Stranyi Division HQ	3
PVO Stranyi Brigade HQ	2
PVO Stranyi Corps Region HQ	1
PVO Stranyi Division Region HQ	14
PVO Stranyi Brigade Region HQ	14
Anti-Aircraft Regiments	29
Anti-Aircraft Machine Gun Regiments	3
Searchlight Regiments	2
Anti-Aircraft Battalions	154

Throughout much of 1941, partisan activity often amounted to little more than seizing food from peasants in a desperate attempt to survive. By the end of the year, a total of 30,000 Communist activists had been given basic training and infiltrated through the Axis lines to organize and expand partisan groups. More than 2000 partisan detachments (with over 90,000 personnel) now operated in German-occupied territories.

Further organization
However, the activities of partisan forces were not centrally coordinated and supplied until the spring of

1942, when a Central Headquarters of the Partisan Movement was set up in Moscow, with subordinate HQs attached to each Front. Stalin still feared that independent-minded partisan units might pose a threat to the Soviet regime and ensured that an NKVD cell was attached to each group to keep it in line. In some cases, industrial-style 'production targets' were set for the partisans – the Yalta Brigade's orders included instructions that 'Each partisan must exterminate at least five fascists or traitors; [and] he must take part in at least three actions a month.'

THIRTY-EIGHTH ARMY (SOUTHWEST FRONT) TANK STRENGTH (JUNE 1942)						
Tank Bde	KV-1	T-34	T-60	Matilda	Valentine	Total
3	1	2	4	–	–	7
13	–	–	–	–	1	1
36	5	1	13	1	9	29
133	–	–	–	–	–	–
156	2	–	–	–	–	2
159	–	–	20	–	28	48
168	3	10	17	–	–	30
92 STB	7	–	7	–	–	14
Total	18	13	61	1	38	131

MOTORIZED RIFLE BRIGADE (APRIL 1942)					
Unit	Personnel	Arm Cars	Motor-cycles	Field Cars	Trucks
Brigade HQ	84	–	2	3	5
HQ Company	105	–	1	–	8
Reconnaissance Coy	148	7	6	–	10
3 x Mot Inf Btns, each	641	–	–	1	59
Sub MG Company	102	–	–	–	9
Anti-Tank Rifle Coy	61	–	–	–	5
Mortar Battalion	195	–	–	1	20
Artillery Battalion	225	–	–	1	23
Anti-Air Battalion	195	–	–	1	20
Trains Company	80	–	1	1	29
Medical Platoon	33	–	–	–	7

Moscow counter-offensive

By early December 1941, it seemed that the *Wehrmacht* was on the point of taking Moscow, but it had outrun its supply lines and was horribly vulnerable to a counterattack …

As the German advance ground to a halt in early December, the Soviet war machine was beginning to show signs of recovery. Despite the loss of 200 divisions and 4.3 million casualties, a ruthless mobilization programme had brought the Red Army's strength up to 4,196,000 men. However, this was at the expense of a further reduction in industrial manpower, which had already been hit by the loss of population (35 million) in territories overrun by Axis forces. Coupled with the disruption caused by the evacuation of war industries, this meant that the newly raised and sketchily trained forces suffered from a dire shortage of all types of weaponry from tanks to small arms.

Armour shortage

In such a crisis, there was no chance to rebuild the grandiose mechanized corps with their official tank strengths of over 1000 vehicles apiece – the tanks simply did not exist, and most surviving commanders were too inexperienced to cope with anything other than the simplest units. The small tank brigades that had replaced all larger formations from August 1941 shrank steadily – in December they were reduced to 46 tanks each, with a further reduction to 42 in January 1942 and a final cut to 27 tanks in February 1942. (These were all 'official strengths' – in practice, many brigades were significantly weaker.)

By 5 December 1941, average temperatures around Moscow had dropped to -12°C (10°F) and the *Wehrmacht* lay horribly exposed at the end of tenuous supply lines, with frostbite casualties climbing to 100,000 during the month. It was the ideal time for a Soviet counterattack and the Red Army had managed to assemble a force totalling eight tank brigades, 15 rifle divisions and three cavalry divisions, many of which had been transferred

KALININ FRONT (1 NOV 1941)	
Army	**Tank & Mechanized Units**
Twenty-Ninth	8 Tank Bde
Thirtieth	58 Tank Div 107 Motorized Rgt 21 Tank Bde 2, 11 Motorcycle Rgts
Front HQ	46 Motorcycle Rgt

WESTERN FRONT (1 NOV 1941)	
Army	**Tank & Mechanized Units**
Fifth	18, 19, 20, 22, 25 Tank Bdes 27 STB, 36 Motorcycle Rgt
Sixteenth	107 Motorized Rgt 4, 27, 28 Tank Bdes 2, 11 Motorcycle Rgts
Thirty-Third	5 Tank Bde
Forty-Third	9, 17, 24 Tank Bdes, 31 STB
Front HQ	23, 26 Tank Bdes

BRYANSK FRONT (1 NOV 1941)	
Army	**Tank & Mechanized Units**
Third	42, 121, 133 Tank Bdes
Thirteenth	141, 150 Tank Bdes 38 Motorcycle Rgt
Fiftieth	108 Tank Div 11, 32 Tank Bdes

SOVIET ARMOURED UNITS (JANUARY 1942)						
Front	TD	T Bde	Rfl Rgt	Mcl Rgt	STB	Train
Kalinin	1	2	1	3	–	–
Western	–	14	1	3	2	–
Bryansk	1	7	–	1	–	–

CAVALRY REGIMENT (JANUARY 1942)						
Unit	Officers	Pol Offs & WOs	NCOs	Other Ranks	Horse	Wagon
Rgtl HQ	9	12	1	–	17	–
Signal Ptn	–	–	12	22	44	4
Pioneer Ptn	1	–	3	16	22	–
Anti-Air Ptn	1	–	3	9	–	–
4 x Mntd Sqds, each						
Sqd HQ	2	1	3	1	7	–
4 x Line Ptns, each	1	–	3	24	30	–
Mortar Ptn	1	–	4	16	29	–
AT Platoon	1	–	7	31	41	2
Trains Sctn	–	–	–	5	6	3
MG Sqd	–	–	–	–	–	–
Sqd HQ	2	1	3	2	8	–
4 x MG Ptns, each	1	–	5	13	23	4
Trains Sctn	–	–	–	5	6	3
Mortar Sqd						
Sqd HQ	2	1	3	2	8	–
2 x Ptns, each	1	–	4	16	24	3
Supply Sctn	–	–	1	13	23	11
Rgtl Battery						
Battery HQ	2	1	3	2	8	–
HQ Section	1	–	2	12	12	1
2 x Gun Ptns, each	1	–	5	28	46	–
AT Platoon	1	–	9	37	63	–
Supply Sctn	–	1	2	16	27	13
Trains Group	1	4	5	13	15	4

Moscow. Buoyed up by this success, Stalin started to become overconfident. On 17 December 1941, he ordered more attacks:

- The Leningrad, Volkhov and Northwest Fronts were to break the siege of Leningrad.
- An offensive by Fourth Shock Army to split Army Groups North and Centre and retake Smolensk.
- An amphibious operation to seize the Kerch Peninsula in the Crimea as a prelude to raising the Axis siege of Sevastopol.

To say the least, these aims were highly ambitious, but on 5 January, Stalin went further, announcing to a horrified meeting of *Stavka* that the current operations were to be supplemented by a general offensive from the Baltic to the Black Sea, with the objectives of decisively defeating Army Group North, destroying Army Group Centre and recapturing the Donbass and the Crimea. Zhukov protested that the resources simply did not exist to support such operations, but was overruled.

High cost

Throughout the rest of January and February, the general offensive was maintained at the cost of appalling

January–March 1942

The *Wehrmacht*'s ability to survive the Soviet winter offensives of 1941/42 was largely due to Hitler's insistence that units should dig in and hold out rather than retreat. As he scathingly replied to his generals' advice to withdraw to more readily defensible lines: 'Is it any less cold 50 miles [80km] back?' The *Luftwaffe*'s maintenance of air superiority was a crucial factor in riding out the Red Army's attacks – the small numbers of fighters which could be kept operational in the worst Russian winter for many years were enough to ensure that isolated German pockets could be resupplied by air without interference from the Red Air Force.

Stalin's determination to keep launching over-ambitious offensives culminated in the disastrous Second Battle of Kharkov (12–28 May 1942), which cost the Red Army 22 rifle divisions, seven cavalry divisions and 15 tank brigades and allowed the Axis to seize the strategic initiative for the summer campaigning season.

from the Far East. (Stalin was prepared to risk weakening his forces in Siberia and Mongolia as intelligence reports indicated that Japanese attention was focused on Southeast Asia and the Pacific. However, his innate caution led him to keep substantial formations in the Far East, including roughly 2000 of the 4500 operational AFVs left in the Red Army.)

Soviet success

Shortages of tanks and artillery, combined with sheer inexperience, led to heavy Soviet casualties, but the initial counterattacks succeeded in pushing back Army Group Centre and eliminating the immediate threat to

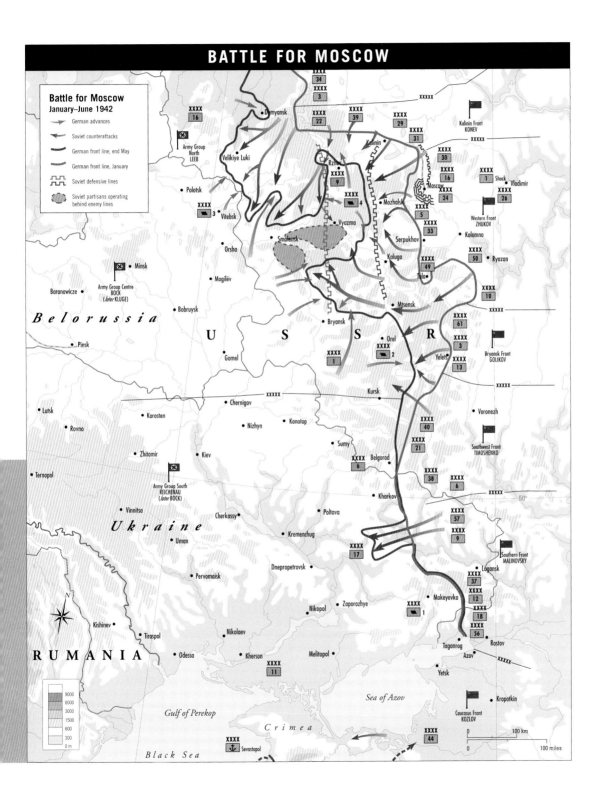

BATTLE FOR MOSCOW

Battle for Moscow
January–June 1942

→ German advances
→ Soviet counterattacks
〰 Army Group North LEEB
〰 German front line, end May
〰 German front line, January
⊔⊓ Soviet defensive lines
▨ Soviet partisans operating behind enemy lines

Demyansk

XXXX 34
XXXX 3
XXXXX

XXXX 16

XXXX 22
XXXX 39
XXXX 29
XXXX 31

Kalinin Front KONEV
XXXXX

Velikiye Luki

Kalinin

XXXX 30
XXXX 16
XXXX 1 Shock
Vladimir

Rzhev
XXXX 9

XXXX 4

Moscow
XXXX 24
XXXX 26

Western Front ZHUKOV

Mozhaisk
XXXX 5
XXXX 33

Kolomna

Polotsk

XXXX 3 Vitebsk

Orsha

Smolensk

Vyazma

Serpukhov
XXXX 50
Ryazan

Kaluga
XXXX 49

Tula
XXXX 10
XXXXX

Minsk

Army Group Centre BOCK (later KLUGE)

Mogilëv

Baranowicze

Bobruysk

Mtsensk

Bryansk
XXXX 61
XXXX 3

Belorussia

Pinsk

Gomel

U   S   S   R

Orel
XXXX 1
XXXX 2
Yelets
XXXX 13

Bryansk Front GOLIKOV
XXXXX

Lutsk

Korosten

Chernigov
XXXXX

Kursk

Voronezh

Rovno

Nizhyn

Konotop

Zhitomir

Kiev

Sumy

Army Group South REICHENAU (later BOCK)

Ternopol

Vinnitsa

Cherkassy

Poltava

Belgorod
XXXX 6

XXXX 40
XXXX 21

Southwest Front TIMOSHENKO

Kharkov
XXXX 38
XXXX 6
XXXXX

XXXX 57
XXXX 9

Ukraine

Uman

Kremenchug

XXXX 17

Southern Front MALINOVSKY

Pervomaisk

Dnepropetrovsk

Lugansk
XXXX 37
XXXX 12
XXXX 18
XXXX 56

Nikopol

Zaporozhye

Makeyevka
XXXX 1

Kishinev

Nikolaev

Melitopol

Taganrog

Rostov

Azov
XXXXX

Tiraspol

R U M A N I A

Odessa

Kherson

Yetsk

XXXX 11

Sea of Azov

Kropotkin

9000
6000
3000
1500
600
300
0 m

Gulf of Perekop

C r i m e a

Caucasus Front KOZLOV

0   100 km
0   100 miles

XXXX Sevastopol

XXXX 44

Black Sea

casualties, which were worsened by continuing acute shortages of the most basic weapons and ammunition. Zhukov, the former Chief of the General Staff, recalled that this was a time of acrimonious *Stavka* meetings, at which furious discussions were held to decide which units should be allotted a dozen or so anti-tank rifles or mortars. Debates on the allocation of artillery ammunition were even more heated – at times, batteries were limited to one or two rounds per gun per day.

The restoration of Soviet power
Nonetheless, the Axis forces were pushed back between 80km and 300km (50–188 miles), and Red Army morale was further boosted by the arrival of Lend-Lease

equipment, including the first Matilda and Valentine infantry tanks.

The NKVD closely followed the Red Army's advance in the winter of 1941/42 to 'restore revolutionary order' in territory 'newly liberated from enemy forces'. The organization's head, Beria, supervised the drafting of plans for the identification and arrest of 'wreckers, traitors and provocateurs' who had either worked for the Germans or carried out anti-Soviet activities. Special efforts were to be put into tracking down and arresting deserters. (The NKVD were particularly alarmed at the welcome given to Axis forces in the Ukraine and at reports of the Germans recruiting anti-Soviet units from the huge numbers of prisoners taken in 1941.)

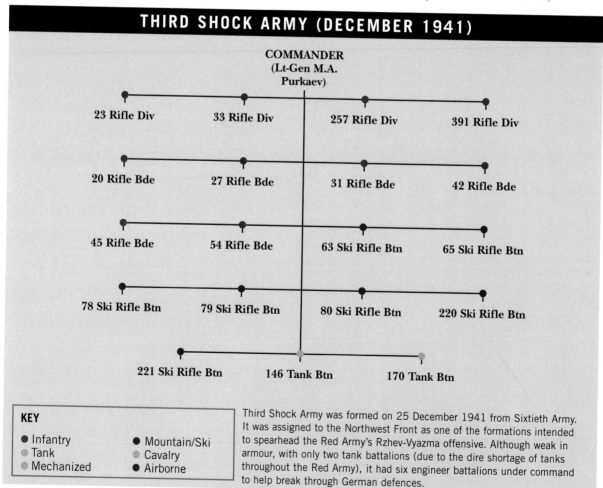

THIRD SHOCK ARMY (DECEMBER 1941)

COMMANDER
(Lt-Gen M.A. Purkaev)

23 Rifle Div	33 Rifle Div	257 Rifle Div	391 Rifle Div
20 Rifle Bde	27 Rifle Bde	31 Rifle Bde	42 Rifle Bde
45 Rifle Bde	54 Rifle Bde	63 Ski Rifle Btn	65 Ski Rifle Btn
78 Ski Rifle Btn	79 Ski Rifle Btn	80 Ski Rifle Btn	220 Ski Rifle Btn
221 Ski Rifle Btn	146 Tank Btn	170 Tank Btn	

KEY
- Infantry
- Tank
- Mechanized
- Mountain/Ski
- Cavalry
- Airborne

Third Shock Army was formed on 25 December 1941 from Sixtieth Army. It was assigned to the Northwest Front as one of the formations intended to spearhead the Red Army's Rzhev-Vyazma offensive. Although weak in armour, with only two tank battalions (due to the dire shortage of tanks throughout the Red Army), it had six engineer battalions under command to help break through German defences.

Rzhev-Vyazma offensive

The Rzhev-Vyazma offensive was intended to destroy Army Group Centre, building on earlier Soviet advances towards Rzhev. The main operation was begun on 8 January 1942 with assaults by two Soviet Fronts.

The forces involved, the Western and Kalinin Fronts, launched pincer attacks that threatened the Warsaw to Moscow highway within a few days. This was one of the very few all-weather roads in the region and was especially vital as it formed Fourth Panzer Army's *Rollbahn* (main supply route). By 19 January, Soviet forces had cut this route and were preparing for the next stage in the operation.

Whilst the Western and Kalinin Fronts were pushing their limited armoured forces to the limit, it was clear, even to Stalin, that these were not strong enough to achieve decisive results. It was decided to drop a full parachute corps – IV Airborne Corps – south of Vyazma to link up with Soviet partisans and seal off the Rzhev-Vyazma salient, trapping Ninth Army and Fourth Panzer Army. Such airborne operations were always highly risky, even with the benefit of complete air superiority, and in early 1942, it was the *Luftwaffe* that ruled the skies, threatening to massacre the slow, unwieldy Soviet transport aircraft.

Two battalions from 21st Parachute Brigade and 250th Air Assault Regiment formed the first wave of this part of the operation, but had to be dropped over a period of several days (18–22 January). After I Guards Cavalry Corps again cut the Warsaw to Moscow highway on 27 January, the most that could be done was to drop 8th Airborne Brigade in support – only a third of the intended force. Ironically this was not due to the *Luftwaffe*, but to the diversion of Soviet aircraft to supply Red Army formations, notably Thirty-Ninth Army, which had been cut off by German counterattacks.

The limited airborne forces that could be deployed were too weak to be effective – immense efforts reopened supply routes to Ninth Army and Fourth Panzer Army. Well-executed German counterattacks were able to turn the tables, eliminating the threat from 8th Airborne Brigade and trapping a number of other

RIFLE BRIGADE (1942)				
Unit	Officers	Political Officers	NCOs	Other Ranks
Brigade Headquarters	43	16	30	58
Signal Company	4	1	10	21
Bicycle Recon Coy	4	1	12	99
4 x Infantry Btns, each	34	8	86	544
Artillery Battalion	22	6	30	114
Pioneer Company	5	1	12	64
AA Machine Gun Coy	5	1	8	25
Total	219	58	446	2557

Soviet formations (the final tally included Twenty-Second, Twenty-Ninth and Thirty-Ninth Armies) until the front became a complex mass of isolated pockets separated by wide gaps, which neither side had the strength to exploit.

As the Soviet operation wound down, it was possible to make some assessment of the results. Army Group Centre had been mauled and pushed back between 80km and 250km (50–156 miles), but had inflicted over 750,000 casualties, three to four times its own losses. Soviet forces had also lost 957 tanks, almost 7300 guns and 550 aircraft. Several factors contributed to their failure to achieve a decisive victory:

- Dire equipment shortages following the loss of so much matériel in the summer and autumn battles – at one *Stavka* conference, Stalin bluntly told his generals that for the moment there were simply no more tanks.
- The crisis in weapons production caused by the evacuation of much of the Soviet arms industry.
- Inexperience, coupled with poor, sometimes non-existent, training, which led to units launching costly frontal attacks on well-fortified German positions.

Kharkov and the Crimea

Fired by the success of Soviet winter offensives in the Ukraine, Stalin was only too ready to approve Marshal Semyon Timoshenko's plans for a massive attack to seize Kharkov and drive on to the Dnieper.

The spring thaws of 1942 gave both sides a chance to take stock and plan their summer campaigns. Stalin turned his attention to the south and ordered Marshal Timoshenko to prepare an attack to recapture Kharkov and disrupt German preparations for their own offensive. These objectives were ambitious enough, but Timoshenko was soon expanding them to include the recapture of a great swathe of territory as far west as the Dnieper – a total advance of roughly 250km (156 miles). *Stavka*'s planning staff were concerned that the proposed offensive was dangerously over-ambitious, but Stalin angrily dismissed such reservations, asking 'Are we supposed to sit in defence, idling away our time and wait for the Germans to attack first?'

German intelligence was aware of the build-up of Soviet forces, coming up with an accurate estimate of 620,000 men, 1300 AFVs, 10,000 guns and mortars, supported by 926 aircraft. The majority of the tanks were concentrated in new tank corps, each with 20 KV-1s, 40 T-34s and 40 light tanks of various types. Shortly before the offensive, many of these corps were strengthened and grouped into tank armies, which were supposed to have 200–300 tanks each.

76TH RIFLE DIVISION (TWENTY-FIRST ARMY)
Unit structure
93 Rifle Regiment
207 Rifle Regiment
216 Rifle Regiment
80 Artillery Regiment
560 Howitzer Artillery Regiment
100 Independent Anti-Tank Artillery Battalion
404 Independent Anti-Aircraft Artillery Battalion
528 Mortar Battalion
36 Reconnaissance Company
95 Sapper Battalion
230 Independent Signals Battalion
150 Medical Battalion
148 Motor Transport Company
133 Field Bakery
123 Divisional Veterinary Clinic
206 Field Post Office
232 Field Cash Office of the State Bank

New offensive

The Soviet offensive opened on 12 May, with a thrust by Southwest Front from Volchansk to the north of Kharkov, whilst the Southern Front attacked from the Barvenkovo salient to the south of the city. The operation was spearheaded by 15 of the Red Army's 20 operational tank brigades, whose initial objective was to envelop Kharkov before driving westwards to the Dnieper. Timoshenko achieved initial successes by sheer weight of numbers, but after making advances averaging 25km (15.6 miles) in the first 48 hours, he was unable to maintain the tempo of the offensive. One factor in delaying the Soviet progress was a plethora of local counterattacks by Axis forces, backed up by repeated *Luftwaffe* air strikes. However, the Red Army's poor logistic support and planning also played a part in this, as was apparent on 15 May when an opportunity to achieve a decisive breakthrough was missed because XXI and XXIII Tank Corps were 25km (15.6 miles) behind the front. They took a further 48 hours to assemble and move up, by which time German reinforcements had arrived to stabilize the threatened sector.

Kleist's counter-offensive

Nonetheless, Timoshenko's forces were still advancing on 17 May when Kleist's Army Group A (First Panzer

Army and Seventeenth Army) launched a devastating counter-offensive against the southern flank of the Barvenkovo salient. Over the next few days, Stalin rejected increasingly urgent requests from Timoshenko to call off the offensive, and a bizarre situation developed as Soviet armour continued to advance westwards as Kleist's Panzers were cutting through the neck of the salient.

By the time that Timoshenko received belated authorization to retreat, it was too late – the salient was sealed off on 23 May, and during the next six days the bulk of the trapped units were virtually wiped out. Red Army losses probably totalled 208,000 men – 22 rifle divisions, seven cavalry divisions and 15 tank brigades were destroyed. Equipment losses were equally severe – 1200 tanks, 1600 guns, 3200 mortars and 540 aircraft.

The disaster at Kharkov vividly demonstrated the fragility of the Red Army at this stage of the war. Its ranks were full of barely trained conscripts, and the officer corps, emasculated by Stalin's Purges, was struggling to learn the basics of armoured warfare in the midst of campaigning against a sophisticated enemy.

Political interference

All ranks went in fear of the NKVD, whose malign influence was personified by Lev Mekhlis, the *Stavka* representative to the Crimean Front, who was also Head of the Main Political Administration of the Red Army. He was an arrogant bully who quarrelled with General Dmitri Kozlov, the Front commander, and engineered the dismissal of his highly competent chief of staff, the future Marshal Fyodor Tolbukhin. Mekhlis was largely

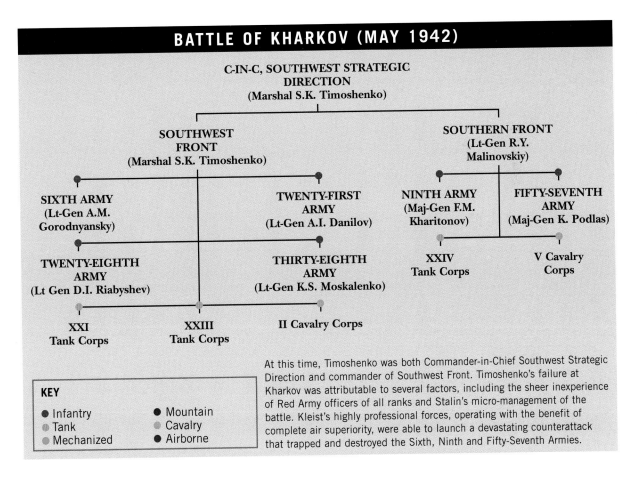

BATTLE OF KHARKOV (MAY 1942)

C-IN-C, SOUTHWEST STRATEGIC DIRECTION
(Marshal S.K. Timoshenko)

SOUTHWEST FRONT
(Marshal S.K. Timoshenko)

SOUTHERN FRONT
(Lt-Gen R.Y. Malinovskiy)

SIXTH ARMY
(Lt-Gen A.M. Gorodnyansky)

TWENTY-FIRST ARMY
(Lt-Gen A.I. Danilov)

NINTH ARMY
(Maj-Gen F.M. Kharitonov)

FIFTY-SEVENTH ARMY
(Maj-Gen K. Podlas)

TWENTY-EIGHTH ARMY
(Lt Gen D.I. Riabyshev)

THIRTY-EIGHTH ARMY
(Lt-Gen K.S. Moskalenko)

XXIV Tank Corps

V Cavalry Corps

XXI Tank Corps

XXIII Tank Corps

II Cavalry Corps

At this time, Timoshenko was both Commander-in-Chief Southwest Strategic Direction and commander of Southwest Front. Timoshenko's failure at Kharkov was attributable to several factors, including the sheer inexperience of Red Army officers of all ranks and Stalin's micro-management of the battle. Kleist's highly professional forces, operating with the benefit of complete air superiority, were able to launch a devastating counterattack that trapped and destroyed the Sixth, Ninth and Fifty-Seventh Armies.

KEY

- Infantry
- Tank
- Mechanized
- Mountain
- Cavalry
- Airborne

RIFLE COMPANY (DECEMBER 1942)

By late 1942, rifle companies were gaining significant extra firepower as the number of support weapons was increased. Each company now fielded 18 LMGs, one MMG and two 50mm (2in) mortars. Even at lower levels, firepower was still impressive and included SMGs, LMGs and a range of rifles, including the Moisin-Nagant and SVT40 semi-automatic.

Company HQ (2 x officers, 1 x political officer, 2 x NCOs)

Medical Squad (1 x NCO, 4 x ORs)

Rifle Platoon 1
HQ (1 x officer, 1 x NCO, 2 x ORs)

MG Squad (2 x NCOs, 2 x ORs)

Mortar Platoon (1 x officer, 4 x NCOs, 2 x ORs)

2 x Light Squads (2 x NCOs, 7 x ORs)

2 x Heavy Squads (2 x NCOs, 7 x ORs)

Rifle Platoon 2
HQ (1 x officer, 1 x NCO, 2 x ORs)

MG Squad (2 x NCOs, 2 x ORs)

Mortar Platoon (1 x officer, 4 x NCOs, 2 x ORs)

2 x Light Squads (2 x NCOs, 7 x ORs)

2 x Heavy Squads (2 x NCOs, 7 x ORs)

Rifle Platoon 3
HQ (1 x officer, 1 x NCO, 2 x ORs)

MG Squad (2 x NCOs, 2 x ORs)

Mortar Platoon (1 x officer, 4 x NCOs, 2 x ORs)

2 x Light Squads (2 x NCOs, 7 x ORs)

2 x Heavy Squads (2 x NCOs, 7 x ORs)

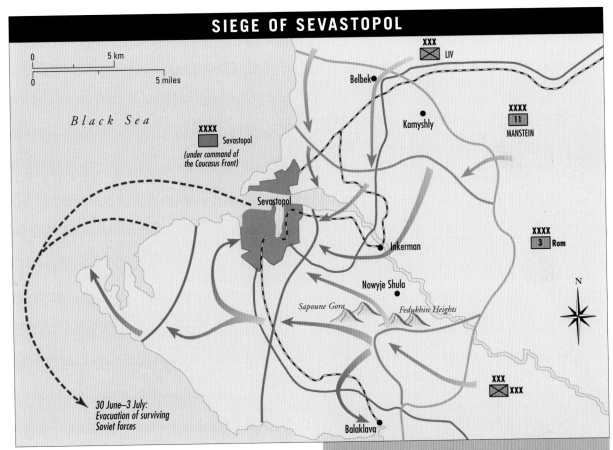

SIEGE OF SEVASTOPOL

Black Sea

XXXX
Sevastopol
(under command of
the Caucasus Front)

XXX
LIV

Belbek

Kamyshly

XXXX
11
MANSTEIN

Sevastopol

Inkerman

XXXX
3 Rom

Nowyje Shula

Sapoune Gora

Fedukhin Heights

N

XXX
XXX

30 June–3 July:
Evacuation of surviving
Soviet forces

Balaklava

0   5 km
0   5 miles

responsible for failing effectively to attack Manstein's force besieging Sevastopol when it was at its most vulnerable in early 1942, and when the Germans counterattacked on 8 May his incompetence contributed to the destruction of the Crimean Front in barely 10 days.

Crimean disaster

As at Kharkov, there was little coordination between the Soviet tank brigades. Their 350 AFVs were committed to action piecemeal, thus negating their numerical superiority over the sole German armoured formation, the understrength 22nd Panzer Division, which was largely equipped with obsolescent Panzer 38(t)s.

Once again, Soviet losses were staggering – three armies (Forty-Fourth, Forty-Seventh and Fifty-First) totalling 21 divisions had been broken and Manstein's

December 1941–July 1942

After destroying the Crimean Front, von Manstein was able to concentrate on the siege of Sevastopol. The city and harbour were protected by extensive field defences and the pre-war forts 'Stalin', 'Molotov', 'Siberia' and 'Maxim Gorky'. In all, the garrison had 600 guns, including 8 massive 30.5cm (12in) guns.

The German attack commenced with a concentrated five-day barrage, which reminded some older members of the army staff of Verdun, 25 years before. The German Eleventh Army's experts used every piece of artillery they could bring to bear.

Included in the heavy artillery pounding the Russian positions were two of the massive 'Karl' siege mortars with a calibre of 60cm (24in), and the largest gun ever made – the 80cm (32in) 'Gustav' railway gun.

forces had taken 170,000 prisoners, besides capturing 258 tanks and over 1100 guns. Fortunately for the Red Army, there were indications that Stalin was beginning to appreciate the realities of combat – when Mekhlis attempted to make Kozlov the scapegoat for the disaster, Stalin retorted: 'You are taking a strange position as an outside observer who has no responsibility for the Crimean Front. This position may be comfortable, but it is utterly disgraceful. You are not some outside observer … but the Stavka representative responsible for all the Front's successes and failures and obliged to correct the command's mistakes on the spot.'

Retreat to the Don

In April 1942, Hitler had chosen to make his main effort for that year at the southern end of the Eastern Front. Under Plan Blue, he aimed to take Stalingrad and drive deep into the Caucasus to seize the oilfields of Maikop, Grozny and Baku.

Timoshenko's offensive at Kharkov had disrupted preparations for the offensive, but the sheer scale of the Soviet disaster (almost 75 per cent of the Red Army's tanks were destroyed) meant that there was very little left to oppose the Panzers as they struck deep into southern Russia on 28 June. By 5 July, Hoth's Fourth Panzer Army had taken Voronezh, reinforcing Stalin's instinctive belief that Moscow was still the primary German objective. Whilst *Stavka* concentrated on directing reserves to counter the illusory threat to Moscow, *General der Panzertruppe* Friedrich Paulus' Sixth Army was making for Stalingrad and Kleist's First Panzer Army was well on its way to the oilfields of the Caucasus.

The psychological impact of these events was sharpened by the first indications that the *Panzerwaffe* was regaining lost ground in the gun/armour race. As a first step to combat the T-34 and KV-1, production of the 50mm (2in) L/60 and its tungsten-cored APCR ammunition was increased to ensure that the Panzer III stood some chance against these opponents. Frantic

RIFLE BRIGADE (JULY 1942)												
Unit	Officers	NCOs	Other Ranks	AT Rifles	AT Mortars	50mm Mortars	82mm Mortars	120mm Mortars	45mm AT Guns	76mm Guns	Horses
Brigade HQ	51	14	23	–	–	–	–	–	–	–	5
Signal Battalion	22	30	85	–	–	–	–	–	–	–	8
Reconnaissance Coy	6	15	74	–	–	–	–	–	–	–	6
4 x Inf Btn, each	58	193	677	8	7	12	6	–	–	–	89
Heavy Mortar Btn	18	26	101	–	–	–	–	8	–	–	77
Artillery Battalion	35	66	240	–	–	–	–	–	–	12	244
Anti-Tank Battalion	30	73	170	48	–	–	–	–	12	–	–
Submachine Gun Coy	6	20	74	–	–	–	–	–	–	–	17
Pioneer Company	8	18	80	–	–	–	–	–	–	–	–
Motor Transport Coy	12	18	47	–	–	–	–	–	–	–	–
NKVD Platoon	1	4	13	–	–	–	–	–	–	–	–
Bakery	2	3	28	–	–	–	–	–	–	–	–

INFANTRY REGIMENT (OCTOBER 1942)						
Unit	Officers	Political Officers	Warrant Officers	NCOs	Other Ranks	Weapons, Equipment & Notes
Regimental HQ & Platoon	15	4	10	6	10	2 Wagons
Mounted Recon Platoon	1	1	–	3	13	(2 Squads) 2 SMGs
Infantry Recon Platoon	1	1	–	5	43	(4 Squads) 2 SMGs
Signal Company	5	1	–	9	35	(Radio Sctn & 2 Wire Ptns) 2 Radios, 6 Wire Equipment Carts
Anti-Aircraft MG Company	1	–	–	6	9	3 HMGs, 3 Trucks
Chemical Platoon	1	–	–	4	25	6 Wagons
Pioneer Platoon	1	–	–	5	33	1 Wagon
Anti-Tank Mortar Platoon	1	–	–	8	14	6 AT Mortars, 2 Wagons
Band	–	–	1	1	11	
3 x Infantry Battalions, each						
Battalion HQ	4	1	–	–	–	
Signal Platoon	1	–	–	4	12	1 Radio, 1 Wire Equipment Cart
3 x Rifle Companies, each	6	1	–	39	144	(3 Rifle & 1 Mort Ptns) 11 Sniper Rifles, 9 SMGs, 12 LMGs, 4 50mm Morts
Machine Gun Company	5	1	–	19	51	(3 Ptns, each 3 Sqds) 9 MGs, 6 Wagons
AT Rifle Company	4	1	–	19	24	(2 Ptns, each 4 Sqds) 16 AT Rifles
Mortar Company	6	1	–	29	60	(6 ptns) 12 82mm Morts, 12 Wagons
Medical Platoon	–	–	1	1	5	1 Cart
Trains Platoon	1	–	–	3	19	14 Wagons
Submachine Gun Company	5	1	–	20	74	(3 Ptns, each 3 Sqds) 100 SMGs, 1 Wagon
Anti-Tank Rifle Company	5	1	–	22	48	(3 Ptns, each 3 Sqds) 27 AT Rifles, 3 Wagons
Anti-Tank Battery	5	1	–	13	38	(3 Ptns) 6 45mm AT Guns, 6 Caissons
Infantry Gun Battery	6	1	–	15	62	(2 Gun Ptns) 4 76mm Inf Guns, 2 Carts, 16 Wagons
Mortar Company	6	1	–	21	43	(4 Ptns) 8 82mm Morts, 11 Wagons
Mortar Battery	5	1	–	13	37	(3 Ptns) 6 120mm Morts, 7 Trucks
Medical Company	–	–	7	7	34	2 Carts, 9 Wagons
Supply Company	4	1	–	8	46	(2 Ptns) 43 Wagons
Other Services	–	–	4	9	6	1 Wagon

efforts also went into replacing the Panzer IV's 75mm (2.9in) L/24 with a long-barrelled L/43 version, but it was mid-1942 before the first deliveries were made to front-line units. At the same time, work was in hand to rearm the StuG III with the L/43, and up-gunned versions were produced alongside the new Panzer IVs.

At the end of June, General Y.N. Fedorenko, head of the Red Army's armoured force, issued a directive on the principles for its future employment. Whilst hardly original, they represented a willingness to learn from German practice, calling for the use of armour en masse against strategic targets. There was new emphasis on the importance of surprise, the exploitation of favourable terrain and a call for logistic support capable of sustaining prolonged advances. For the time being, these were little more than hopes for the future – the pressing issue was whether the Red Army could survive long enough to put them into practice. A further disaster was in the making as First Tank Army and Sixty-Second Army were pinned against the Don in a double envelopment by Paulus' Sixth Army. Both the Stalingrad Front and the Southern Front temporarily collapsed, with the loss of 350,000 men and over 2000 AFVs.

On 20 July, Hitler joyously announced, 'The Russian is finished!' and even the cautious, scholarly General Franz Halder, OKH's Chief of Staff, agreed: 'I must admit, it looks like it.' Such impressions were not confined to the high command – a Panzer NCO commented that the situation on the ground was different from that in 1941. 'It's more like Poland. The Russians aren't nearly so thick on the ground. They fire their guns like madmen, but they don't hurt us.'

Penal units

Although evidence is sketchy, it seems likely that penal units (one battalion per army) had existed in the Red Army since the Winter War. Following the issue of Stalin's 'No Retreat' Order No 227 in July 1942, the numbers of such units greatly increased and they were far more extensively used for the remainder of the war. The first penal battalion deployed under this new policy was sent to the Stalingrad Front on 22 August 1942, shortly before German troops reached the Volga. After three days in combat, there were only 300 survivors from the 929 former officers who were assigned to the unit.

Penal battalions, or *shtrafbats*, had an official strength of 360, and penal companies, 100 to 150 men. Each penal unit also had a small, heavily armed guard detachment; initially these contained regular troops but were later manned by the NKVD. Approximately 600,000 military personnel and perhaps one million Gulag prisoners were transferred to penal units during the war. The number of such units grew rapidly – there were ultimately 1049 penal companies in the Red Army.

Offenders were sentenced to between one and three months service in infantry penal units and were eligible for early release and transfer to a Red Army line unit if they sustained a combat wound (the crime was considered to be 'cleansed in blood') or if they had shown outstanding heroism. They could theoretically receive military decorations and were officially fully rehabilitated at the end of their sentences.

Penal battalion service was understandably viewed by many Soviet prisoners as tantamount to a death sentence. The official view was that such unreliable personnel were expendable and should be used to reduce losses in regular units by, for example, spearheading attacks on enemy defences, crossing minefields ahead of the main assault and taking part in decoy assaults to draw enemy fire. By May 1943, each Soviet Front commander had 10 to 15 penal battalions at his disposal and it became standard practice for any Soviet offensive to be preceded by the advance of several such battalions, which were usually wiped out.

Stalingrad and the Caucasus

In a matter of weeks, Kleist's First Panzer Army had taken Maikop, whilst Hoth's Fourth Panzer Army led the drive on Stalingrad. The sheer scale of the advance soon began to cause problems as the Panzers outran their overstretched supply lines.

Hitler's interference had also delayed the advance. Fourth Panzer Army had been temporarily diverted from its assigned role of spearheading the advance on Stalingrad to 'assist the early passage of the lower Don'. Logistic problems were causing far more delay to First

Panzer Army than the shaky Soviet defence, and these were compounded by the arrival of Fourth Panzer Army, which created a monumental traffic jam at the Don crossings. In Hoth's absence, the advance on Stalingrad slowed, allowing the Soviets just enough time to

SOVIET GROUND FORCES (JULY 1942)	
Unit Type	**Number**
AIRBORNE	
Airborne Brigades	30
ARTILLERY	
Separate Artillery Regiments	323
Separate Mortar Regiments	75
Separate Anti-Tank Regiments	151
Separate Rocket Regiments	70
Separate Anti-Aircraft Regiments	35
Separate Artillery Battalions	24
Separate Anti-Aircraft Battalions	126
Separate Rocket Battalions	52
Separate Anti-Tank Battalions	–
Separate Mortar Battalions	1
PVO STRANYI	
PVO Stranyi Corps HQ	–
PVO Stranyi Division HQ	2
PVO Stranyi Brigade HQ	2
PVO Stranyi Corps Region HQ	2
PVO Stranyi Division Region HQ	13
PVO Stranyi Brigade Region HQ	14
Anti-Aircraft Regiments	56
Anti-Aircraft MG Regiments	5
Searchlight Regiments	9
Anti-Aircraft Battalions	118

SOVIET GROUND FORCES (JULY 1942)	
Unit Type	**Number**
HEADQUARTERS	
Fronts	14
Armies	76
Rifle Corps	19
Cavalry Corps	12
Tank Corps	22
Mechanized Corps	–
INFANTRY	
Rifle Divisions (inc Mountain & Motorized)	425
Rifle Brigades	144
Ski Brigades	2
Tank Destroyer Brigades	17
Separate Rifle Regiments	8
Fortified Regions	53
Ski Battalions	25
CAVALRY	
Cavalry Divisions	46
Cavalry Brigades	–
Separate Cavalry Regiments	5
ARMOUR	
Tank Divisions	2
Motorized Divisions	–
Armoured Car Brigades	1
Tank Brigades	192
Assault Gun Brigades	–
Mechanized Brigades	–
Motor Rifle Brigades	29
Motorcycle Brigades	1
Separate Tank Regiments	–
Separate Assault Gun Regiments	–
Motorcycle Regiments	5
Separate Tank Battalions	80
Separate Aerosan Battalions	–
Special Motorized Battalions	–
Armoured Train Battalions	64
Separate Arm Car & Motorcycle Battalions	22

reinforce the city's garrison before the Germans arrived in August. (The Russian Sixty-Second Army defending Stalingrad had 54,000 men, 900 guns and 110 tanks.) Thus, instead of taking a largely undefended city, more and more German forces were sucked in to fierce street fighting, in which their rate of advance slowed to no more than a few hundred metres a day.

As Sixth Army and Fourth Panzer Army became ever more deeply committed to fighting in Stalingrad itself, responsibility for protection of their long, vulnerable flanks had to be assigned to comparatively weak and ill-equipped satellite armies. Eighth Italian Army and Third Rumanian Army held a long sector of front northwest of

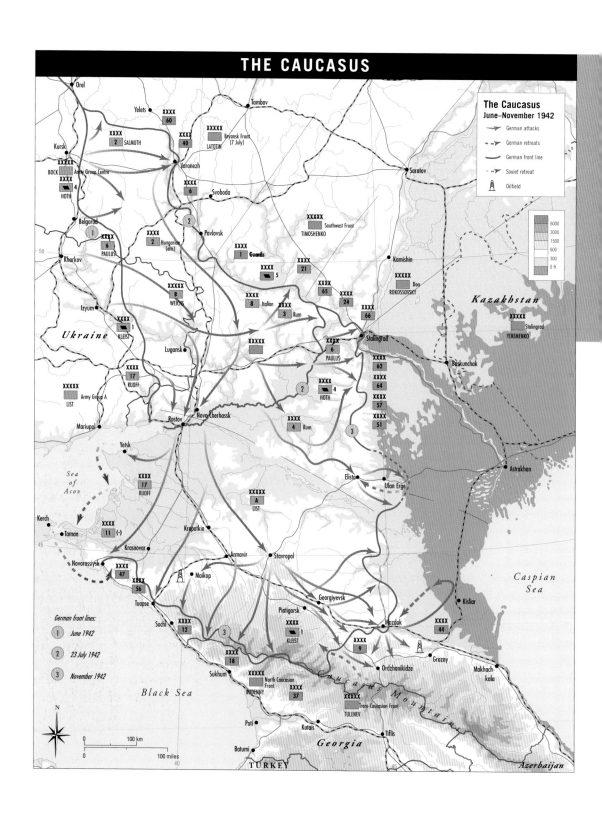

THE CAUCASUS

The Caucasus
June–November 1942

→ German attacks
- - → German retreats
—— German front line
··→ Soviet retreat
⛽ Oilfield

6000
3000
1500
600
300
0 ft

German front lines:
① June 1942
② 23 July 1942
③ November 1942

Orel

Yelets

XXXX
60

Tambov

Kursk

XXXX
2 SALMUTH

XXXX
40

XXXXX
LATOTIN

Bryansk Front
(7 July)

Saratov

XXXXX
BOCK Army Group Centre

XXXX
4 HOTH

Voronezh

XXXX
6

Svoboda

Belgorod

①

XXXX
6 PAULUS

XXXX
2 Hungarian
(elts)

Pavlovsk

②

XXXXX
Southwest Front
TIMOSHENKO

Kamishin

Kharkov

XXXX
1 Guards

XXXX
21

XXXXX
Don
ROKOSSOVSKY

Kazakhstan

50

XXXX
8 B
WEICHS

XXXX
8 Italian

XXXX
5

XXXX
65

XXXX
24

Ukraine

Izyum

XXXX
1
KLEIST

XXXX
3 Rum

XXXX
66

XXXXX
Stalingrad
YEREMENKO

Lugansk

XXXXX

XXXX
6 PAULUS

Stalingrad

XXXX
62

XXXX
17 RUOFF

XXXX
2

XXXX
4 HOTH

XXXX
64

Baskunchak

XXXXX
Army Group A
LIST

XXXX
57

Mariupol

Rostov

Nova Cherhassk

XXXX
4 Rum

③

XXXX
51

Yetsk

Elista

Astrakhan

*Sea
of
Asov*

XXXX
17 RUOFF

XXXXX
A
LIST

Ulan Erge

Kerch

XXXX
11 (-)

Krasnovar

Kropotkin

Taman

Armavir

Stavropol

*Caspian
Sea*

45

Novorossiysk

XXXX
47

Maikop

Georgiyevsk

Kisliar

XXXX
56

Tuapse

Piatigorsk

Mozdok

XXXX
44

Sochi

XXXX
12

XXXX
3

XXXX
1
KLEIST

XXXX
9

Grozny

Makhach-
kala

XXXX
18

Ordzhonikidze

Sukhum

XXXXX
North Caucasian
Front
BUDENNY

XXXX
37

XXXXX
Trans-Caucasian Front
TULENEV

Caucasus Mountains

Black Sea

N

Poti

Kutais

Tiflis

Batumi

Georgia

0   100 km
0   100 miles

TURKEY

40

45

Azerbaijan

June–November 1942

The spectacular Axis advance into the Caucasus posed a major threat to the Soviet capacity to continue the war. The loss of the region's oilfields would have been a serious blow to the Soviet war economy, but the political impact was likely to be far worse. A successful German offensive in the region could well induce Turkey to join the Axis and possibly tempt Japan to attack Siberia or Mongolia.

Fortunately for the Red Army, Hitler's overconfidence led him to attempt to take Stalingrad and the Caucasus simultaneously with totally inadequate resources. Kleist's advance came tantalizingly close to overrunning the entire region but was starved of vital logistic and air support by the ever-increasing demands of Sixth Army in its efforts to take Stalingrad. The theatre of operations was so vast that both sides could not hope to hold a continuous front line – the vast expanse of the Kalmyk Steppe was 'held' by patrols operating from isolated bases.

the city, whilst Fourth Rumanian Army held the line south of Stalingrad.

The Caucacus

At first, Kleist's drive into the Caucasus achieved spectacular results – First Panzer Army took the first of the oilfields at Maikop on 9 August and pushed on towards Grozny and Baku. In a propaganda coup, a team of *Gebirgsjäger* planted a swastika flag on the summit of Mount Elbrus, the highest mountain in the Caucasus. Stalin was conscious of the potentially disastrous political implications of the German advance – Turkey might well join the Axis and launch an attack that would almost certainly destroy the hard-pressed Trans-Caucasian Front. There was also the possibility of a revolt against Soviet rule throughout the region, which was taken so seriously that Beria was sent there to supervise an urgent programme of repression.

This fear of a major revolt was soundly based – parts of Chechnya had been in rebellion since February 1940 and many Cossacks had welcomed Axis units as they advanced into the Caucasus. The Germans attempted to exploit the situation, infiltrating Special Forces detachments from the *Abwehr*'s *Nordkaukasische Sonderkommando* 'Schamil' to assist the Chechen rebels and prevent Soviet sabotage of the Maikop oilfields.

This operation fanned the flames of the revolt in Chechnya and encouraged the desertion of many of the Red Army's Chechen conscripts. The total of such desertions may have reached 62,000.

However, the dire consequences of Hitler's decision to take Stalingrad and the Caucasus simultaneously rapidly became apparent. Essential supplies could only be brought up by continual improvisation – quartermasters resorted to a motley collection of pack animals to move vital ammunition, spares and rations. Distances in this region were so vast that in many areas there were no conventional front lines. Armoured patrols from both sides roamed the Kalmyk Steppe, the Soviets seeking Kleist's vulnerable supply lines, whilst the Germans attacked targets such as the Baku–Astrakhan railway.

However, the Axis advance faltered in the face of rapidly stiffening Soviet resistance, dwindling supplies, disease and severe manpower shortages – on average, each German division was 4000 troops below strength. Ultimately, so many resources were diverted to the interminable battle of attrition in Stalingrad that Kleist was robbed of any chance of taking the remaining oilfields and was left stranded deep in the Caucasus in a dangerously exposed salient.

TANK DESTROYER BRIGADE (1942)		
Unit	Personnel	Weapons
Brigade Headquarters	94	–
AT Artillery Rgt		
4 x Heavy Batteries, each	–	4 x 76mm
3 x Light Batteries, each	–	4 x 45mm
Anti-Aircraft Battery	–	4 x 37mm
2 x AT Rifle Btns, each	200	–
3 x AT Rifle Coys, each	–	24 x ATR
Mortar Battalion	134	–
2 x Medium Companies	–	4 x 82mm Mtrs
Heavy Company	–	4 x 120mm Mtrs
Tank Battalion	143	–
Light Tank Company	–	11 x T-40/T-60s
2 x Medium Tank Coys	–	10 x T-34s each
Engineer Minelaying Btn	330	–
3 x Eng Mine Coys	–	–
Submachine Gun Coy	100	–
Services	34	

Operation Uranus

In September 1942, Stalin approved plans for Operation Uranus, an ambitious counter-offensive intended to punch through the Third and Fourth Rumanian Armies, before enveloping the German Sixth Army and Fourth Panzer Army.

Throughout the autumn of 1942, the Red Army built up reserves around Stalingrad whilst feeding in just enough reinforcements to prevent any decisive German breakthrough. General Vasily Chuikov's Sixty-Second

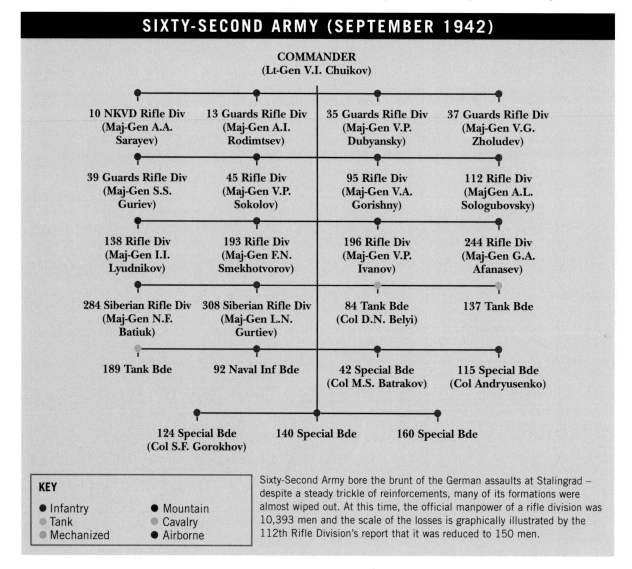

SIXTY-SECOND ARMY (SEPTEMBER 1942)

COMMANDER
(Lt-Gen V.I. Chuikov)

10 NKVD Rifle Div (Maj-Gen A.A. Sarayev)	**13 Guards Rifle Div** (Maj-Gen A.I. Rodimtsev)	**35 Guards Rifle Div** (Maj-Gen V.P. Dubyansky)	**37 Guards Rifle Div** (Maj-Gen V.G. Zholudev)
39 Guards Rifle Div (Maj-Gen S.S. Guriev)	**45 Rifle Div** (Maj-Gen V.P. Sokolov)	**95 Rifle Div** (Maj-Gen V.A. Gorishny)	**112 Rifle Div** (MajGen A.L. Sologubovsky)
138 Rifle Div (Maj-Gen I.I. Lyudnikov)	**193 Rifle Div** (Maj-Gen F.N. Smekhotvorov)	**196 Rifle Div** (Maj-Gen V.P. Ivanov)	**244 Rifle Div** (Maj-Gen G.A. Afanasev)
284 Siberian Rifle Div (Maj-Gen N.F. Batiuk)	**308 Siberian Rifle Div** (Maj-Gen L.N. Gurtiev)	**84 Tank Bde** (Col D.N. Belyi)	**137 Tank Bde**
189 Tank Bde	**92 Naval Inf Bde**	**42 Special Bde** (Col M.S. Batrakov)	**115 Special Bde** (Col Andryusenko)
124 Special Bde (Col S.F. Gorokhov)	**140 Special Bde**	**160 Special Bde**	

KEY
- ● Infantry
- ● Tank
- ● Mechanized
- ● Mountain
- ● Cavalry
- ● Airborne

Sixty-Second Army bore the brunt of the German assaults at Stalingrad – despite a steady trickle of reinforcements, many of its formations were almost wiped out. At this time, the official manpower of a rifle division was 10,393 men and the scale of the losses is graphically illustrated by the 112th Rifle Division's report that it was reduced to 150 men.

Army held the city itself, steadily wearing down Sixth Army and Fourth Panzer Army. At the same time, Zhukov assembled his forces, including 894 tanks and 13,500 guns, to strike at the Rumanian forces on either side of Stalingrad. When the Southwest Front launched its attack on Third Rumanian Army on 19 November, the 80-minute Soviet barrage by at least 3000 guns could be heard 50km (31 miles) away.

A 12km (7.5-mile) gap was ripped in the Rumanian defences, which was rapidly exploited by Fifth Tank Army. Twenty-four hours later, the Stalingrad Front's offensive hit Fourth Rumanian Army, tearing a 30km (19-mile) hole in its line before IV Mechanized and IV Cavalry Corps were launched into the breach to link up with Fifth Tank Army.

Surprise, disbelief

Most German planners had simply not believed that the Red Army had the resources or the skill to conduct an offensive on this scale. Soviet armour was now being employed – and most effectively – in accordance with the principles laid down by General Fedorenko earlier

in the year. In contrast, the German response was clumsy and ineffective. XLVIII Panzer Corps had been assigned to act as an armoured reserve for Third Rumanian Army, but it was an exceptionally weak formation, comprising 22nd Panzer Division with only 45 operational tanks and 1st Rumanian Tank Division with 40 R-2 tanks – obsolete Panzer 35(t)s. Despite being massively outnumbered by Soviet armour, these two divisions managed to break out to the west. The understrength elements of Fourth Panzer Army that attempted to block Fifth Tank Army's advance at the Don crossings near Kalach were not so fortunate. They were inadequately briefed and committed to an understandably rushed deployment with low stocks of fuel and ammunition. Although they reached Kalach just ahead of the Soviets, their small ad hoc combat teams lacked infantry support to hold vital ground and were quickly overrun by armour operating en masse.

On 23 November, the Soviet pincers closed at Sovietskiy, 20km (12.5 miles) southeast of Kalach, trapping an estimated 300,000 Axis troops in Stalingrad. The tables had been decisively turned.

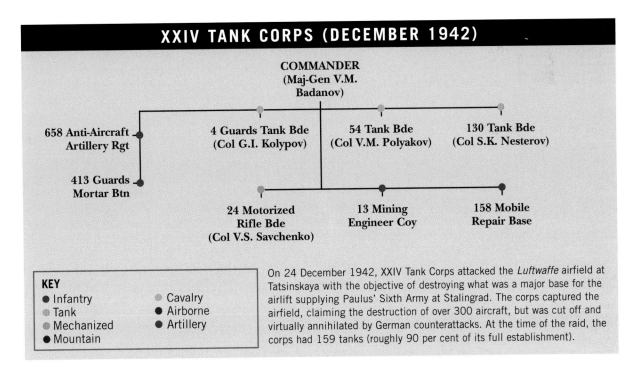

XXIV TANK CORPS (DECEMBER 1942)

COMMANDER
(Maj-Gen V.M. Badanov)

658 Anti-Aircraft Artillery Rgt

413 Guards Mortar Btn

4 Guards Tank Bde (Col G.I. Kolypov)

54 Tank Bde (Col V.M. Polyakov)

130 Tank Bde (Col S.K. Nesterov)

24 Motorized Rifle Bde (Col V.S. Savchenko)

13 Mining Engineer Coy

158 Mobile Repair Base

KEY
- Infantry
- Tank
- Mechanized
- Mountain
- Cavalry
- Airborne
- Artillery

On 24 December 1942, XXIV Tank Corps attacked the *Luftwaffe* airfield at Tatsinskaya with the objective of destroying what was a major base for the airlift supplying Paulus' Sixth Army at Stalingrad. The corps captured the airfield, claiming the destruction of over 300 aircraft, but was cut off and virtually annihilated by German counterattacks. At the time of the raid, the corps had 159 tanks (roughly 90 per cent of its full establishment).

TANK BRIGADE (NOVEMBER 1942)

By this time, tank brigades were receiving more T-34s, although there were still too few to dispense with the light tanks. However, more and more of these light tanks were T-70s, which were far better armed than the earlier T-60s. The tactical flexibility of tank formations was still hampered since only the company and platoon HQ vehicles were fitted with radios.

Brigade HQ

HQ, Medium Tank Battalion

HQ, Light Tank Battalion

1 Medium Tank Company (10 x T-34)

2 Medium Tank Company (10 x T-34)

3 Medium Tank Company (10 x T-34)

1 Light Tank Company (10 x T-70)

2 Light Tank Company (10 x T-70)

Final battle for Stalingrad

Marshal Georgi Zhukov launched Operation Uranus on 19 November 1942, and within days a massive Soviet pincer movement had isolated Sixth Army fighting in Stalingrad. All attempts to relieve the trapped German soldiers failed, and the *Luftwaffe* was never able to make good Hermann Göring's boasts that he would sustain the city from the air. As January progressed, the noose around Stalingrad was tightened. The German forces retreated to the city, losing control of important airfields. The fighting was less fierce than it had been in September and October – the Soviets could let cold, starvation and disease do most of the work. Stalin ordered the pocket eliminated in January, and by the end of the month the surviving Germans were pressed into two small pockets on the Volga.

Final battle for Stalingrad
November 1942–February 1943

⤙ Soviet attacks

⤙ German counterattacks

⤙ German retreats

— German front line

— Limit of Soviet artillery

Soviet air support

BATTLE OF STALINGRAD

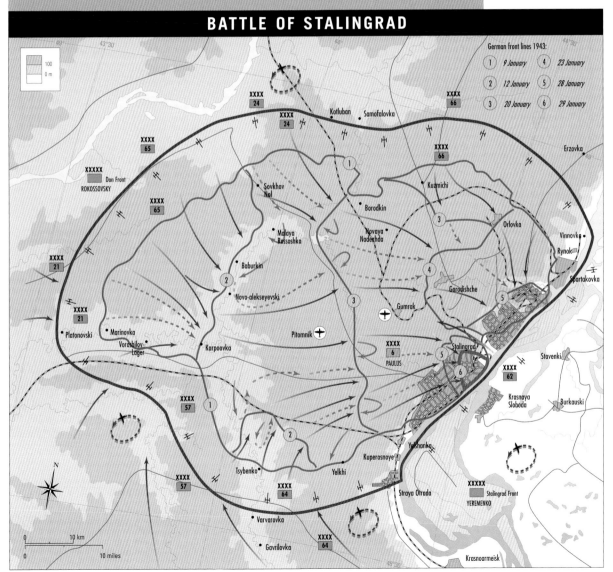

German front lines 1943:

① 9 January   ④ 23 January
② 12 January ⑤ 28 January
③ 20 January ⑥ 29 January

100
0 m

XXXX 24
XXXX 24
XXXX 65
XXXX 65
XXXX 66
XXXX 66
XXXXX Don Front ROKOSSOVSKY
XXXX 21
XXXX 21
XXXX 57
XXXX 57
XXXX 64
XXXX 64
XXXX 6 PAULUS
XXXX 62
XXXXX Stalingrad Front YEREMENKO

Kotluban Samofalovka
Erzovka
Sovkhov Nol
Kuzmichi
Borodkin
Novaya Nadezhda
Orlovka
Malaya Rossoshka
Vinnovka
Rynok
Baburkin
Gorodishche
Spartakovka
Novo-alekseyevski
Gumrak
Marinovka
Pitomnik
Stalingrad
Stavenki
Platonovski
Voroshilov-Lager
Karpoovka
Krasnaya Sloboda
Burkauski
Tsybenko
Yelkhi
Kuporosnoye
Yelshanka
Varvarovka
Straya Otrada
Gavrilovka
Krasnoarmeisk

N

0   10 km
0   10 miles

85

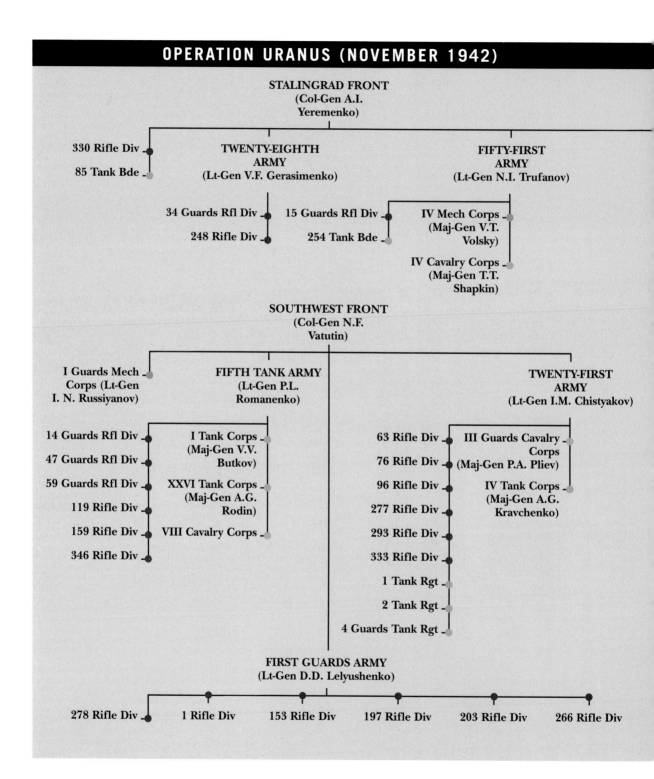

OPERATION URANUS (NOVEMBER 1942)

STALINGRAD FRONT
(Col-Gen A.I. Yeremenko)

330 Rifle Div

85 Tank Bde

TWENTY-EIGHTH ARMY
(Lt-Gen V.F. Gerasimenko)

FIFTY-FIRST ARMY
(Lt-Gen N.I. Trufanov)

34 Guards Rfl Div

248 Rifle Div

15 Guards Rfl Div

254 Tank Bde

IV Mech Corps
(Maj-Gen V.T. Volsky)

IV Cavalry Corps
(Maj-Gen T.T. Shapkin)

SOUTHWEST FRONT
(Col-Gen N.F. Vatutin)

I Guards Mech Corps (Lt-Gen I. N. Russiyanov)

FIFTH TANK ARMY
(Lt-Gen P.L. Romanenko)

TWENTY-FIRST ARMY
(Lt-Gen I.M. Chistyakov)

14 Guards Rfl Div

47 Guards Rfl Div

59 Guards Rfl Div

119 Rifle Div

159 Rifle Div

346 Rifle Div

I Tank Corps
(Maj-Gen V.V. Butkov)

XXVI Tank Corps
(Maj-Gen A.G. Rodin)

VIII Cavalry Corps

63 Rifle Div

76 Rifle Div

96 Rifle Div

277 Rifle Div

293 Rifle Div

333 Rifle Div

1 Tank Rgt

2 Tank Rgt

4 Guards Tank Rgt

III Guards Cavalry Corps
(Maj-Gen P.A. Pliev)

IV Tank Corps
(Maj-Gen A.G. Kravchenko)

FIRST GUARDS ARMY
(Lt-Gen D.D. Lelyushenko)

278 Rifle Div   1 Rifle Div   153 Rifle Div   197 Rifle Div   203 Rifle Div   266 Rifle Div

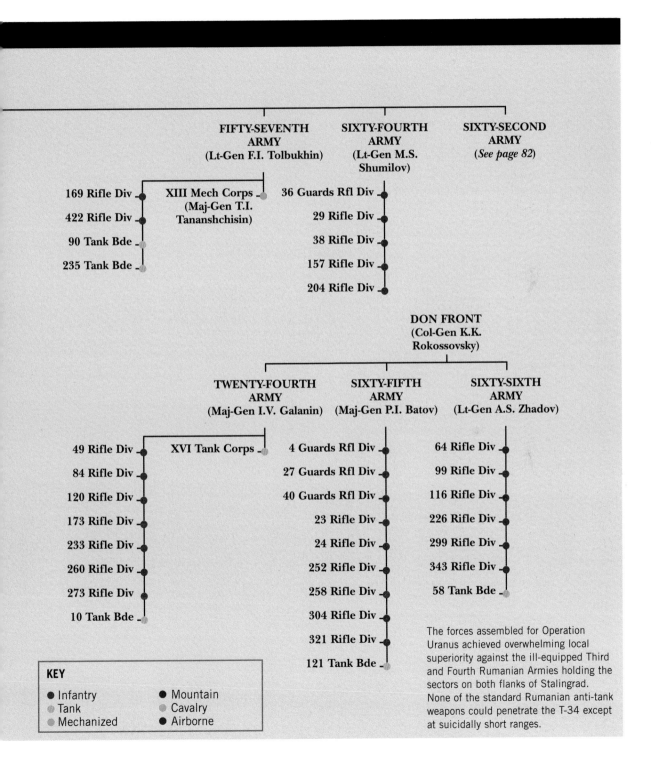

FIFTY-SEVENTH ARMY
(Lt-Gen F.I. Tolbukhin)

169 Rifle Div
422 Rifle Div
90 Tank Bde
235 Tank Bde

XIII Mech Corps
(Maj-Gen T.I. Tananshchisin)

SIXTY-FOURTH ARMY
(Lt-Gen M.S. Shumilov)

36 Guards Rfl Div
29 Rifle Div
38 Rifle Div
157 Rifle Div
204 Rifle Div

SIXTY-SECOND ARMY
(*See page 82*)

DON FRONT
(Col-Gen K.K. Rokossovsky)

TWENTY-FOURTH ARMY
(Maj-Gen I.V. Galanin)

49 Rifle Div
84 Rifle Div
120 Rifle Div
173 Rifle Div
233 Rifle Div
260 Rifle Div
273 Rifle Div
10 Tank Bde

XVI Tank Corps

SIXTY-FIFTH ARMY
(Maj-Gen P.I. Batov)

4 Guards Rfl Div
27 Guards Rfl Div
40 Guards Rfl Div
23 Rifle Div
24 Rifle Div
252 Rifle Div
258 Rifle Div
304 Rifle Div
321 Rifle Div
121 Tank Bde

SIXTY-SIXTH ARMY
(Lt-Gen A.S. Zhadov)

64 Rifle Div
99 Rifle Div
116 Rifle Div
226 Rifle Div
299 Rifle Div
343 Rifle Div
58 Tank Bde

The forces assembled for Operation Uranus achieved overwhelming local superiority against the ill-equipped Third and Fourth Rumanian Armies holding the sectors on both flanks of Stalingrad. None of the standard Rumanian anti-tank weapons could penetrate the T-34 except at suicidally short ranges.

KEY

● Infantry   ● Mountain
● Tank   ● Cavalry
● Mechanized ● Airborne

Turning the Tide: 1943

In early 1943, it seemed that the Red Army had finally gained a decisive advantage in the East. The German surrender at Stalingrad was followed by rapid Soviet advances. However, events would show that the *Wehrmacht* was still a force to be reckoned with.

Urrah! A Red Army infantry section goes into the attack armed with Moison-Nagant rifles and PPSh-41 sub-machineguns.

On 25 November 1942, two days after Operation Uranus had trapped Sixth Army at Stalingrad, Zhukov launched Operation Mars, an equally ambitious offensive that was intended to crush Army Group Centre's forces in the Rzhev salient. A total of 83 divisions – over 800,000 men – and 2350 tanks were committed against the German Ninth Army, which had used the relatively quiet months since the conclusion of Operation Seydlitz (the destruction of Soviet forces trapped during the Rzhev-Vyazma offensive) to construct a network of defences around the salient.

Initially, the Soviet attacks made progress through sheer weight of numbers – the Western Front's Twentieth and Thirty-First Armies achieved a local five-to-one superiority when they opened the offensive against the northeastern edge of the salient supported by 500 tanks. Even so, they succeeded in making only a small breach in the German defences at the cost of horrendous losses. Under immense pressure from *Stavka*, General Ivan Konev, commanding the Western Front, ordered VIII Guards Rifle Corps and its mobile group (VI Tank and II Guards Cavalry Corps) into the breach to enlarge the bridgehead and exploit the breakthrough.

Any thoughts of a decisive victory quickly faded as stubbornly resisting strongpoints on the flanks of the Soviet penetration funnelled the advancing units into a congested, narrow front where they could not exploit their numerical superiority and provided a concentrated target for German artillery.

By 28 November, the attack in this sector had broken down with the encirclement of VI Tank and II Guards Cavalry Corps. Although the remnants of both formations managed to break out of the trap on the night of 29 November, virtually all their armour and heavy equipment was abandoned or destroyed.

Red Army success

On the western face of the salient, Soviet attacks had greater initial success. On 25 November, Forty-First Army launched a major assault near Belyi, opening the way for the 224 tanks of I Mechanized Corps, which by the following day had advanced almost 30km (19 miles) on a 20km (12.5-mile) front. On their left flank, Twenty-Second Army's III Mechanized Corps achieved similar success, advancing up the Luchesa valley towards Twentieth Army and threatening to seal off the north of the salient, potentially trapping the German XXVII and XXXIII Corps, plus 14th Panzergrenadier Division. This advance was finally halted after five days of fierce fighting, but neither side was strong enough to break through in this area.

The determined German defence of Belyi drew Soviet resources into a battle of attrition for the town, preventing I Mechanized Corps from exploiting its early success and giving vital time for Army Group Centre's reserves to arrive. On 7 December, a total of four Panzer divisions attacked Forty-First Army's flanks and swiftly achieved a double encirclement, trapping roughly 40,000 Soviet troops.

Failed campaign

News of this drove Zhukov to order further attacks to try to stave off the impending disaster. On 11 December, Twentieth and Twenty-Ninth Armies, including V and VI Tank Corps were ordered to renew attacks against the northeast of the salient. German anti-tank defences had been reinforced and a near massacre ensued as 300 Soviet tanks were destroyed in 48 hours. Some T-34s of the newly reconstituted VI Tank Corps were thrown into action straight from *Stavka* reserve stocks without any snow camouflage. Still in their factory-applied green paint, they were little more than appallingly conspicuous targets for well-camouflaged anti-tank guns.

Even Zhukov finally had to admit defeat – on the night of 15/16 December, the survivors of Forty-First Army destroyed their remaining tanks and artillery before breaking out of the pocket around Belyi. Although estimates of Soviet casualties vary wildly, it seems likely that they totalled almost 200,000 men and 1600 tanks. Red Army veterans understandably referred to the battles as 'the Rzhev meatgrinder'.

Breakout or rescue?

Although Operation Mars was a failure, it did ensure that the bulk of Army Group Centre's reserves could not be redeployed against the Soviet forces slowly strangling Paulus' Sixth Army at Stalingrad. Characteristically, Hitler had refused to allow any breakout from Stalingrad, insisting that the city should be held until a

SOVIET GROUND FORCES (JANUARY 1943)	
Unit Type	Number
HEADQUARTERS	
Fronts	15
Armies	67
Rifle Corps	34
Cavalry Corps	10
Tank Corps	20
Mechanized Corps	8
INFANTRY	
Rifle Divisions (inc Mountain & Motorized)	407
Rifle Brigades	177
Ski Brigades	48
Tank Destroyer Brigades	11
Separate Rifle Regiments	7
Fortified Regions	45
Ski Battalions	–
CAVALRY	
Cavalry Divisions	31
Cavalry Brigades	–
Separate Cavalry Regiments	5
ARMOUR	
Tank Divisions	2
Motorized Divisions	–
Armoured Car Brigades	1
Tank Brigades	176
Assault Gun Brigades	–
Mechanized Brigades	26
Motor Rifle Brigades	27
Motorcycle Brigades	–
Separate Tank Regiments	83
Separate Assault Gun Regiments	–
Motorcycle Regiments	5
Separate Tank Battalions	71
Separate Aerosan Battalions	54
Special Motorized Battalions	–
Armoured Train Battalions	62
Separate Arm Car & Motorcycle Battalions	40

relief force could be assembled to raise the siege. The unenviable responsibility for rescuing Sixth Army was given to Manstein, who assumed command of the newly formed Army Group Don on 26 November. It took two

SOVIET GROUND FORCES (JANUARY 1943)	
Unit Type	Number
AIRBORNE	
Airborne Divisions	10
ARTILLERY	
Artillery Divisions	25
Rocket Divisions	4
Anti-Aircraft Divisions	27
Separate Artillery Brigades	–
Separate Anti-Aircraft Brigades	1
Separate Mortar Brigades	7
Separate Rocket Brigades	11
Anti-Tank Brigades	–
Separate Artillery Regiments	273
Separate Mortar Regiments	102
Separate Anti-Tank Regiments	176
Separate Rocket Regiments	91
Separate Anti-Aircraft Regiments	123
Separate Artillery Battalions	25
Separate Anti-Aircraft Battalions	109
Separate Rocket Battalions	59
Separate Anti-Tank Battalions	2
Separate Mortar Battalions	12
PVO STRANYI	
PVO Stranyi Corps Region HQ	2
PVO Stranyi Division Region HQ	15
PVO Stranyi Brigade Region HQ	11
Anti-Aircraft Regiments	76
Anti-Aircraft Machine Gun Regiments	8
Searchlight Regiments	9
Anti-Aircraft Battalions	158
Anti-Aircraft Machine Gun Battalions	7
Searchlight Battalions	1

weeks of frantic efforts to assemble a force that had any chance of breaking through to Stalingrad.

The end at Stalingrad

During much of the winter of 1942/43, it seemed that the Red Army was on the verge of achieving a decisive victory. Hitler insisted that Kleist's Army Group A should remain in the Caucasus, despite the threat of being cut off. Even Manstein's genius could not compensate for this folly – his attempt to relieve Stalingrad was beaten

back and the last remnants of the garrison surrendered on 2 February 1943. Field Marshal Paulus and in the region of 100,000 German troops were taken into captivity by the Soviets.

The Soviet advance threatened to cut off Army Group A, which was forced to retreat to the Taman Peninsula. Within a week of the surrender at Stalingrad, the Voronezh and Southwest Fronts had retaken Kursk and Belgorod. Kharkov fell on the 14th and Soviet armour was threatening the Dnieper crossings at Zaporozhe.

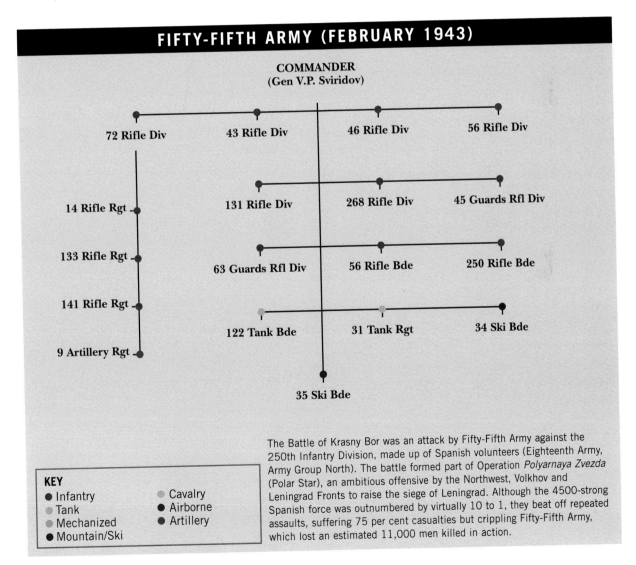

FIFTY-FIFTH ARMY (FEBRUARY 1943)

COMMANDER
(Gen V.P. Sviridov)

72 Rifle Div — 43 Rifle Div — 46 Rifle Div — 56 Rifle Div

14 Rifle Rgt — 131 Rifle Div — 268 Rifle Div — 45 Guards Rfl Div

133 Rifle Rgt — 63 Guards Rfl Div — 56 Rifle Bde — 250 Rifle Bde

141 Rifle Rgt — 122 Tank Bde — 31 Tank Rgt — 34 Ski Bde

9 Artillery Rgt

35 Ski Bde

KEY
- Infantry
- Tank
- Mechanized
- Mountain/Ski
- Cavalry
- Airborne
- Artillery

The Battle of Krasny Bor was an attack by Fifty-Fifth Army against the 250th Infantry Division, made up of Spanish volunteers (Eighteenth Army, Army Group North). The battle formed part of Operation *Polyarnaya Zvezda* (Polar Star), an ambitious offensive by the Northwest, Volkhov and Leningrad Fronts to raise the siege of Leningrad. Although the 4500-strong Spanish force was outnumbered by virtually 10 to 1, they beat off repeated assaults, suffering 75 per cent casualties but crippling Fifty-Fifth Army, which lost an estimated 11,000 men killed in action.

Third Battle of Kharkov

The seemingly irresistible Red Army winter offensive of 1942/43 was pushed too far, outrunning its supply lines and providing an opportunity for a devastating German counterattack.

2–23 March 1943

The German winter counter-offensive achieved both strategic and tactical surprise. On the strategic level, this was due to the fact that all the operational planning was carried out at Manstein's HQ, which gave immunity from the Soviet 'Lucy' spy ring which had infiltrated OKH.

At the tactical level, on the other hand, the Red Army had become overconfident, believing that the *Wehrmacht*'s losses at Stalingrad had left it incapable of making any significant counterattacks.

KHARKOV (FEBRUARY–MARCH 1943)

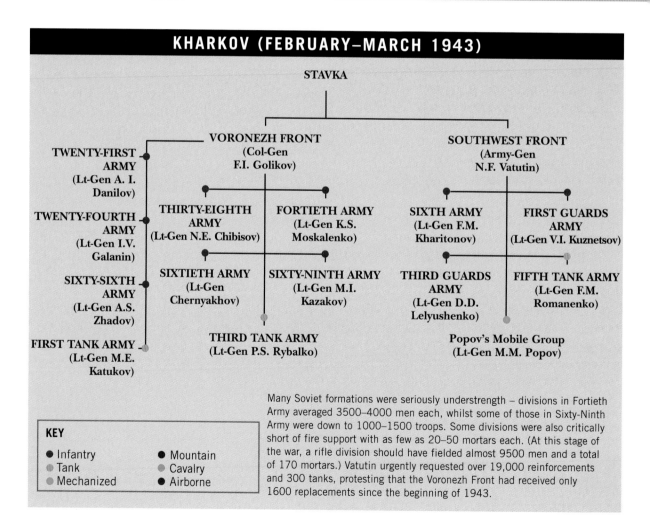

STAVKA

VORONEZH FRONT (Col-Gen F.I. Golikov)

SOUTHWEST FRONT (Army-Gen N.F. Vatutin)

TWENTY-FIRST ARMY (Lt-Gen A. I. Danilov)

THIRTY-EIGHTH ARMY (Lt-Gen N.E. Chibisov)

FORTIETH ARMY (Lt-Gen K.S. Moskalenko)

SIXTH ARMY (Lt-Gen F.M. Kharitonov)

FIRST GUARDS ARMY (Lt-Gen V.I. Kuznetsov)

TWENTY-FOURTH ARMY (Lt-Gen I.V. Galanin)

SIXTIETH ARMY (Lt-Gen Chernyakhov)

SIXTY-NINTH ARMY (Lt-Gen M.I. Kazakov)

THIRD GUARDS ARMY (Lt-Gen D.D. Lelyushenko)

FIFTH TANK ARMY (Lt-Gen F.M. Romanenko)

SIXTY-SIXTH ARMY (Lt-Gen A.S. Zhadov)

FIRST TANK ARMY (Lt-Gen M.E. Katukov)

THIRD TANK ARMY (Lt-Gen P.S. Rybalko)

Popov's Mobile Group (Lt-Gen M.M. Popov)

KEY

- ● Infantry
- ● Tank
- ● Mechanized
- ● Mountain
- ● Cavalry
- ● Airborne

Many Soviet formations were seriously understrength – divisions in Fortieth Army averaged 3500–4000 men each, whilst some of those in Sixty-Ninth Army were down to 1000–1500 troops. Some divisions were also critically short of fire support with as few as 20–50 mortars each. (At this stage of the war, a rifle division should have fielded almost 9500 men and a total of 170 mortars.) Vatutin urgently requested over 19,000 reinforcements and 300 tanks, protesting that the Voronezh Front had received only 1600 replacements since the beginning of 1943.

THIRD BATTLE OF KHARKOV

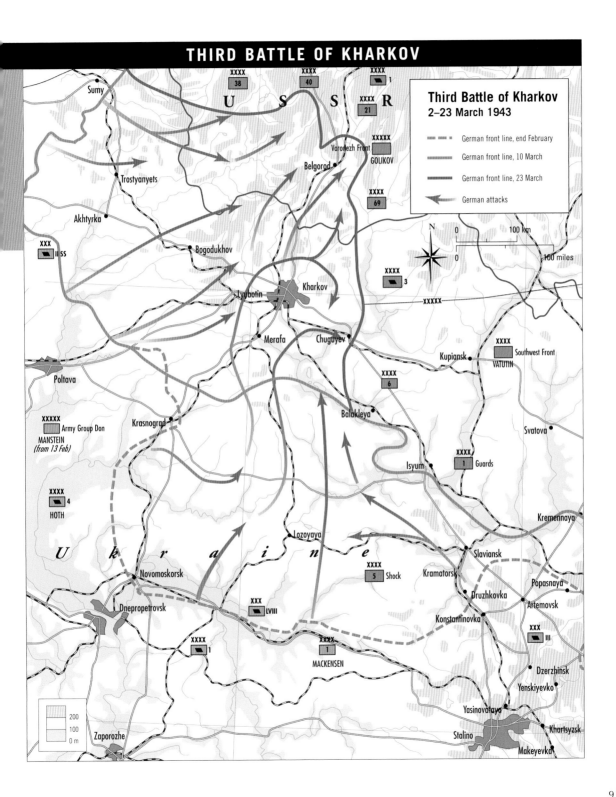

Third Battle of Kharkov
2–23 March 1943

- German front line, end February
- German front line, 10 March
- German front line, 23 March
- German attacks

USSR

Sumy

Trostyanyets

Akhtyrka

Bogodukhov

XXXX 38

XXXX 40

XXXX 1

XXXX 21

Varonezh Front
GOLIKOV

Belgorod

XXXX 69

XXX II SS

XXXX 3

Lyubotin

Kharkov

Merafa

Chuguyev

Kupiansk

Southwest Front
VATUTIN

XXXX 6

XXXX Balakleya

XXXXX Army Group Don
MANSTEIN
(from 13 Feb)

Krasnograd

Poltava

Svatova

Isyum

XXXX 1 Guards

XXXX 4
HOTH

Kremennaya

Lozovaya

Slaviansk

XXXX 5 Shock

Kramatorsk

Popasnaya

Novomoskorsk

XXX LVIII

Druzhkovka

Artemovsk

Konstantinovka

Dneprovetrovsk

XXXX 1

XXXX 1
MACKENSEN

XXX III

Dzerzhinsk

Yenskiyevko

200
100
0 m

Zaporozhe

Yasinovataya

Stalino

Khartsyzsk

Makeyevka

Ukraine

N

0   100 km
0   100 miles

EASTERN FRONT

Eastern Front
Beginning of
March 1943

1500
1000
500
200
100
0 m

0   100 km
0   100 miles

Leningrad
Leningrad Front
XXXX 18
Army Group North
Volkhov Front
Northwest Front
XXXX 16
Kalinin Front
XXXX 3   Velikiye Luki
Army Group Centre
Western Front
MOSCOW
N
Smolensk
Russia
XXXX 4
Belorussia
Bryansk Front
Bryansk
XXXX 2
Orel
U   S   S   R
XXXX 9
Kursk
Voronezh
Voronezh Front
XXXX 2
Kiev
Ukraine
Kharkov
XXXX 4
Southwest Front
Army Group South
Dnepropetrovsk
XXXX 8
XXXX 1
XXXX 6   Southern Front
Sea of Azov
North Caucasian Front
Army Group A
Black Sea   Crimea   XXXX 17
Sevastopol
Novorossiysk

By mid-February, there was very little time left before the mud of the spring thaw made major operations impossible, but Manstein showed just what could be achieved in a most threatening situation. By getting a shaken Hitler to authorize a mobile defence and release the necessary resources (the SS Panzer Corps, five *Wehrmacht* Panzer divisions and the elite *Grossdeutschland* Division), he was able to shorten his front and concentrate the Panzers to take advantage of Russian overconfidence. This overconfidence was understandable – Soviet armour had advanced as much as 300km (188 miles) in a month and seemed poised to reconquer the entire Ukraine.

However, the Soviet offensive was far more fragile than it seemed – General Nikolai Vatutin, commanding the Southwest Front, assembled four of his tank corps (III, X, XVIII, and IV Guards) under a single HQ (Group Popov) as a prototype Soviet Front mobile group to spearhead the advance. To help the group hold newly won territory, motorized rifle divisions were attached to each of the tank corps. To a large degree, however, the group's effectiveness was compromised by the weakness of its tank corps, which totalled only 160 AFVs, a figure that shrank rapidly due to breakdowns as much as enemy action. The group's advance deep into the German rear areas had great psychological impact,

March 1943

In March 1943, the *Wehrmacht* was still reeling from the disaster at Stalingrad, and on the southern battlefront the Red Army was advancing westwards at a headlong pace. However, the Soviet lines of communications were extended, and spearhead units were rapidly coming to the end of their resources. German divisions were, however, regrouping, slowing the Soviet advance and allowing time for a counterstrike to be prepared.

To the north, Army Group Centre had stopped a series of Soviet attacks around the Rzhev salient, inflicting a stinging reverse on Marshal Georgi Zhukov, and was now retiring to prepared defensive positions. Army Group North was still investing Leningrad, managing to blunt most Soviet attempts to break through to the city, although it could not cut the tenuous supply lines that ensured the city's survival.

MEDIUM ASSAULT GUN REGIMENT (APRIL 1943)															
Unit	Offs	Pol Offs	WOs	NCOs	Other Ranks	Pistol	Carbine	SMG	BA-64	T-34	SU-122	Motor-cycle	Car	Truck	Tractor
Regimental HQ	15	3	2	13	26	20	11	28	1	1	–	5	1	–	–
4 x Batteries, each	6	–	–	10	12	8	–	20	–	–	4	–	–	–	–
Medical Section	2	–	–	2	3	4	3	–	–	–	–	–	–	1	–
Trains Elements	8	–	–	19	43	9	30	31	–	–	–	–	–	36	2

but Manstein kept his nerve, noting the steady attrition of Lieutenant-General Popov's mobile group as its attached rifle divisions failed to keep pace with the tanks, which had also outrun their supply columns.

Panzer attack

On 20 February 1943, Manstein unleashed four Panzer corps supported by a 'maximum effort' from the *Luftwaffe*, which rapidly established air superiority over the battlefield, flying up to 1000 sorties per day. By this time, Popov's mobile group was reduced to 53 serviceable tanks with totally inadequate reserves of fuel and ammunition.

The concentrated Panzer thrusts achieved massive local superiority over the scattered and depleted Red Army armoured forces, rapidly defeating each in detail. The SS Panzer Corps recaptured Kharkov on 15 March, going on to take Belgorod three days later before the

thaw and the exhaustion of the German forces combined to end the counter-offensive.

After coming tantalizingly close to winning a major victory, the Red Army had been badly mauled – the Southwest Front had lost 23,000 men, 615 AFVs and 354 guns, whilst the Voronezh Front's casualties were even worse, totalling 40,000 men, 600 tanks and 500 guns. German forces once again held much of the territory lost during the winter except for a large salient centred on the small provincial city of Kursk.

By the spring of 1943, the numerical odds were very much in the Red Army's favour – it fielded six million men, between 12,000 and 15,000 AFVs and 33,000 guns against Axis totals of 2.7 million men, 2200 AFVs and 6360 guns. However, the loss ratios were still running strongly in favour of the Germans, as they had since the opening of Barbarossa. The figures for AFVs were: 1941 – 1:7; 1942 – 1:6; 1943 – 1:4.

Kursk, July 1943

From the German perspective, the Kursk salient was an obvious target for a summer offensive in 1943 – unfortunately for them, it was just as obvious to the Red Army that they would attack.

An attack to 'pinch out' the Kursk salient would shorten the German front by 250km (156 miles), freeing up to 20 divisions for use elsewhere, besides destroying what was seen as a 'gateway for the invasion of the Ukraine'. Typically, Field Marshal Manstein proposed a radical alternative, a new offensive on the same principles as his

recent operations, which had led to the recapture of Kharkov and Belgorod. He intended to lure the Southern and Southwest Fronts into attacks against the newly reconstituted Sixth Army, drawing them into the eastern Ukraine. A counter-offensive would then be launched from the Kharkov area towards Rostov, with

SOVIET GROUND FORCES (JULY 1943)	
Unit Type	Number
HEADQUARTERS	
Fronts	18
Armies	81
Rifle Corps	82
Cavalry Corps	9
Tank Corps	24
Mechanized Corps	13
INFANTRY	
Rifle Divisions (inc Mountain & Motorized)	462
Rifle Brigades	98
Ski Brigades	3
Tank Destroyer Brigades	6
Separate Rifle Regiments	6
Fortified Regions	45
Ski Battalions	–
CAVALRY	
Cavalry Divisions	27
ARMOUR	
Tank Divisions	2
Motorized Divisions	–
Armoured Car Brigades	–
Tank Brigades	182
Assault Gun Brigades	–
Mechanized Brigades	42
Motor Rifle Brigades	21
Motorcycle Brigades	–
Separate Tank Regiments	118
Separate Assault Gun Regiments	57
Motorcycle Regiments	8
Separate Tank Battalions	45
Separate Aerosan Battalions	57
Special Motorized Battalions	–
Armoured Train Battalions	66
Separate Armoured Car & Motorcycle Btns	44

the aim of trapping most of the two Fronts against the Sea of Azov.

Predictably, this 'Manstein plan' was vetoed by Hitler, who ordered an offensive against the Kursk salient,

SOVIET GROUND FORCES (JULY 1943)	
Unit Type	Number
AIRBORNE	
Airborne Divisions	10
Airborne Brigades	21
ARTILLERY	
Artillery Divisions	25
Rocket Divisions	7
Anti-Aircraft Divisions	63
Separate Artillery Brigades	17
Separate Anti-Aircraft Brigades	3
Separate Mortar Brigades	11
Separate Rocket Brigades	10
Anti-Tank Brigades	27
Separate Artillery Regiments	235
Separate Mortar Regiments	171
Separate Anti-Tank Regiments	199
Separate Rocket Regiments	113
Separate Anti-Aircraft Regiments	212
Separate Artillery Battalions	41
Separate Anti-Aircraft Battalions	112
Separate Rocket Battalions	37
Separate Anti-Tank Battalions	44
Separate Mortar Battalions	5
PVO STRANYI	
PVO Stranyi Corps Region HQ	5
PVO Stranyi Division Region HQ	13
PVO Stranyi Brigade Region HQ	11
Anti-Aircraft Regiments	106
Anti-Aircraft Machine Gun Regiments	14
Searchlight Regiments	4
Anti-Aircraft Battalions	168
Anti-Aircraft Machine Gun Battalions	21
Searchlight Battalions	13

which seemed to invite the sort of Panzer-led pincer attack that had been so successful in the past. This was equally obvious to the Soviets, who were busily fortifying the area, and almost all the German commanders urged Hitler to strike quickly before the odds became too great.

Fortunately for the Red Army, Hitler was convinced that only the new Elefants and Panthers could guarantee to break the strengthening Russian defences and imposed delay after delay until he felt that the *Panzerwaffe* was strong enough for the task. German commanders were appalled at the prospect of a head-on attack against the deep belts of minefields and *Pakfronten* – massed anti-tank gun batteries – which showed up all too clearly in air reconnaissance photographs. They were also well aware of the security risks that grew with each successive delay (in fact, the so-called 'Red Orchestra' spy ring was busily sending Moscow complete details of the German plans).

The last German offensive

On 5 July, the German attack, codenamed Citadel, went in against the flanks of the salient. *Generaloberst* Walter Model's Ninth Army struck south to meet *Generaloberst* Hermann Hoth's Fourth Panzer Army moving north on Kursk. A total of 16 Panzer and Panzergrenadier divisions with 2700 AFVs were fielded with the support

July 1943

Kursk was such an obvious objective that the Soviets began fortifying it almost as soon as the Germans decided to attack it. As early as March, Marshal Georgi Zhukov and his Front commanders were presenting Stalin with their expectations of likely German plans for the coming campaigning season. Their predictions proved to be remarkably accurate when the battle started in July.

In addition, the Red Army planned new offensives of its own, scheduled to open the moment the German attack stalled. Stalin and his most senior commanders gambled that they could hold Kursk against the elite Panzer divisions, absorb the full strength of the German blow, then unleash a multi-Front offensive that would liberate the Ukraine.

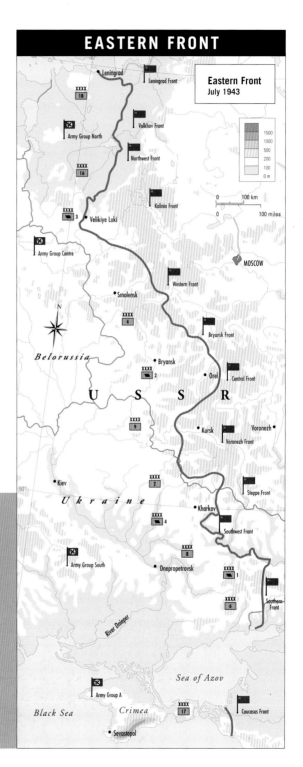

of 10,000 guns and 2000 aircraft. The Red Army had the advantage of eight defensive belts, six within the salient itself, backed by a final two covering the River Don and the approaches to Voronezh. These defences were covered by 3600 AFVs, 20,000 guns and 2400 aircraft.

The massive field defences gave the defenders a vital advantage and the German offensive soon ran into trouble – the first attacks quickly bogged down in huge

minefields of up to 3200 mines per kilometre (1093 yards) frontage, which were swept by fire from up to 100 guns and mortars per kilometre (1093 yards). At Kursk, each battalion of Seventh Guards Army's XXV Guards Rifle Corps was protected by an average of 1.6km (1750 yards) of barbed wire covering its position, plus 1500 anti-tank mines and 1700 anti-personnel mines per kilometre (1093 yards) of defensive frontage. On the

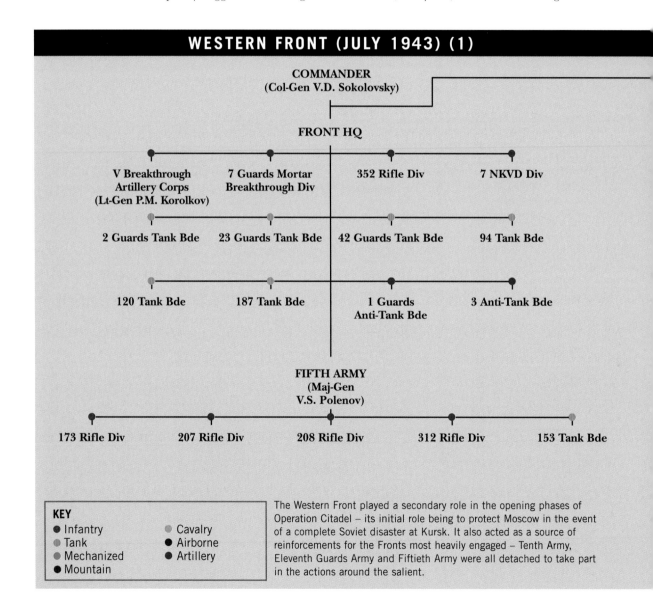

WESTERN FRONT (JULY 1943) (1)

COMMANDER
(Col-Gen V.D. Sokolovsky)

FRONT HQ

| V Breakthrough Artillery Corps (Lt-Gen P.M. Korolkov) | 7 Guards Mortar Breakthrough Div | 352 Rifle Div | 7 NKVD Div |

| 2 Guards Tank Bde | 23 Guards Tank Bde | 42 Guards Tank Bde | 94 Tank Bde |

| 120 Tank Bde | 187 Tank Bde | 1 Guards Anti-Tank Bde | 3 Anti-Tank Bde |

FIFTH ARMY
(Maj-Gen
V.S. Polenov)

| 173 Rifle Div | 207 Rifle Div | 208 Rifle Div | 312 Rifle Div | 153 Tank Bde |

KEY
● Infantry
● Cavalry
● Tank
● Airborne
● Mechanized
● Artillery
● Mountain

The Western Front played a secondary role in the opening phases of Operation Citadel – its initial role being to protect Moscow in the event of a complete Soviet disaster at Kursk. It also acted as a source of reinforcements for the Fronts most heavily engaged – Tenth Army, Eleventh Guards Army and Fiftieth Army were all detached to take part in the actions around the salient.

section of front occupied by Fifteenth Army's 81st Rifle Division, the anti-tank mines accounted for the destruction or crippling of 17 of the 40 AFVs that took part in the initial German assault.

Minefields

Overall, mines were especially important at Kursk given the limitations of most Soviet anti-tank guns against the newer, better-protected German AFVs. The 6000 mines on Thirteenth Army's section of front accounted for 98 German tanks on the first day of battle. On 6 July, the eight mobile obstacle detachments of Thirteenth Army laid 9000 additional mines, which cost the Germans 88 tanks and assault guns on the second day of battle. The following day, 8000 newly laid mines accounted for a further 93 tanks.

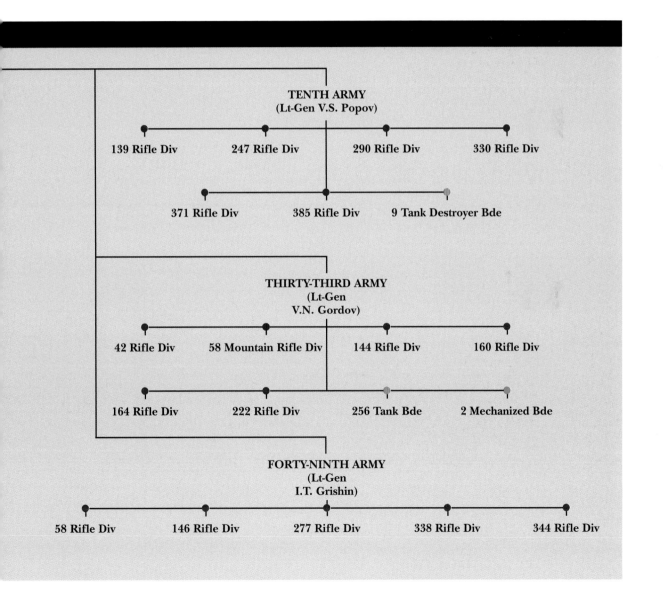

WESTERN FRONT (JULY 1943) (2)

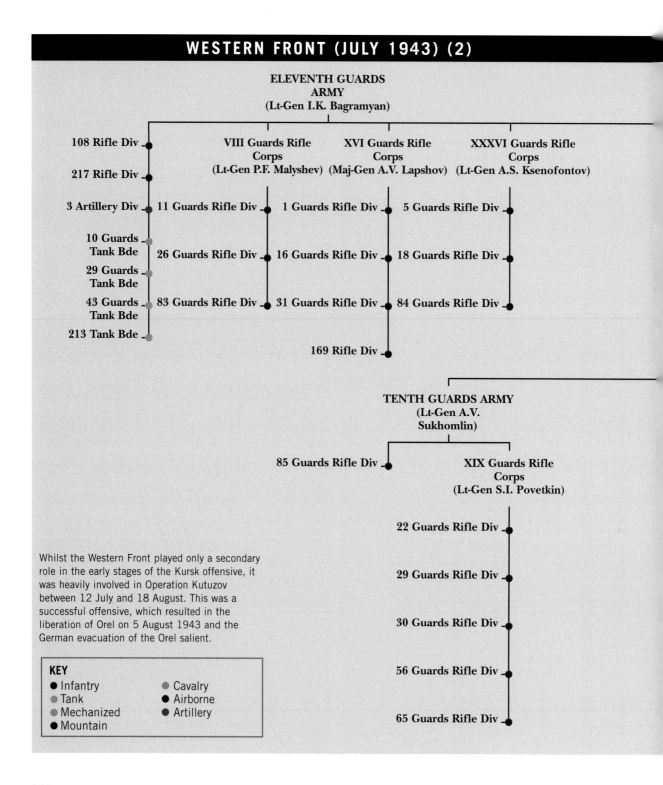

ELEVENTH GUARDS ARMY
(Lt-Gen I.K. Bagramyan)

108 Rifle Div

217 Rifle Div

3 Artillery Div

10 Guards Tank Bde

29 Guards Tank Bde

43 Guards Tank Bde

213 Tank Bde

VIII Guards Rifle Corps
(Lt-Gen P.F. Malyshev)

11 Guards Rifle Div

26 Guards Rifle Div

83 Guards Rifle Div

XVI Guards Rifle Corps
(Maj-Gen A.V. Lapshov)

1 Guards Rifle Div

16 Guards Rifle Div

31 Guards Rifle Div

169 Rifle Div

XXXVI Guards Rifle Corps
(Lt-Gen A.S. Ksenofontov)

5 Guards Rifle Div

18 Guards Rifle Div

84 Guards Rifle Div

TENTH GUARDS ARMY
(Lt-Gen A.V. Sukhomlin)

85 Guards Rifle Div

XIX Guards Rifle Corps
(Lt-Gen S.I. Povetkin)

22 Guards Rifle Div

29 Guards Rifle Div

30 Guards Rifle Div

56 Guards Rifle Div

65 Guards Rifle Div

Whilst the Western Front played only a secondary role in the early stages of the Kursk offensive, it was heavily involved in Operation Kutuzov between 12 July and 18 August. This was a successful offensive, which resulted in the liberation of Orel on 5 August 1943 and the German evacuation of the Orel salient.

KEY
- Infantry
- Tank
- Mechanized
- Mountain
- Cavalry
- Airborne
- Artillery

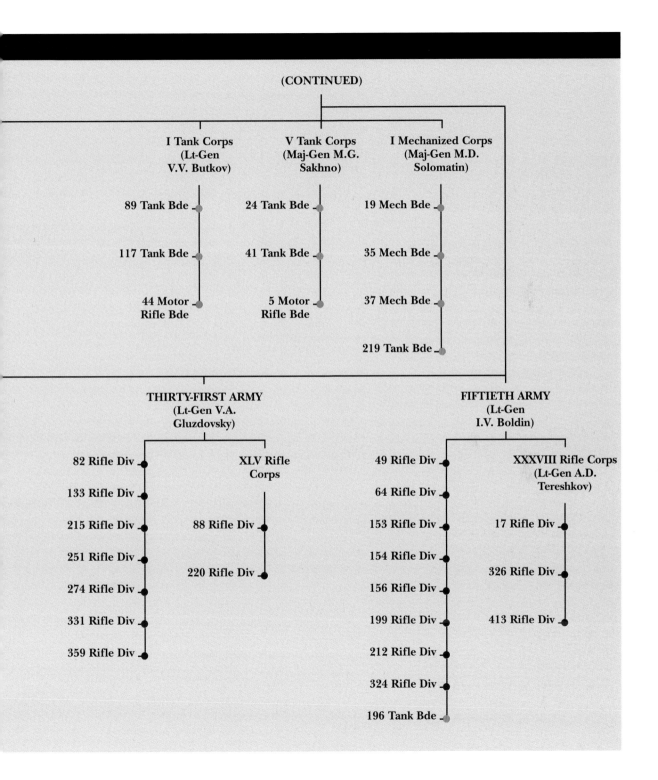

(CONTINUED)

I Tank Corps
(Lt-Gen
V.V. Butkov)

V Tank Corps
(Maj-Gen M.G.
Sakhno)

I Mechanized Corps
(Maj-Gen M.D.
Solomatin)

89 Tank Bde

117 Tank Bde

44 Motor
Rifle Bde

24 Tank Bde

41 Tank Bde

5 Motor
Rifle Bde

19 Mech Bde

35 Mech Bde

37 Mech Bde

219 Tank Bde

THIRTY-FIRST ARMY
(Lt-Gen V.A.
Gluzdovsky)

82 Rifle Div

133 Rifle Div

215 Rifle Div

251 Rifle Div

274 Rifle Div

331 Rifle Div

359 Rifle Div

**XLV Rifle
Corps**

88 Rifle Div

220 Rifle Div

FIFTIETH ARMY
(Lt-Gen
I.V. Boldin)

49 Rifle Div

64 Rifle Div

153 Rifle Div

154 Rifle Div

156 Rifle Div

199 Rifle Div

212 Rifle Div

324 Rifle Div

196 Tank Bde

XXXVIII Rifle Corps
(Lt-Gen A.D.
Tereshkov)

17 Rifle Div

326 Rifle Div

413 Rifle Div

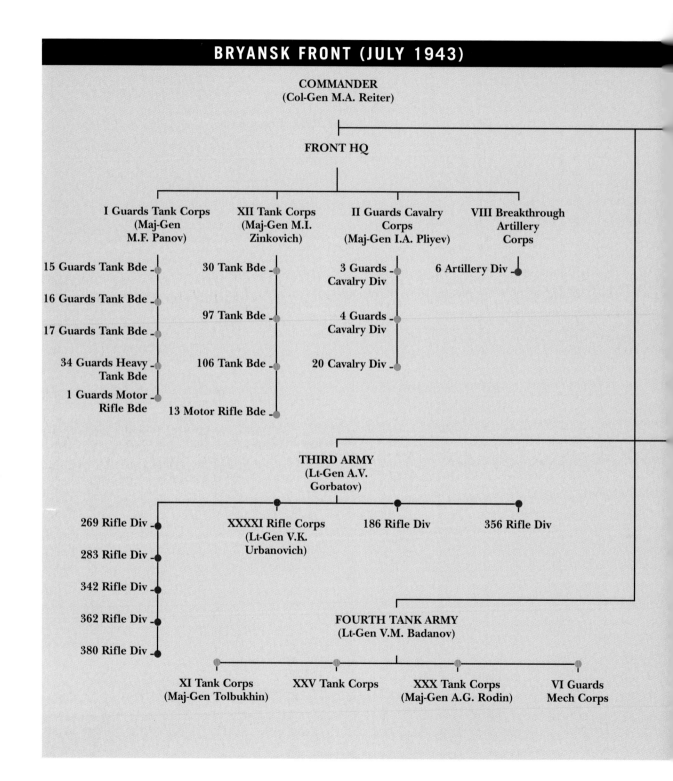

BRYANSK FRONT (JULY 1943)

COMMANDER
(Col-Gen M.A. Reiter)

FRONT HQ

I Guards Tank Corps
(Maj-Gen
M.F. Panov)

XII Tank Corps
(Maj-Gen M.I.
Zinkovich)

**II Guards Cavalry
Corps**
(Maj-Gen I.A. Pliyev)

**VIII Breakthrough
Artillery
Corps**

15 Guards Tank Bde

16 Guards Tank Bde

17 Guards Tank Bde

34 Guards Heavy
Tank Bde

1 Guards Motor
Rifle Bde

30 Tank Bde

97 Tank Bde

106 Tank Bde

13 Motor Rifle Bde

3 Guards
Cavalry Div

4 Guards
Cavalry Div

20 Cavalry Div

6 Artillery Div

THIRD ARMY
(Lt-Gen A.V.
Gorbatov)

269 Rifle Div

283 Rifle Div

342 Rifle Div

362 Rifle Div

380 Rifle Div

XXXXI Rifle Corps
(Lt-Gen V.K.
Urbanovich)

186 Rifle Div

356 Rifle Div

FOURTH TANK ARMY
(Lt-Gen V.M. Badanov)

XI Tank Corps
(Maj-Gen Tolbukhin)

XXV Tank Corps

XXX Tank Corps
(Maj-Gen A.G. Rodin)

**VI Guards
Mech Corps**

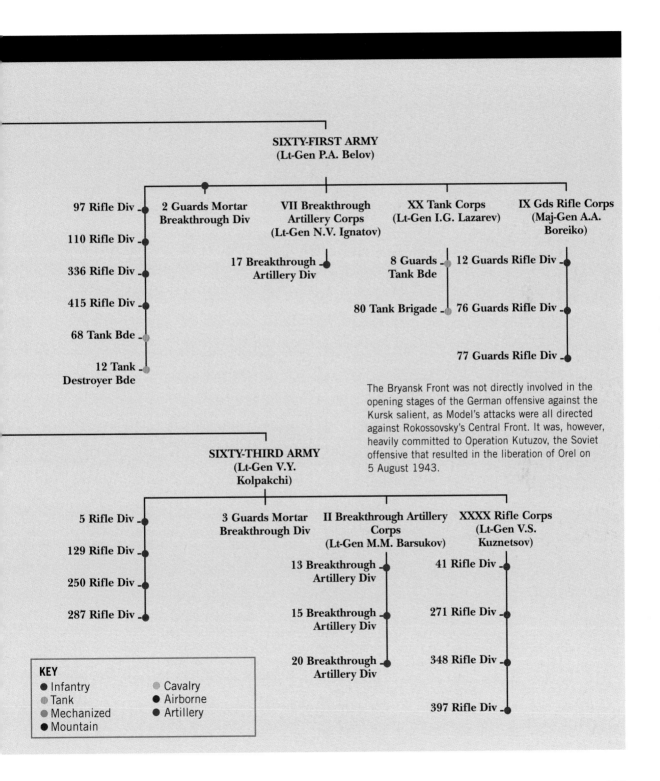

SIXTY-FIRST ARMY
(Lt-Gen P.A. Belov)

97 Rifle Div

110 Rifle Div

336 Rifle Div

415 Rifle Div

68 Tank Bde

12 Tank
Destroyer Bde

**2 Guards Mortar
Breakthrough Div**

**VII Breakthrough
Artillery Corps**
(Lt-Gen N.V. Ignatov)

17 Breakthrough
Artillery Div

XX Tank Corps
(Lt-Gen I.G. Lazarev)

8 Guards
Tank Bde

80 Tank Brigade

IX Gds Rifle Corps
(Maj-Gen A.A.
Boreiko)

12 Guards Rifle Div

76 Guards Rifle Div

77 Guards Rifle Div

The Bryansk Front was not directly involved in the
opening stages of the German offensive against the
Kursk salient, as Model's attacks were all directed
against Rokossovsky's Central Front. It was, however,
heavily committed to Operation Kutuzov, the Soviet
offensive that resulted in the liberation of Orel on
5 August 1943.

SIXTY-THIRD ARMY
(Lt-Gen V.Y.
Kolpakchi)

5 Rifle Div

129 Rifle Div

250 Rifle Div

287 Rifle Div

**3 Guards Mortar
Breakthrough Div**

**II Breakthrough Artillery
Corps**
(Lt-Gen M.M. Barsukov)

13 Breakthrough
Artillery Div

15 Breakthrough
Artillery Div

20 Breakthrough
Artillery Div

XXXX Rifle Corps
(Lt-Gen V.S.
Kuznetsov)

41 Rifle Div

271 Rifle Div

348 Rifle Div

397 Rifle Div

KEY
● Infantry
● Tank
● Mechanized
● Mountain
● Cavalry
● Airborne
● Artillery

CENTRAL FRONT (JULY 1943) (1)

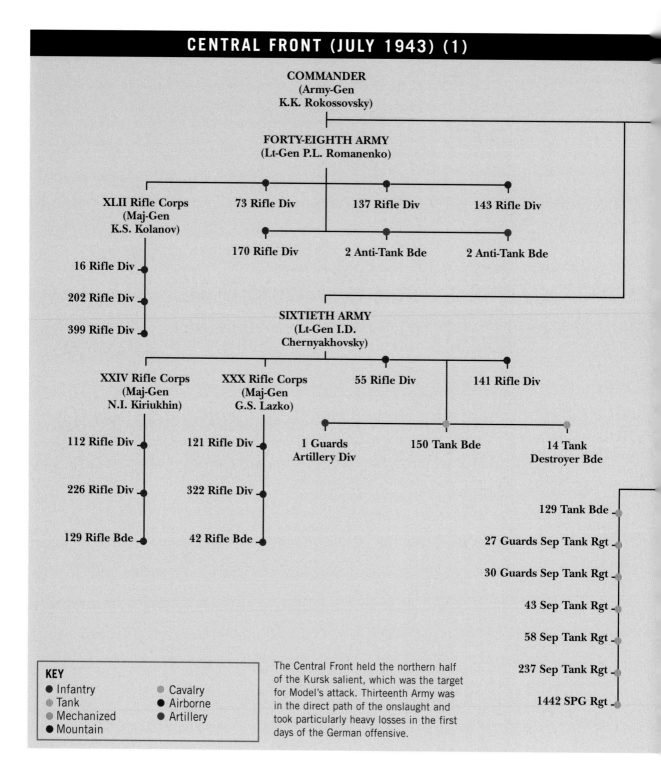

COMMANDER
(Army-Gen
K.K. Rokossovsky)

FORTY-EIGHTH ARMY
(Lt-Gen P.L. Romanenko)

XLII Rifle Corps
(Maj-Gen
K.S. Kolanov)

73 Rifle Div

137 Rifle Div

143 Rifle Div

170 Rifle Div

2 Anti-Tank Bde

2 Anti-Tank Bde

16 Rifle Div

202 Rifle Div

399 Rifle Div

SIXTIETH ARMY
(Lt-Gen I.D.
Chernyakhovsky)

XXIV Rifle Corps
(Maj-Gen
N.I. Kiriukhin)

XXX Rifle Corps
(Maj-Gen
G.S. Lazko)

55 Rifle Div

141 Rifle Div

112 Rifle Div

121 Rifle Div

1 Guards
Artillery Div

150 Tank Bde

14 Tank
Destroyer Bde

226 Rifle Div

322 Rifle Div

129 Tank Bde

129 Rifle Bde

42 Rifle Bde

27 Guards Sep Tank Rgt

30 Guards Sep Tank Rgt

43 Sep Tank Rgt

58 Sep Tank Rgt

237 Sep Tank Rgt

1442 SPG Rgt

KEY
- Infantry
- Tank
- Mechanized
- Mountain
- Cavalry
- Airborne
- Artillery

The Central Front held the northern half of the Kursk salient, which was the target for Model's attack. Thirteenth Army was in the direct path of the onslaught and took particularly heavy losses in the first days of the German offensive.

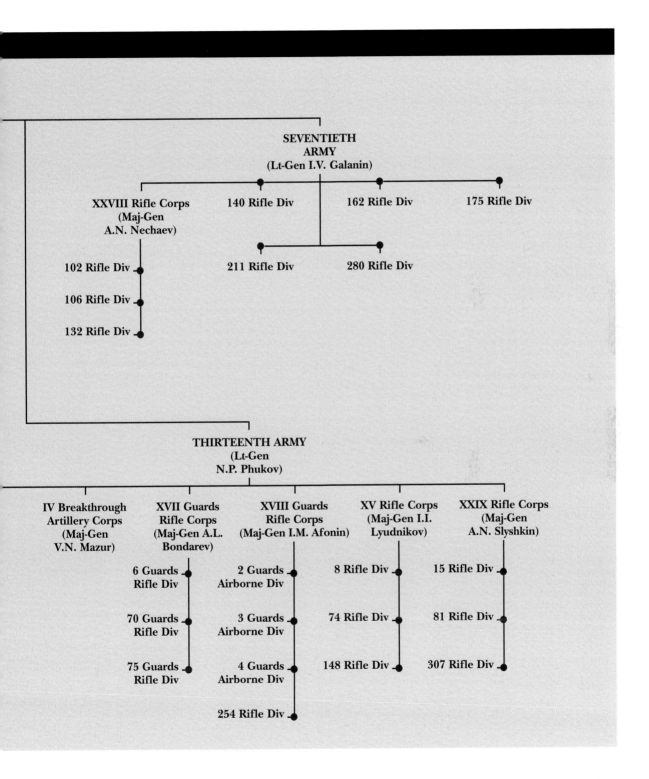

SEVENTIETH ARMY
(Lt-Gen I.V. Galanin)

XXVIII Rifle Corps
(Maj-Gen A.N. Nechaev)

140 Rifle Div

162 Rifle Div

175 Rifle Div

102 Rifle Div

106 Rifle Div

132 Rifle Div

211 Rifle Div

280 Rifle Div

THIRTEENTH ARMY
(Lt-Gen N.P. Phukov)

IV Breakthrough Artillery Corps
(Maj-Gen V.N. Mazur)

XVII Guards Rifle Corps
(Maj-Gen A.L. Bondarev)

XVIII Guards Rifle Corps
(Maj-Gen I.M. Afonin)

XV Rifle Corps
(Maj-Gen I.I. Lyudnikov)

XXIX Rifle Corps
(Maj-Gen A.N. Slyshkin)

6 Guards Rifle Div

70 Guards Rifle Div

75 Guards Rifle Div

2 Guards Airborne Div

3 Guards Airborne Div

4 Guards Airborne Div

254 Rifle Div

8 Rifle Div

74 Rifle Div

148 Rifle Div

15 Rifle Div

81 Rifle Div

307 Rifle Div

During the course of the battle in this sector, Soviet engineers laid 35,000 anti-tank and 4000 anti-personnel mines, which destroyed or disabled 420 German tanks and assault guns. In the areas in which Fourth Panzer Army and Army Detachment 'Kempf' were operating, mines took a toll of 355 German tanks and 30 assault guns – a very significant number and critical in the Red Army's successful defence.

The attackers frequently used the *Panzerkeil*, or armoured wedge, a formation in which Elefants or Tigers formed the point of the wedge and Panthers the sides in order to protect the lighter AFVs – Panzer IIIs

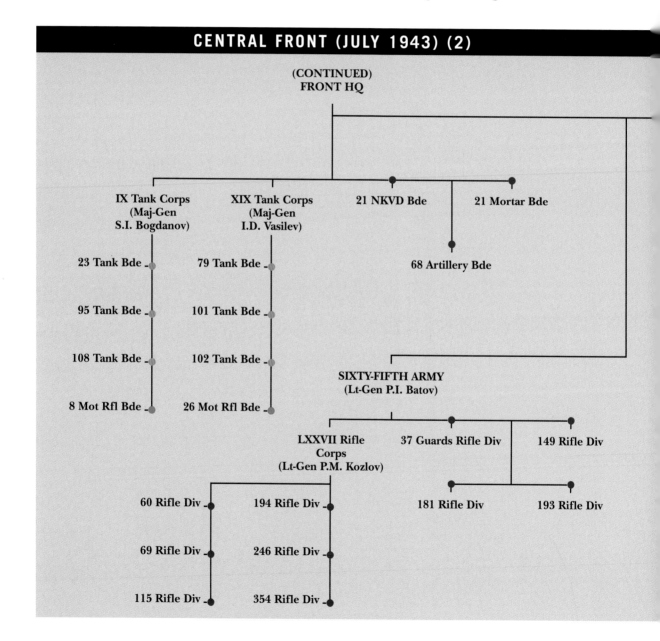

CENTRAL FRONT (JULY 1943) (2)

(CONTINUED)
FRONT HQ

IX Tank Corps (Maj-Gen S.I. Bogdanov)
- 23 Tank Bde
- 95 Tank Bde
- 108 Tank Bde
- 8 Mot Rfl Bde

XIX Tank Corps (Maj-Gen I.D. Vasilev)
- 79 Tank Bde
- 101 Tank Bde
- 102 Tank Bde
- 26 Mot Rfl Bde

21 NKVD Bde

21 Mortar Bde
- 68 Artillery Bde

SIXTY-FIFTH ARMY (Lt-Gen P.I. Batov)

LXXVII Rifle Corps (Lt-Gen P.M. Kozlov)
- 60 Rifle Div
- 69 Rifle Div
- 115 Rifle Div
- 194 Rifle Div
- 246 Rifle Div
- 354 Rifle Div

37 Guards Rifle Div

149 Rifle Div

181 Rifle Div

193 Rifle Div

and IVs – from the withering anti-tank fire. Even this formation was only partially successful in the face of such massive Soviet defences – the Tigers and Elefants might well get through, but all too often the lighter vehicles and infantry were destroyed as they attempted to follow. This left the 'heavies' unsupported and horribly vulnerable to Soviet infantry anti-tank teams using demolition charges or flamethrowers.

Air battle
The Red Air Force was able to match the *Luftwaffe* for the first time in a major battle. The close support

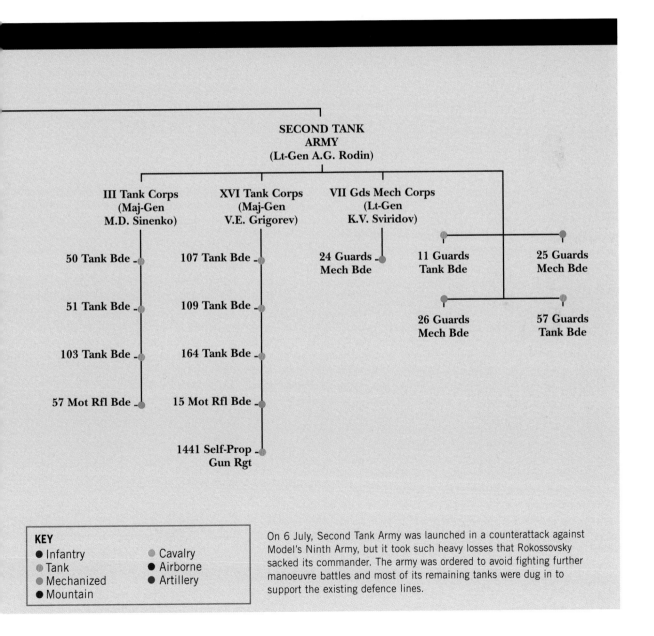

SECOND TANK ARMY
(Lt-Gen A.G. Rodin)

III Tank Corps (Maj-Gen M.D. Sinenko)

50 Tank Bde
51 Tank Bde
103 Tank Bde
57 Mot Rfl Bde

XVI Tank Corps (Maj-Gen V.E. Grigorev)

107 Tank Bde
109 Tank Bde
164 Tank Bde
15 Mot Rfl Bde
1441 Self-Prop Gun Rgt

VII Gds Mech Corps (Lt-Gen K.V. Sviridov)

24 Guards Mech Bde
11 Guards Tank Bde
25 Guards Mech Bde
26 Guards Mech Bde
57 Guards Tank Bde

KEY
● Infantry
● Tank
● Mechanized
● Mountain
● Cavalry
● Airborne
● Artillery

On 6 July, Second Tank Army was launched in a counterattack against Model's Ninth Army, but it took such heavy losses that Rokossovsky sacked its commander. The army was ordered to avoid fighting further manoeuvre battles and most of its remaining tanks were dug in to support the existing defence lines.

VORONEZH FRONT (JULY 1943) (1)

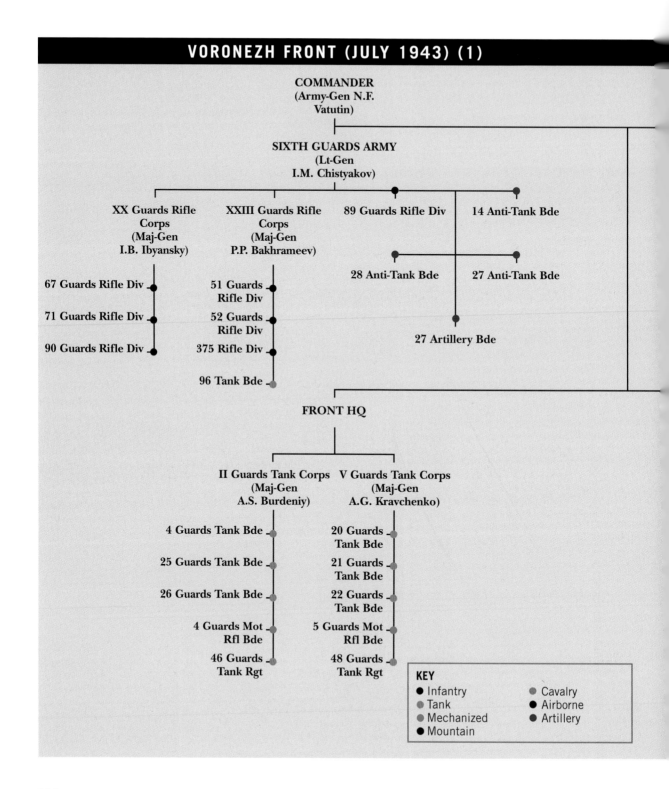

COMMANDER
(Army-Gen N.F. Vatutin)

SIXTH GUARDS ARMY
(Lt-Gen I.M. Chistyakov)

XX Guards Rifle Corps
(Maj-Gen I.B. Ibyansky)

XXIII Guards Rifle Corps
(Maj-Gen P.P. Bakhrameev)

89 Guards Rifle Div

14 Anti-Tank Bde

28 Anti-Tank Bde

27 Anti-Tank Bde

67 Guards Rifle Div

71 Guards Rifle Div

90 Guards Rifle Div

51 Guards Rifle Div

52 Guards Rifle Div

375 Rifle Div

96 Tank Bde

27 Artillery Bde

FRONT HQ

II Guards Tank Corps
(Maj-Gen A.S. Burdeniy)

V Guards Tank Corps
(Maj-Gen A.G. Kravchenko)

4 Guards Tank Bde

25 Guards Tank Bde

26 Guards Tank Bde

4 Guards Mot Rfl Bde

46 Guards Tank Rgt

20 Guards Tank Bde

21 Guards Tank Bde

22 Guards Tank Bde

5 Guards Mot Rfl Bde

48 Guards Tank Rgt

KEY
- Infantry
- Tank
- Mechanized
- Mountain
- Cavalry
- Airborne
- Artillery

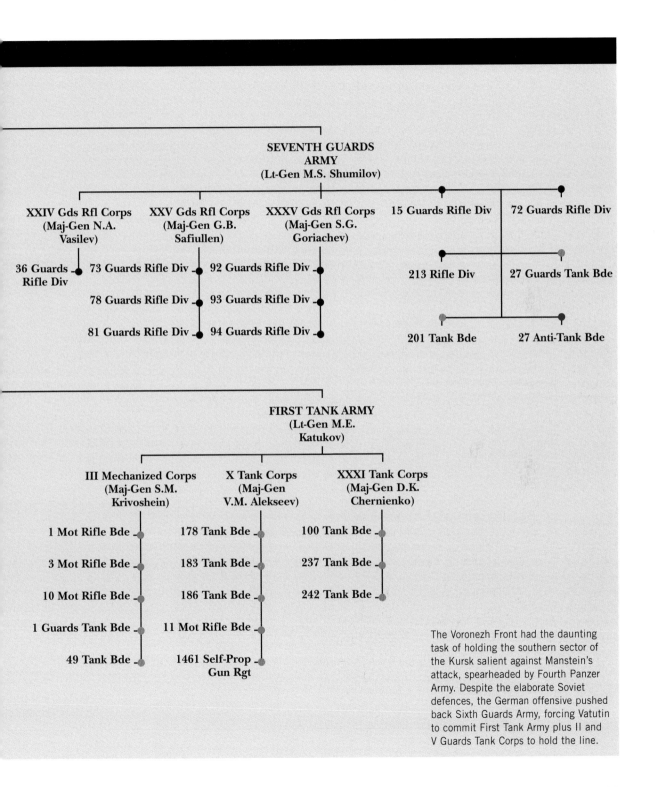

SEVENTH GUARDS ARMY
(Lt-Gen M.S. Shumilov)

XXIV Gds Rfl Corps
(Maj-Gen N.A. Vasilev)

XXV Gds Rfl Corps
(Maj-Gen G.B. Safiullen)

XXXV Gds Rfl Corps
(Maj-Gen S.G. Goriachev)

15 Guards Rifle Div

72 Guards Rifle Div

36 Guards Rifle Div

73 Guards Rifle Div

92 Guards Rifle Div

213 Rifle Div

27 Guards Tank Bde

78 Guards Rifle Div

93 Guards Rifle Div

81 Guards Rifle Div

94 Guards Rifle Div

201 Tank Bde

27 Anti-Tank Bde

FIRST TANK ARMY
(Lt-Gen M.E. Katukov)

III Mechanized Corps
(Maj-Gen S.M. Krivoshein)

X Tank Corps
(Maj-Gen V.M. Alekseev)

XXXI Tank Corps
(Maj-Gen D.K. Chernienko)

1 Mot Rifle Bde

178 Tank Bde

100 Tank Bde

3 Mot Rifle Bde

183 Tank Bde

237 Tank Bde

10 Mot Rifle Bde

186 Tank Bde

242 Tank Bde

1 Guards Tank Bde

11 Mot Rifle Bde

49 Tank Bde

1461 Self-Prop Gun Rgt

The Voronezh Front had the daunting task of holding the southern sector of the Kursk salient against Manstein's attack, spearheaded by Fourth Panzer Army. Despite the elaborate Soviet defences, the German offensive pushed back Sixth Guards Army, forcing Vatutin to commit First Tank Army plus II and V Guards Tank Corps to hold the line.

VORONEZH FRONT (JULY 1943) (2)

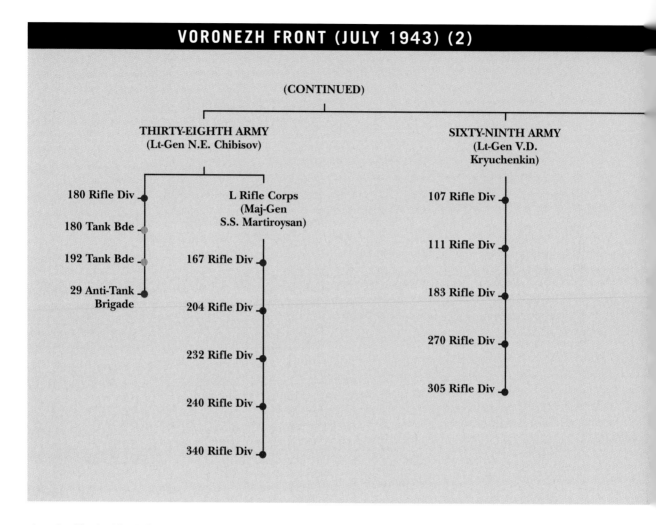

(CONTINUED)

THIRTY-EIGHTH ARMY
(Lt-Gen N.E. Chibisov)

SIXTY-NINTH ARMY
(Lt-Gen V.D. Kryuchenkin)

180 Rifle Div

180 Tank Bde

192 Tank Bde

29 Anti-Tank Brigade

L Rifle Corps
(Maj-Gen S.S. Martiroysan)

167 Rifle Div

204 Rifle Div

232 Rifle Div

240 Rifle Div

340 Rifle Div

107 Rifle Div

111 Rifle Div

183 Rifle Div

270 Rifle Div

305 Rifle Div

aircraft of both sides inflicted heavy damage, and although German fighters and AA units shot down large numbers of Soviet aircraft, the Red Air Force proved that it could absorb these losses and continue to operate effectively.

The IL-2 Sturmovik ground-attack aircraft had been a threat to German armour since the opening stages of *Barbarossa* but had rarely been deployed in sufficient numbers to be fully effective. Now that it was available in substantial quantities, the situation was far more dangerous for the Germans – in a single action against XXXXVII Panzer Corps, Sturmoviks destroyed 20 AFVs and damaged a further 40 for the loss of just a single aircraft.

On 6 July, General Konstantin Rokossovsky's Central Front, holding the north of the salient, launched a counterattack through Second Tank Army; it broke down after sustaining heavy losses (in part from Soviet minefields that had been strengthened by German engineers).

In contrast, Vatutin's Voronezh Front in the south did not commit major armoured formations against the initial German attacks, relying on the minefields and *Pakfronten* to blunt the offensive. Although the advance of Model's Ninth Army was halted after little more than 15km (9.4 miles) – well short of Kursk – Hoth beat off all counterattacks, cut deeply into the Soviet defences and threatened to make a decisive breakthrough.

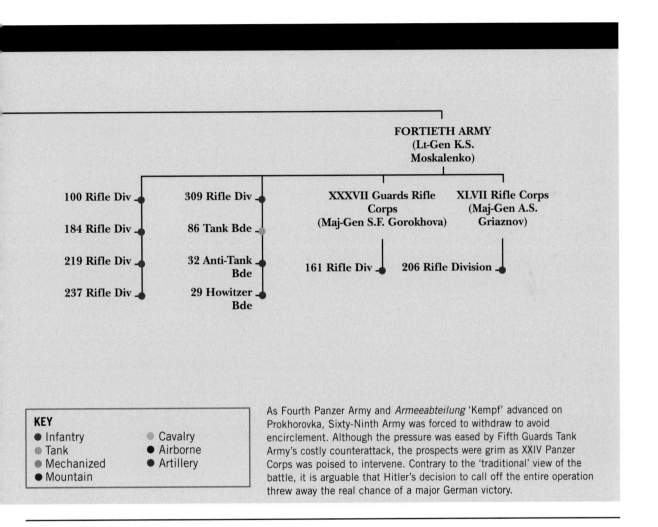

FORTIETH ARMY
(Lt-Gen K.S. Moskalenko)

100 Rifle Div

184 Rifle Div

219 Rifle Div

237 Rifle Div

309 Rifle Div

86 Tank Bde

32 Anti-Tank Bde

29 Howitzer Bde

XXXVII Guards Rifle Corps
(Maj-Gen S.F. Gorokhova)

161 Rifle Div

XLVII Rifle Corps
(Maj-Gen A.S. Griaznov)

206 Rifle Division

KEY
- Infantry
- Tank
- Mechanized
- Mountain
- Cavalry
- Airborne
- Artillery

As Fourth Panzer Army and *Armeeabteilung* 'Kempf' advanced on Prokhorovka, Sixty-Ninth Army was forced to withdraw to avoid encirclement. Although the pressure was eased by Fifth Guards Tank Army's costly counterattack, the prospects were grim as XXIV Panzer Corps was poised to intervene. Contrary to the 'traditional' view of the battle, it is arguable that Hitler's decision to call off the entire operation threw away the real chance of a major German victory.

Prokhorovka

Although the German advance from the north of the Kursk salient was halted, Hoth's attack from the south was making progress, and desperate measures were called for.

By 11 July, Hoth's Fourth Panzer Army was threatening to capture Prokhorovka, securing a bridgehead over the River Psel, the last natural barrier between the Panzers and Kursk. The German attack was led by *SS Obergruppenführer und General der Waffen SS* Paul Hausser's II SS Panzer Corps, which had begun the offensive with over 300 tanks.

Vatutin believed that the situation was critical and committed the 650 tanks of Lieutenant-General Pavel Rotmistrov's Fifth Guards Tank Army, which had been intended to spearhead the Soviet 'post-Kursk' offensive, Operation Rumyantsev. On 11 July, Fifth Guards Tank Army arrived in the Prokhorovka area, after a four-day march from assembly areas 300km (188 miles) to the east. It was reinforced by II Tank Corps and II Guards Tank Corps, increasing its strength to about 850 tanks, 500 of which were T-34s.

These forces faced 211 German tanks, including only 15 Tigers, when the battle opened on 12 July with massed Soviet tank attacks from Prokhorovka. Waves of 40–50 T-34s and T-70s carrying infantry were launched against the German armour in frontal charges, which were broken up with heavy losses. The Germans resumed their advance on Prokhorovka and were engaged by Rotmistrov's reserves, including 181st Tank Regiment, which was virtually wiped out when it took on a handful of Tigers of 1st SS Panzer Regiment. It was only late in the day that the intervention of the Soviet V Mechanized Corps finally stabilized the situation.

Great tank battle

The first day's fighting had resulted in massive Soviet casualties – almost 650 tanks were destroyed, whilst II SS Panzer Corps' casualties totalled 70 AFVs, of which 22 were repaired and serviceable by the following day. The subsequent Soviet General Staff study was highly critical of Rotmistrov's performance: '…Fifth Guards Tank Army delivered a frontal attack against crack German panzer divisions which, without an essential superiority in forces, could at best result in driving the enemy back … Thus on 12 July Fifth Guards Tank Army failed to accomplish its assigned mission.'

In contrast to the traditional view that Fifth Guards Tank Army 'saved the day' at Prokhorovka, it seems more likely that Rotmistrov was saved from complete annihilation by the fierce resistance of the rifle divisions manning the defence lines along the southern face of the Kursk salient. These formations absorbed the full impact of Manstein's initial attacks, buying time for the deployment of Fifth Guards Tank Army and inflicting losses on II SS Panzer Corps, which may well have been the decisive factor at Prokhorovka.

ANTI-TANK ARTILLERY REGIMENT (APRIL 1943)													
Unit	Offs	Pol Offs	WOs	NCOs	Other Ranks	LMG	AT Rifle	76mm AT Gun	Field Car	GAZ-AA Truck	ZIL-5 Truck	Special Truck	Tractor
REGIMENTAL HEADQUARTERS													
Personnel/Equipment	7	3	7	2	4	–	–	–	1	1	–	–	–
HEADQUARTERS PLATOON													
Personnel/Equipment	1	–	–	6	28	–	–	–	–	2	–	–	–
5 X ANTI–TANK BATTERIES, EACH													
Battery Headquarters	2	1	–	2	–	–	–	–	–	–	–	–	–
Headquarters Platoon	1	–	–	5	14	–	1	–	–	1	–	–	–
Firing Battery Firing Battery Group	–	–	–	2	1	–	–	–	–	–	–	–	1
2 x Platoons, each	1	–	–	6	11	1	1	2	–	–	1	–	2
AMMUNITION PLATOON													
Personnel/Equipment	1	–	–	2	18	–	–	–	–	–	12	–	–
LOGISTICS SECTION													
Personnel/Equipment	–	–	2	5	13	–	–	–	–	4	2	2	–
OTHER TRAINS ELEMENTS													
Personnel/Equipment	–	–	4	9	15	–	–	–	–	2	3	3	–
TOTAL													
Personnel/Equipment	34	8	13	129	263	10	10	20	1	14	27	5	25

BATTLE OF PROKHOROVKA

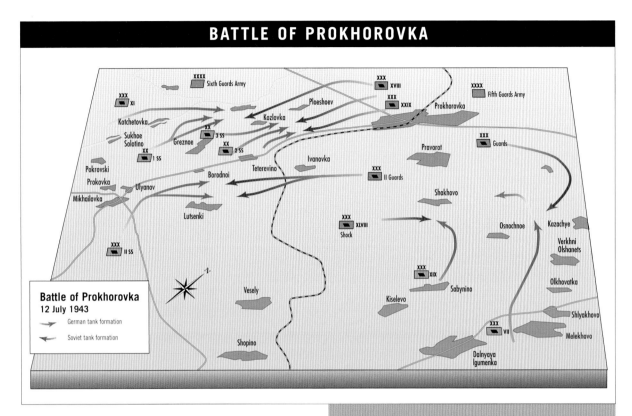

Battle of Prokhorovka
12 July 1943

→ German tank formation

← Soviet tank formation

When combat resumed on 13 July, Fifth Guards Tank Army was reduced to 150–200 operational tanks and was incapable of effective offensive action. (The surviving armour was deployed in dug-in positions in support of the infantry defending Prokhorovka.) Hausser's forces continued to attack but were unable to make a decisive breakthrough. There was still a chance of a German victory – Manstein urged Hitler to commit the three experienced Panzer divisions of XXIV Panzer Corps, which he believed could destroy Fifth Guards Tank Army and take Kursk itself. Despite these forceful arguments, Hitler called off the operation to free up units for Italy, as the Allied landings in Sicily were on the point of causing the collapse of Mussolini's regime.

Technological lessons

Although the Kursk offensive had failed, it showed that the Red Army was in danger of losing the technological battle – the T-34 and KVs were outgunned by the Tiger and Panther, whilst their 76.2mm (3in) armament was

12 July 1943

The tank battles fought through the duration of Operation Citadel culminated in the celebrated action near the small town of Prokhorovka. On 10 July, the SS vanguard, led by *Totenkopf*, tore through the Soviet First Tank Army, overrunning the 71st Guards Rifle Division. Stalin sat at his desk in the Kremlin day and night, demanding hourly situation reports. He consented to the release of the Fifth Guards Tank Army and the Fifth Guards Army from the reserve: they moved up, ready to counterattack. Here, they encountered the Germans in the largest and most bloody tank action of the whole battle, which can be described as a tactical loss but an operational draw for the Soviets. The Fifth Guards Tank Army did not achieve its mission of destroying the SS units, but they did stop the German advance.

ineffective against both German types, except at suicidally short ranges. The new SU-152 had proved to be a highly effective tank destroyer, but was, at best, only a partial solution to the problem. It was a time of frantic activity for Soviet tank design teams.

FIFTH GUARDS TANK ARMY (JULY 1943)

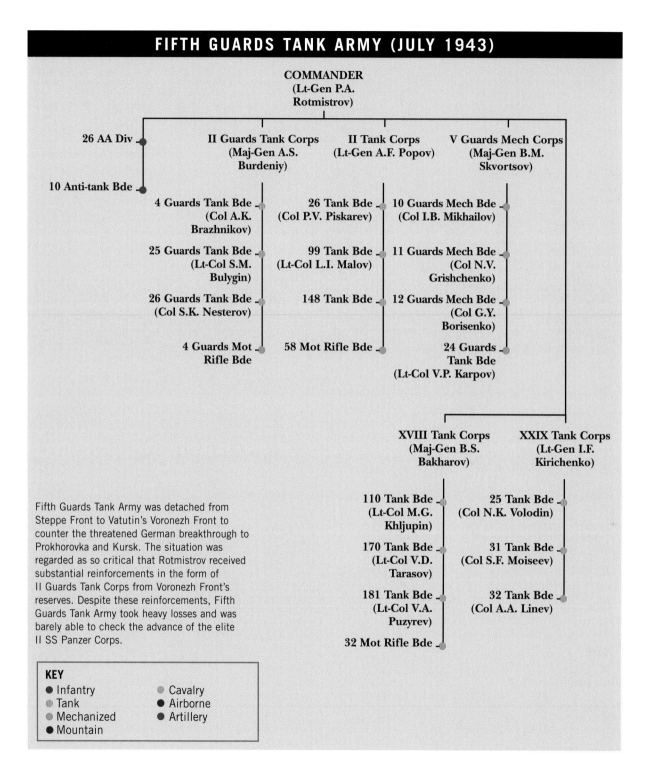

COMMANDER
(Lt-Gen P.A. Rotmistrov)

26 AA Div

10 Anti-tank Bde

II Guards Tank Corps
(Maj-Gen A.S. Burdeniy)

- 4 Guards Tank Bde (Col A.K. Brazhnikov)
- 25 Guards Tank Bde (Lt-Col S.M. Bulygin)
- 26 Guards Tank Bde (Col S.K. Nesterov)
- 4 Guards Mot Rifle Bde

II Tank Corps
(Lt-Gen A.F. Popov)

- 26 Tank Bde (Col P.V. Piskarev)
- 99 Tank Bde (Lt-Col L.I. Malov)
- 148 Tank Bde
- 58 Mot Rifle Bde

V Guards Mech Corps
(Maj-Gen B.M. Skvortsov)

- 10 Guards Mech Bde (Col I.B. Mikhailov)
- 11 Guards Mech Bde (Col N.V. Grishchenko)
- 12 Guards Mech Bde (Col G.Y. Borisenko)
- 24 Guards Tank Bde (Lt-Col V.P. Karpov)

XVIII Tank Corps
(Maj-Gen B.S. Bakharov)

- 110 Tank Bde (Lt-Col M.G. Khljupin)
- 170 Tank Bde (Lt-Col V.D. Tarasov)
- 181 Tank Bde (Lt-Col V.A. Puzyrev)
- 32 Mot Rifle Bde

XXIX Tank Corps
(Lt-Gen I.F. Kirichenko)

- 25 Tank Bde (Col N.K. Volodin)
- 31 Tank Bde (Col S.F. Moiseev)
- 32 Tank Bde (Col A.A. Linev)

Fifth Guards Tank Army was detached from Steppe Front to Vatutin's Voronezh Front to counter the threatened German breakthrough to Prokhorovka and Kursk. The situation was regarded as so critical that Rotmistrov received substantial reinforcements in the form of II Guards Tank Corps from Voronezh Front's reserves. Despite these reinforcements, Fifth Guards Tank Army took heavy losses and was barely able to check the advance of the elite II SS Panzer Corps.

KEY
- ● Infantry
- ● Tank
- ● Mechanized
- ● Mountain
- ● Cavalry
- ● Airborne
- ● Artillery

Push into the Ukraine

Soviet forces in the north of the Kursk salient recovered quickly from the German attack and launched their own offensive – Operation Kutuzov – against Orel on 12 July.

Orel was strongly defended, falling only on 3/4 August after Third Guards Tank Army and Fourth Tank Army had been committed to the assault. Further south, the battering that Hoth's Fourth Panzer Army had inflicted meant that Operation Rumyantsev, the Soviet attack on Belgorod and Kharkov, could not begin until 3 August.

Battle for Kharkov

Belgorod fell on 5 August, but Kharkov was far more strongly defended, with its garrison reinforced by 2nd SS Panzer Division *Das Reich* boasting some 96 Panthers, 32 Tigers and 25 assault guns. When Rotmistrov's newly re-equipped Fifth Guards Tank Army attacked in an attempt to encircle the city, its initial assaults were beaten off with the loss of 420 tanks. It was not until 22 August that the defenders withdrew from Kharkov to avoid being cut off.

The Red Army now held the strategic initiative, but its advances were to be costly affairs as German forces fought a series of highly effective rearguard actions. In the aftermath of the Red Army's capture of Orel and Kharkov, even Hitler recognized that there was little chance of holding any line east of the Dnieper River. Orders to construct the Dnieper defence line, which formed part of the Panther-Wotan Line, or the Eastern Wall, had been issued as early as 11 August 1943 and work began immediately.

Although in theory fortifications were to be erected along the length of the Dnieper, the resources simply did not exist to undertake such a massive project and defence works were concentrated in sectors where Soviet assault crossings were most likely to be attempted, especially Kremenchug, Zaporozhe and Nikopol. (The line was particularly weak in the area just north of the

MECHANIZED BRIGADE (SEPTEMBER 1943)										
	Officers	NCOs	Others	Motor-cycle	Field Car	Truck	Arm Truck	AC	Light Tank	Med Tank
Brigade Headquarters	39	15	26	–	2	4	–	–	–	–
Headquarters Company	5	17	51	6	–	5	–	–	–	–
Reconnaissance Company	7	72	62	6	–	4	10	7	–	–
Tank Regiment	89	194	187	4	2	70	–	3	7	32
3 x Motorized Rifle Btn, each	48	212	389	1	1	26	–	–	–	–
Submachine Gun Company	4	22	68	1	–	1	–	–	–	–
Anti-Tank Rifle Company	4	20	45	–	–	–	–	–	–	–
Mortar Battalion	23	47	127	–	–	20	–	–	–	–
Artillery Battalion	24	67	123	–	1	25	–	–	–	–
AA Machine Gun Coy	4	23	21	–	–	12	–	–	–	–
Pioneer Mine Company	8	23	90	–	–	6	–	–	–	–
Trains Company	6	28	38	1	–	31	–	–	–	–
Medical Platoon	8	5	19	–	–	5	–	–	–	–

TANK BRIGADE (NOVEMBER 1943)						
Unit	Men	Motor-cycle	Field Car	Truck	Arm Car	Med Tank
Brigade HQ	54	3	–	1	–	2
HQ Company	164	9	–	10	3	–
3 x Tank Btn, each	148	–	1	12	–	21
Mot SMG Btn	507	–	–	30	–	–
AAMG Company	48	–	–	9	–	–
Trains Company	123	–	1	58	–	–
Medical Platoon	14	–	–	2	–	–

KONSTANTIN ROKOSSOVSKY (1896–1968)

Born in Warsaw, Rokossovsky enlisted in an Imperial Russian Army dragoon regiment at the outbreak of World War I. During the Russian Civil War, he commanded a Red Army cavalry regiment and was steadily promoted to corps command by 1937. That year, he was caught up in Stalin's purge of the Red Army officer corps, tortured and imprisoned until March 1940, when he was suddenly released and appointed to the command of a corps in the Kiev Special Military District.

- Rokossovsky commanded IX Mechanized Corps at Brody-Dubno in 1941, Sixteenth Army in the defence of Moscow during the winter of 1941/42, and the Don Front in the Battle of Stalingrad from September 1942 to February 1943.
- In February 1943, Rokossovsky took command of the Central Front and played a key role in the preparations for the Battle of Kursk and the subsequent Soviet offensives.
- During 1944–45, Rokossovsky commanded the 1st and 2nd Belorussian Fronts and was largely responsible for the success of Operation Bagration, as well as the East Prussian and East Pomeranian offensives. He was promoted to the rank of Marshal of the Soviet Union on 29 June 1944.

Black Sea, which allowed Tolbukhin's 4th Ukrainian Front to breach it relatively easily, cutting off the German Seventeenth Army in the Crimea.)

Crossing the Dnieper

On 15 September 1943, Hitler finally authorized Army Group South to fall back to the Dnieper defence line and a deadly race ensued, with the Red Army attempting to cut off the German retreat. *Stavka* assigned Third Tank Army to spearhead the drive to the river, which it reached on the night of 21/22 September. Small bridgeheads were secured, but they were desperately vulnerable and it was decided to expand them by an airborne operation using 1st, 3rd and 5th Guards Airborne Brigades. The operation on the night of 24/25 September was rushed and ill-planned, with transport aircraft taking off as they were ready, rather than in properly organized formations. This was a major factor in scattering the 10,000 paratroops over a wide area on the west bank of the Dnieper. Most of 5th Guards Airborne Brigade was slaughtered when it was dropped on 19th Panzer Division, which was moving up to reinforce the Dnieper defences. Whilst the operation was a disaster, German efforts to eliminate the pockets of airborne forces did distract attention from the build-up of Soviet forces for a decisive breakthrough of the Panther-Wotan Line.

The handful of initial bridgeheads were slowly enlarged and new ones secured until, by the end of September, there were no less than 23, some of them 10km (6.25 miles) wide and 2km (1.25 miles) deep. All these attracted fierce German counterattacks but

SOVIET ADVANCE TO THE DNIEPER

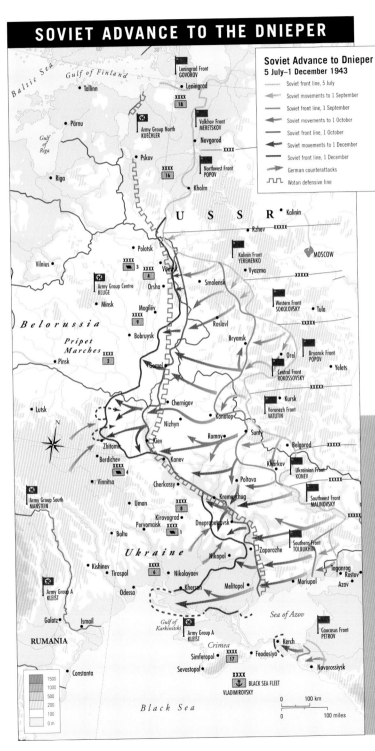

Soviet Advance to Dnieper
5 July–1 December 1943

- Soviet front line, 5 July
- Soviet movements to 1 September
- Soviet front line, 1 September
- Soviet movements to 1 October
- Soviet front line, 1 October
- Soviet movements to 1 December
- Soviet front line, 1 December
- German counterattacks
- Wotan defensive line

managed to hold out with massive fire support from Soviet artillery on the east bank of the river.

Securing the bridgeheads

The bridgeheads were generally secured by forward detachments moving at night. These normally comprised a reinforced tank brigade, a self-propelled artillery regiment, plus one or two battalions of artillery, with an engineer unit of up to battalion strength attached. They sometimes included infantry as well and generally operated 40km (25 miles) or so in advance of their parent tank or mechanized corps. The detachments were usually sent out to seize bridgeheads without artillery preparation or air support and had to make their crossings at night on whatever boats or rafts they could find or improvise. If the opposite bank was fortified, they staged false crossings elsewhere to divert German attention. Before dawn, they

5 July–1 December 1943

After the recapture of Kiev, the Red Army was content to clear the rest of the Dnieper in the south, and recapture a few significant places to the north. Now the ground was frozen, the Russian winter again chilled the hearts of the German forces. The Steppe and Southwest Fronts drove across the river and formed a wide and deep penetration pointing at Krivoï Rog and Kirovograd.

Southern Front reached the mouth of the Dnieper and effectively shut off all German forces left in the Crimea. To the north, Generals Vatutin and Rokossovsky had driven their fronts as far as Korosten and the eastern edge of the Pripet Marshes, and Sokolovsky had taken – at great cost – the massive defensive bastion that the Germans had made of Smolensk.

concealed crossing materials and then withdrew or hid until they could continue the operation the next night. Some of the sites included bridges built just below water level to conceal them from the *Luftwaffe*. In one location, the Soviets waterproofed 60 tanks so that they could cross underwater to the right bank.

One of the most experienced German commanders, General Friedrich von Mellenthin, commented that 'Bridgeheads in the hands of the Russians are grave danger indeed. It is quite wrong not to worry about bridgeheads, and to postpone their elimination. Russian bridgeheads, however small and harmless they may appear, are bound to grow into formidable danger-points in a very brief time and soon become insuperable strong points. A Russian bridgehead, occupied by a company in the evening, is sure to be occupied by at least a regiment the following morning and during the night will become a formidable fortress, well-equipped with heavy weapons and everything necessary to make it almost impregnable. No artillery fire, however violent and well concentrated, will wipe out a Russian bridgehead which has grown overnight. This Russian principle of "bridgeheads everywhere" constitutes a most serious danger and cannot be overrated.'

By mid-October, the forces assembled in the bridgeheads were strong enough to go over to the offensive; diversionary attacks were also launched in the south to draw German forces away from Kiev. At the end of the offensive, the Red Army controlled a bridgehead 300km (188 miles) wide and up to 80km (50 miles) deep, whilst in the far south, Army Group A was now cut off in the Crimea.

Autumn delays
German tactical expertise could still impose serious delays – throughout much of October 1943, Vatutin's forces were penned into the 'Bukrin Bend' of the Dnieper and had to be redeployed northwards to the tiny bridgehead across the river at Lyutlezh, just upstream of Kiev. By 3 November, the move was complete and VII Artillery Breakthrough Corps unleashed a bombardment by 2000 guns, mortars and rocket-launchers before Thirty-Eighth Army went in to the attack to open the way for General Rybalko's Third Guards Tank Army. Rybalko's forces maintained the

advance throughout the night, with the tanks using their headlights and sirens to dazzle and demoralize the defenders. Despite German counterattacks, the momentum of the offensive was sustained and V Guards Tank Corps led a successful assault on Kiev on the night of 5/6 November. (The assault on Kiev was one of the first major combat actions of the 1st Czechoslovak Independent Brigade, which had been formed in June 1943. It included a tank battalion equipped with T-34s, T-70 light tanks and BA-64B light armoured cars. The brigade was subsequently used as the cadre for the formation of I Czechoslovak Army Corps in 1944.)

Manstein counters
Fourth Panzer Army attempted to halt the Soviet advance, but Vatutin's newly redesignated 1st Ukrainian Front took Zhitomir and Korosten, cutting the rail link between Army Groups Centre and South. At this critical point, Manstein counterattacked with XXXXVIII Panzer Corps (1st, 7th, 19th and 25th Panzer Divisions, plus 1st SS Panzer Division and elements of 2nd SS Panzer Division.) This force recaptured Zhitomir, fighting a fierce battle with VII Guards Tank Corps before the deep mud created by the autumn rains temporarily halted operations. Both sides took advantage of the enforced lull to refit, but XXXXVIII Panzer Corps took the initiative. As soon as the ground froze in early December, it launched an attack north of Zhitomir with the aim of encircling Sixtieth Army, which hurriedly withdrew from Korosten. The situation was so critical that *Stavka* transferred First Tank Army and Eighteenth Army to 1st Ukrainian Front. These reinforcements allowed Vatutin to halt the German attack and return to the offensive – by mid-December, it seemed that both sides were exhausted and XXXXVIII Panzer Corps was withdrawn to rest and refit. However, Vatutin was determined to exploit his numerical superiority and renewed his attacks on 24 December – these made good progress and as the year ended, his forward units were approaching the 1939 Polish frontier.

The reverse at Zhitomir raised Stalin's suspicions about Vatutin's competence – Rokossovsky was sent to 1st Ukrainian Front's HQ to check up on Vatutin and if necessary relieve him of command. Rokossovsky was received with understandable suspicion by Vatutin and

ANTI-TANK BRIGADE (JULY 1943)

Anti-tank brigades were a key part of the Soviet defences in the Kursk salient, forming what the Germans termed *Pakfronten*. These were tank-killing zones protected by extensive minefields, in which massed anti-tank guns would concentrate their fire to destroy the nearest or most threatening AFV, before swiftly targeting the next.

1 x 4-gun AA Battery (37mm/1.5in 61-K M1939 AA Gun)

3 x 4-gun Batteries (45mm/1.8in Model 1942 Anti-tank Gun)

4 x 4-gun Batteries (76mm/3in ZiS-3 Field/Anti-tank Gun)

his staff, but they quickly appreciated that he had taken his instructions from the Kremlin with a grain of salt, appreciating that some reverses were inevitable, however much Moscow might be displeased with them. Overall,

things had gone very well for the Red Army in the campaign and there was no reason to do more than examine the mistakes made and ensure that the appropriate lessons were learned.

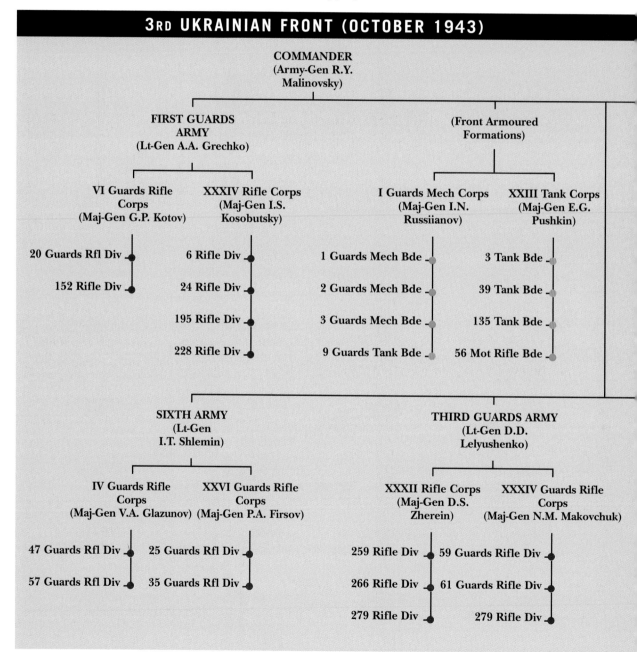

3RD UKRAINIAN FRONT (OCTOBER 1943)

COMMANDER
(Army-Gen R.Y. Malinovsky)

FIRST GUARDS ARMY
(Lt-Gen A.A. Grechko)

(Front Armoured Formations)

VI Guards Rifle Corps
(Maj-Gen G.P. Kotov)

XXXIV Rifle Corps
(Maj-Gen I.S. Kosobutsky)

I Guards Mech Corps
(Maj-Gen I.N. Russiianov)

XXIII Tank Corps
(Maj-Gen E.G. Pushkin)

20 Guards Rfl Div

152 Rifle Div

6 Rifle Div

24 Rifle Div

195 Rifle Div

228 Rifle Div

1 Guards Mech Bde

2 Guards Mech Bde

3 Guards Mech Bde

9 Guards Tank Bde

3 Tank Bde

39 Tank Bde

135 Tank Bde

56 Mot Rifle Bde

SIXTH ARMY
(Lt-Gen I.T. Shlemin)

THIRD GUARDS ARMY
(Lt-Gen D.D. Lelyushenko)

IV Guards Rifle Corps
(Maj-Gen V.A. Glazunov)

XXVI Guards Rifle Corps
(Maj-Gen P.A. Firsov)

XXXII Rifle Corps
(Maj-Gen D.S. Zherein)

XXXIV Guards Rifle Corps
(Maj-Gen N.M. Makovchuk)

47 Guards Rfl Div

57 Guards Rfl Div

25 Guards Rfl Div

35 Guards Rfl Div

259 Rifle Div

266 Rifle Div

279 Rifle Div

59 Guards Rifle Div

61 Guards Rifle Div

279 Rifle Div

The price of victory

Soviet AFV production totalled just under 20,000 vehicles in 1943 compared with almost 6000 in Germany. However, this did not give the Red Army the overwhelming numerical superiority which might have been expected, as the Germans destroyed 22,400 Soviet tanks in the course of the year – approximately four times their own losses.

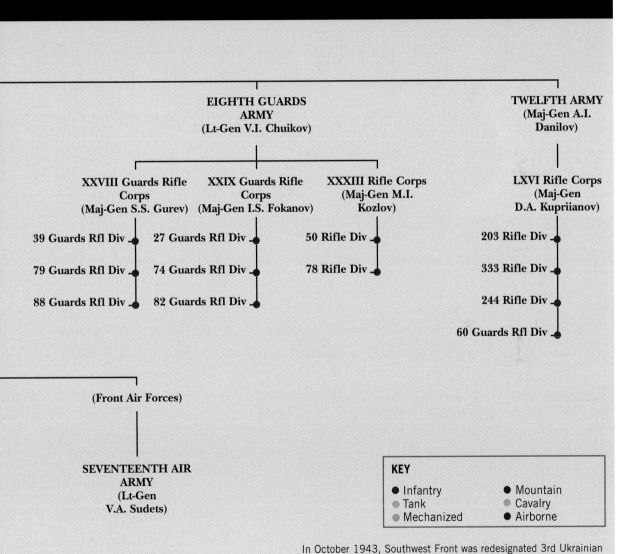

In October 1943, Southwest Front was redesignated 3rd Ukrainian Front. It took part in the Lower Dnieper Offensive, penetrating the German defences of the 'Panther-Wotan Line'. The Front recaptured the huge Dniprostoj Hydro Power Plant on the River Dnieper, but the Germans so thoroughly sabotaged the generating plant and the dam itself that power generation resumed only in 1950.

Year of Victories: 1944

By 1944, the Red Army was becoming increasingly confident and professional. Stalin had learned to curb unnecessary political interference in operational planning and his commanders reaped the benefits.

A column of T-34s waits to move up to the front during the winter of 1943/44.

As 1944 began, the balance of power on the Eastern Front was swinging ever more strongly in favour of the Red Army. Five Tank Armies, each comprising two tank and one mechanized corps, were already in existence and a sixth was forming. A uniquely Russian addition to the more conventional forces was the cavalry-mechanized group (KMG), a combination of a cavalry corps and a mechanized corps. This formation proved to be ideal for 'deep penetration' missions to exploit breakthroughs across thickly forested areas or swamps, such as the Pripet Marshes, which were marginal terrain for tanks.

The *Luftwaffe*'s demonstration of the effectiveness of close air support operations in 1941–43 led to increased resources being devoted to the Red Air Force. An expansion and re-equipment programme provided each Front with its own Air Army of 700–800 aircraft (mainly fighters and ground-attack machines.)

Manpower shortages

Despite the Red Army's increasing success, it was facing significant manpower shortages – there was simply no way that its 500-plus divisions could be maintained at full strength. The tank and mechanized formations tended to receive enough replacement personnel to keep at something approaching their authorized strengths, but rifle divisions fared less well.

Although the official strength of a rifle division had steadily dropped from 14,483 in April 1941 to 9380 in July 1943, even this was almost impossible to meet. At the end of 1943, the Germans began to notice that an increasing percentage of prisoners were either under 18 or in their fifties – the Soviet authorities were 'scraping the bottom of the barrel' in desperate attempts to find more conscripts. This crisis was caused by the heavy casualties sustained by infantry units. Between December 1943 and February 1944, one rifle regiment lost 1638 out of just over 2000 men. This total included 222 killed, 967 wounded, 71 sick and 373 missing. Whilst some of the sick and wounded would have quickly returned to active duty, no unit could take such casualties and retain its combat capability.

By mid-1944, Front commanders were being authorized to issue emergency tables of organization and equipment (TO&Es) for understrength formations.

IVAN STEPANOVICH KONEV (1897–1973)

Born into a peasant family, Konev worked as a lumberjack before being conscripted into the Imperial Russian Army in 1916. Demobilized following the Russian Revolution, he joined the Communist party and the Red Army in 1919, serving in the artillery in the Russian Civil War, where he came to the attention of Voroshilov, a future Commissar for War. After completing advanced officer training at the Frunze Military Academy in 1926, Konev headed the Trans-Baikal and North Caucasus Military Districts, being promoted to Corps Commander (*KomKor*) in 1938.

- At the time of the German invasion, he commanded Nineteenth Army in the retreat from Smolensk to Moscow. He went on to command the Kalinin Front and was promoted to Colonel-General.

- From August 1942 to May 1945, he successively commanded the Western, Northwest and Ukrainian (later redesignated 1st Ukrainian) Fronts, playing key roles in the Soviet offensives in the Ukraine and Poland, besides racing Zhukov's armies to Berlin.

- Konev was promoted to become the twelfth Marshal of the Soviet Union in February 1944.

Whilst there was a fair degree of variation between Fronts, it was not unusual to find provisions for rifle division strengths ranging from 8000 to as low as 4000.

SOVIET GROUND FORCES (JANUARY 1944)	
Unit Type	Number
HEADQUARTERS	
Fronts	17
Armies	75
Rifle Corps	161
Cavalry Corps	8
Tank Corps	24
Mechanized Corps	13
INFANTRY	
Rifle Divisions (inc Mountain & Motorized)	489
Rifle Brigades	57
Ski Brigades	3
Separate Rifle Regiments	10
Fortified Regions	48
CAVALRY	
Cavalry Divisions	26
ARMOUR	
Tank Divisions	2
Motorized Divisions	–
Armoured Car Brigades	–
Tank Brigades	166
Assault Gun Brigades	–
Mechanized Brigades	43
Motor Rifle Brigades	26
Motorcycle Brigades	–
Separate Tank Regiments	122
Separate Assault Gun Regiments	109
Motorcycle Regiments	8
Separate Tank Battalions	26
Separate Aerosan Battalions	57
Special Motorized Battalions	–
Armoured Train Battalions	61
Separate Armoured Car & Motorcycle Btns	44

SOVIET GROUND FORCES (JANUARY 1944)	
Unit Type	Number
AIRBORNE	
Airborne Divisions	16
Airborne Brigades	3
ARTILLERY	
Artillery Divisions	26
Rocket Divisions	7
Anti-Aircraft Divisions	78
Separate Artillery Brigades	22
Separate Anti-Aircraft Brigades	8
Separate Mortar Brigades	11
Separate Rocket Brigades	13
Anti-Tank Brigades	50
Separate Artillery Regiments	229
Separate Mortar Regiments	170
Separate Anti-Tank Regiments	172
Separate Rocket Regiments	108
Separate Anti-Aircraft Regiments	221
Separate Artillery Battalions	28
Separate Anti-Aircraft Battalions	114
Separate Rocket Battalions	42
Separate Anti-Tank Battalions	48
Separate Mortar Battalions	1
PVO STRANYI	
PVO Stranyi Brigade HQ	8
PVO Stranyi Corps Region HQ	7
PVO Stranyi Division Region HQ	14
PVO Stranyi Brigade Region HQ	11
Standard Anti-Aircraft Divisions	15
Searchlight Divisions	4
Anti-Aircraft Regiments	115
Anti-Aircraft Machine Gun Regiments	27
Searchlight Regiments	7
Anti-Aircraft Battalions	214
Anti-Aircraft Machine Gun Battalions	27
Searchlight Battalions	18

Recruitment drive

The Red Army's advance into Poland seemed to be an ideal opportunity to solve the worst of the manpower problem by expanding the Polish People's Army (LWP), a force that could later be used to enforce Communist rule in Poland.

A partial solution to the acute manpower shortage was found with the formation of the first major foreign force under Red Army command. This was the *Ludowe Woisko Polskie* (LWP), or Polish People's Army. This was based on the 1st Polish Infantry Division, which had been formed in the summer of 1943 and was rapidly enlarged to become the Polish I Corps. In March 1944, the corps had expanded to over 30,000 men and became the Polish First Army.

The army's NCOs and other ranks were primarily drawn from Poles who had been deported to the USSR after its invasion of eastern Poland, but almost 40 per

cent of its junior officers were Russian. The proportion of Red Army personnel in command and training posts was as high as 70–85 per cent. This was inevitable, as the cadre of Polish officers who could have filled these posts had been eliminated in the 1940 Katyn Massacre or had escaped to join General Wladyslaw Anders' Polish II Corps fighting in Italy as part of the Eighth Army.

Polish recruiting ground

During 1944, the Soviet conquest of much of pre-war Poland seemed to provide an opportunity to step up

MECHANIZED CORPS (JANUARY 1944)	Strength
PERSONNEL	
Total troops	16,370
ARMOURED VEHICLES	
Light Tanks	21
Medium Tanks	176
Heavy Tanks	–
Light Assault Guns	21
Medium Assault Guns	16
Heavy Assault Guns	12
GUNS & MORTARS	
82mm (3.2in) Mortars	100
120mm (4.7in) Mortars	54
45mm (1.8in) AT Guns	36
57mm (2.2in) AT Guns	8
37mm (1.5in) AA Guns	18
76mm (3in) Guns	36
BM-13 Rocket Launchers	8

TANK CORPS (JANUARY 1944)	Strength
PERSONNEL	
Total troops	12,010
ARMOURED VEHICLES	
T-60 Light Tanks	–
T-70 Light Tanks	–
T-34 Medium Tanks	208
KV Heavy Tanks	1
SU-76s	21
SU-85s	16
SU-152/ISU-152s	12
GUNS & MORTARS	
82mm (3.2in) Mortars	52
120mm (4.7in) Mortars	42
45mm (1.8in) AT Guns	12
57mm (2.2in) AT Guns	16
37mm (1.5in) AA Guns	18
76mm (3in) Guns	12
M-13 Rocket Launchers	8

recruiting for the LWP. Initial plans were drawn up on the assumption that two further armies would be formed, after which all three Polish armies would be grouped to form a Polish Front. It was believed that the Second Polish Army would be ready to go into action by September, but recruitment was slow and it was not operational until January 1945.

In common with the First Polish Army, adequate numbers of Polish NCOs and other ranks could be recruited, but there was an acute shortage of officers. In desperation, Red Army personnel were drafted in to fill about 50 per cent of the officer posts, including that of the army's first commander – Major-General Stanislav Poplavsky – who was transferred from the Soviet XLV

Rifle Corps. The Third Polish Army was little more than a paper formation, and recruiting proved to be so difficult that it was disbanded to provide reinforcements for the existing Polish forces.

Nationalist sentiment

Despite considerable efforts to ensure the political reliability of recruits, age-old anti-Russian sentiments continually resurfaced, with hundreds of incidents of Poles singing 'improper' patriotic songs and dismissing Communist party publications as 'enemy propaganda'. The Soviet authorities were so concerned at the prevalence of Polish nationalist sentiment that they established a special military police and counter-

HEAVY ASSAULT GUN REGIMENT (FEBRUARY 1944)

Although ISU-152 regiments were nominally artillery units, they were almost invariably used to deliver direct fire in the close support role. Many regiments were converted from heavy tank units whose training reinforced the tendency to operate in this way. The vehicle's 152mm (6in) howitzer fired a 40kg (88lb) HE shell, which was highly effective against the fortified buildings encountered in the street fighting of 1944–45. The howitzer was also effective against most German AFVs, as its 51kg (112lb) semi-AP round could penetrate up to 136mm (5.4in) of armour at short range.

Regimental Headquarters

Battery 1

Battery 2

Battery 3

Battery 4

intelligence service, the *Główny Zarzàd Informacji Wojska Polskiego* (GZI WP), or Main Directorate of Information of the Polish Army. The GZI WP was largely staffed by former NKVD and SMERSH (military counter-intelligence) officers, who controlled a massive network of informers within the LWP.

Weapons and equipment
In contrast to the acute manpower shortages, there was a large enough surplus of infantry weapons to allow production to be cut back in 1944 – output of rifles and carbines dropped from 3,850,000 in 1943 to 2,060,000 in the following year, whilst the production of mortars fell even more dramatically in the same period, from 67,900 to only 2000. AFV production also dropped from 19,959 in 1943 to 16,975 in 1944, but this reflected the

final phasing-out of easily produced but vulnerable light tanks in favour of far more effective designs such as the T-34/85 and JS-2.

Motor transport was the one category of equipment in which demand always outstripped supply and the Red Army rapidly came to appreciate the quality of the US vehicles supplied under Lend-Lease, which were far more modern than the vast majority of Soviet vehicles. By 1944–45, US trucks and jeeps represented almost two-thirds of the transport strength of the Red Army. (Well over 400,000 such vehicles were shipped to Russia during the war.) Many units were largely or completely reliant on Lend-Lease vehicles – for example, in March 1944, the 615th Howitzer Regiment had seven GAZ-AA Russian trucks, together with a jeep, 14 Studebaker and 21 International Harvester 2.25-tonne (2.5-ton) trucks.

The Korsun pocket

By 24 December 1943, the 4th Ukrainian Front had sealed off the 150,000 German and Rumanian troops in the Crimea. As the New Year began, cavalry of the 1st Ukrainian Front crossed the 1939 Polish frontier and turned southwards in an attempt to trap the German forces in the Dnieper bend south of Kiev.

The bulk of these forces (elements of 11 divisions of the Eighth Army) held a salient centred on Korsun, west of Cherkassy. *Stavka* quickly appreciated the salient's vulnerability, assigning Vatutin's 1st Ukrainian Front and Konev's 2nd Ukrainian Front to strike at its flanks. By this stage of the war, both were powerful formations, with each fielding three tank armies, plus three to four other armies.

Closing the ring
Konev's Fifth Guards Tank Army and Sixth Tank Army sealed off the salient on 3 February despite appalling weather conditions – intense cold spells broken by brief thaws, which turned the region's dirt roads to thick, clinging mud. Roughly 60,000 men under *General der Artillerie* Wilhelm Stemmermann (*Gruppe Stemmermann*) were trapped in this newly formed

Korsun pocket. A rescue attempt was made by First Panzer Army, which managed to seize small bridgeheads across the River Gniloy Tikich on 11 February but was unable to break through to the pocket 30km (19 miles) away to the east. During the next few days, First Panzer Army was locked in fierce combat with Sixth Tank Army, but the relief force could do no more than hold its ground in the face of such strong opposition.

Breakout
By 15 February, it was clear that the trapped forces would have to attempt a breakout. They had already edged closer to the stalled relief force and launched their main effort on the night of 16/17 February. Elements of three Soviet tank armies lay between *Gruppe Stemmermann* and the forward elements of First Panzer Army only 12km (7.5 miles) away.

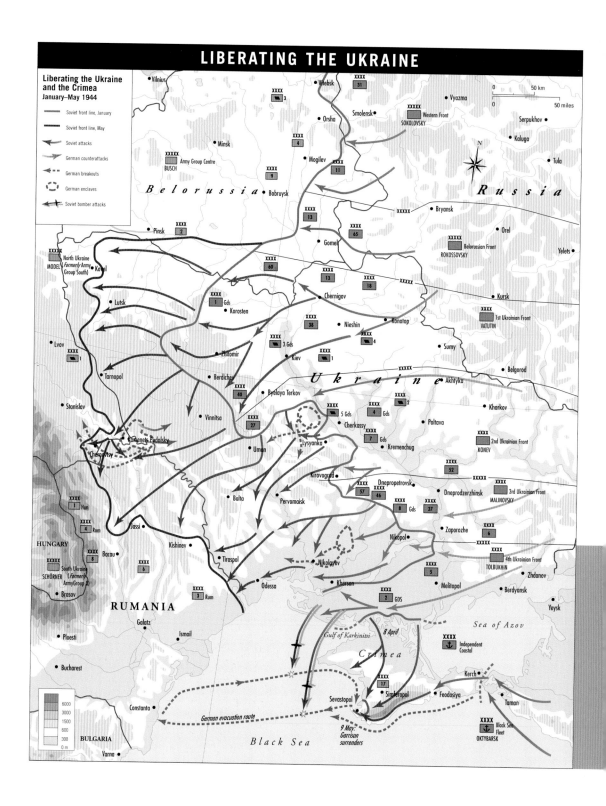

LIBERATING THE UKRAINE

Liberating the Ukraine and the Crimea
January–May 1944

Soviet front line, January
Soviet front line, May
Soviet attacks
German counterattacks
German breakouts
German enclaves
Soviet bomber attacks

Vilnius
Vitebsk
XXXX 31
Smolensk
Vyazma
Serpukhov
XXXXX Western Front SOKOLOVSKY
Orsha
Kaluga
Minsk
XXXX 4
Tula
XXXXX Army Group Centre BUSCH
Mogilev
XXXX 11
R u s s i a
XXXX 9
B e l o r u s s i a • Bobruysk
Pinsk
XXXX 2
XXXX 13
XXXXX Bryansk
XXXX 65
Orel
Gomel
XXXXX Belorussian Front ROKOSSOVSKY
Yelets
XXXXX North Ukraine (*Formerly Army Group South*) MODEL Kovel
XXXX 60
XXXX 13
XXXX 18
Kursk
Lutsk
XXXX 1 Gds
Korosten
Chernigov
XXXX 38
Nieshin
Konotop
XXXX 1st Ukrainian Front VATUTIN
Lvov
XXXX 1
Zhitomir
XXXX 3 Gds
Kiev
XXXX 4
XXXX 1
Sumy
Belgorod
Tarnopol
Berdichev
XXXX 40 • Byelaya Terkov
U k r a i n e • Akhtyka
Stanislav
XXXX 27
Vinnitsa
XXXX 5 Gds
XXXX 4 Gds
XXXX 2
Kharkov
Kamenets Padolsky
Uman
Lysyanka
Cherkassy
XXXX 7 Gds
Poltava
Chernovtsy
XXXX 2nd Ukrainian Front KONEV
XXXX 52
Kirovograd
Dnepropetrovsk
XXXX 57
XXXX 46
Dneprodzerzhinsk
XXXXX 3rd Ukrainian Front MALINOVSKY
XXXX 1 Hun
Balta
Pervomaisk
XXXX 8 Gds
XXXX 37
XXXX 4 Rom
Jassi
Nikopol
Zaporozhe
XXXX 6
HUNGARY
XXXX 1
Bacau
Kishinev
XXXXX 4th Ukrainian Front TOLBUKHIN
XXXX South Ukraine (*Formerly Army Group A*) SCHÖRNER
XXXX 6
Tiraspol
Nikolayev
XXXX 5
Melitopol
Zhdanov
Brasov
Odessa
Kherson
Berdyansk
RUMANIA
XXXX 3 Rum
XXXX 2 GDS
Yeysk
Galatz
Ismail
Sea of Azov
Ploesti
Gulf of Karkinitsi
8 April
XXXX Independent Coastal
C r i m e a
Kerch
Taman
Bucharest
XXXX 17
Simferopol
Feodosiya
Constanta
German evacuation route
Sevastopol
XXXX Black Sea Fleet OKTYABRSK
BULGARIA
9 May: Garrison surrenders
Black Sea
Varna

0   50 km
0   50 miles

N

6000
3000
1500
600
300
0 m

TANK BATTALION (APRIL 1944)

Three of these tank battalions formed the main striking force of each 1944 tank brigade. Ever-increasing numbers of tank brigades were equipped with T-34/85s with much greater firepower and a far more efficient turret layout than earlier T-34s. Their support elements were also rapidly improving as many elderly Soviet-designed trucks were replaced by modern US 4x4 and 6x6 trucks supplied under Lend-Lease.

Tank Battalion (1 x Staff Car, 21 x T-34/85s, 12 x Trucks)

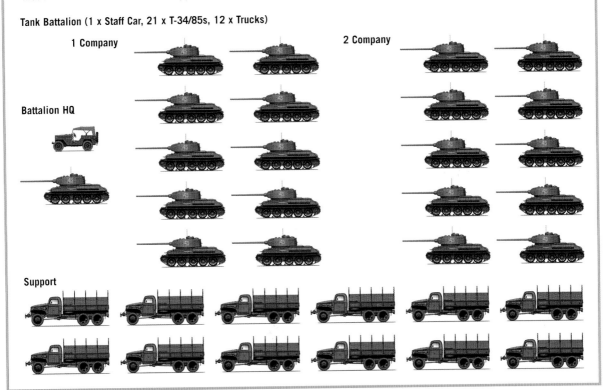

January–May 1944

The first half of 1944 saw enormous Soviet territorial gains, including the reconquest of the Ukraine and the Crimea. Initial Red Army operations such as the Korsun-Shevchenkovsky Offensive inflicted heavy casualties on Axis forces and the abandonment of much heavy equipment, which the bomb-damaged factories of the *Reich* found increasingly difficult to replace. The advance into the Ukraine was not without its problems – the Germans were fighting against ever-lengthening odds, but were still inflicting severe losses on the Red Army, whose rear areas were also subject to attacks from Ukrainian nationalist guerrillas. (General Vatutin, the commander of 1st Ukrainian Front, was mortally wounded in one such attack on 28 February 1944.) Soviet battlefield successes were beginning to bring significant political benefits as the Red Army's advance towards the Balkans undermined the authority of the pro-Axis regimes in Rumania, Bulgaria and Hungary.

Konev reacted furiously to the German breakout attempts – he had rashly promised Stalin a second Stalingrad – and threw in all available units, including the new JS-2s of XX Tank Corps.

Lacking infantry support, Soviet tanks initially stood off, firing into the escaping units from a distance, but once it became obvious that there were very few anti-tank weapons to oppose them, the T-34s charged into the German columns. Although as many as 35,000 German troops eventually fought their way clear after abandoning all their artillery and heavy equipment, Eighth Army had been badly mauled and First Panzer Army had lost large numbers of AFVs, which were increasingly difficult to replace.

Professional soldiers

Korsun marked a further stage in the growing professionalism of the Red Army: with increasing numbers of 6x6 and 4x4 Lend-Lease vehicles, its supply services were able to sustain the offensive

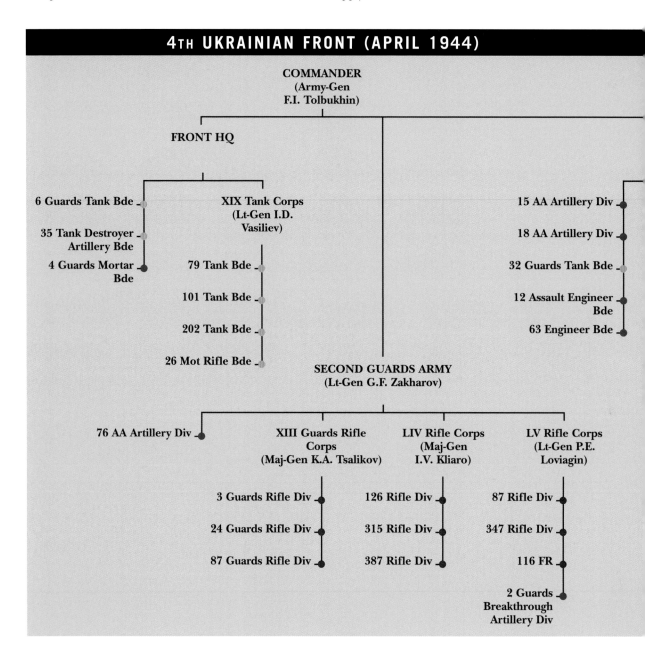

despite appalling terrain conditions. In contrast, German forces were handicapped by a stark lack of transport vehicles with similar cross-country performance. The decline of the *Luftwaffe* meant that, at best, it could manage only 70 supply flights per day

into the pocket's only airfield at Korsun itself. Both the transport aircraft and the trapped ground forces suffered heavy losses from an increasingly capable Red Air Force, which could no longer be held at bay by the dwindling number of German fighters.

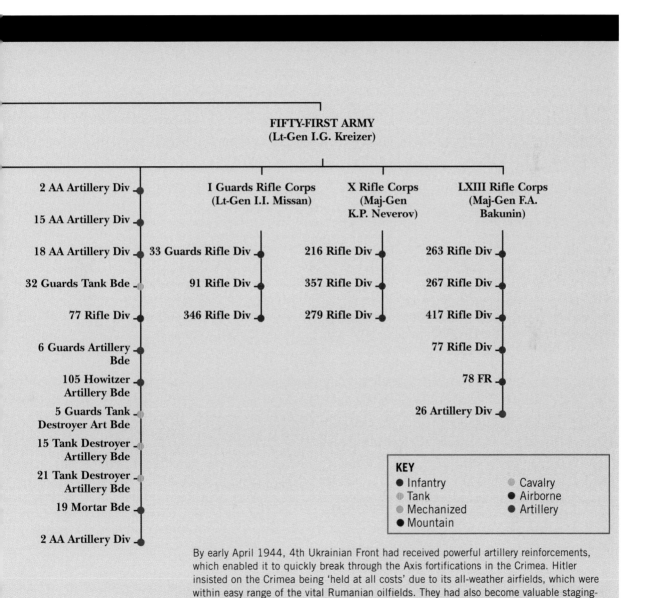

FIFTY-FIRST ARMY
(Lt-Gen I.G. Kreizer)

2 AA Artillery Div

15 AA Artillery Div

18 AA Artillery Div — 33 Guards Rifle Div

32 Guards Tank Bde — 91 Rifle Div

77 Rifle Div — 346 Rifle Div

6 Guards Artillery Bde

105 Howitzer Artillery Bde

5 Guards Tank Destroyer Art Bde

15 Tank Destroyer Artillery Bde

21 Tank Destroyer Artillery Bde

19 Mortar Bde

2 AA Artillery Div

I Guards Rifle Corps (Lt-Gen I.I. Missan)

X Rifle Corps (Maj-Gen K.P. Neverov)
216 Rifle Div
357 Rifle Div
279 Rifle Div

LXIII Rifle Corps (Maj-Gen F.A. Bakunin)
263 Rifle Div
267 Rifle Div
417 Rifle Div
77 Rifle Div
78 FR
26 Artillery Div

KEY
● Infantry   ● Cavalry
◐ Tank   ● Airborne
● Mechanized   ● Artillery
● Mountain

By early April 1944, 4th Ukrainian Front had received powerful artillery reinforcements, which enabled it to quickly break through the Axis fortifications in the Crimea. Hitler insisted on the Crimea being 'held at all costs' due to its all-weather airfields, which were within easy range of the vital Rumanian oilfields. They had also become valuable staging-points for ultra-long-range aircraft flying high-value cargoes between Germany and Japan.

Operation Bagration

In March 1944, *Stavka* began planning Operation Bagration. By now, Stalin had recognized the dangers of 'general offensives', even when the Red Army had such a marked numerical superiority over its opponents, and accepted Rokossovsky's proposal for a concentrated attack against Army Group Centre.

Throughout April and May 1944, *Stavka* planned Operation Bagration, a massive offensive intended to destroy Army Group Centre and drive German forces from Soviet territory. A remarkable example of Stalin's increasing readiness to listen to expert military advice occurred at one planning meeting, when he ordered Rokossovsky's 1st Belorussian Front to make a single attack north of the River Berezina. Rokossovsky argued strongly that two attacks, one on either side of the river, would be far more effective. Stalin twice sent him out to 'think again', but each time he came back and maintained that he was right. To the amazement of everyone present, Stalin accepted his judgment, commenting that such steadfastness was 'a reliable guarantee of success'.

Elaborate deception measures were employed to convince the Germans that the forthcoming offensive would exploit earlier Soviet advances in the south by retaking the remaining occupied areas of the Ukraine and driving into the Balkans to knock Rumania out of the war. *Luftwaffe* reconnaissance flights were allowed to glimpse the huge dummy assembly areas that had been created away to the south, whilst German intelligence monitored the accompanying false radio traffic and concluded that six Soviet tank armies were concentrating in the Ukraine. The estimated 143,000 partisans operating in Belorussia also played an

important role in the Soviet deception plan, attacking German communications so effectively that 147 trains were derailed in a single night. *Stavka* then called a temporary halt to partisan attacks in Army Group Centre's rear areas whilst the Red Army made a diversionary attack in the Ukraine. German reserves were moved south without interference from partisan groups, but were subjected to heavy attacks as soon as attempts were made to move them back when the real offensive began.

Railway demolitions

Immediately before Operation Bagration began, the partisans attempted 15,000 demolitions on the region's railways and were successful in 10,500 cases, all in the course of a single night. Their main effort was directed

OPERATION BAGRATION: COMPARATIVE STRENGTHS

Area	Army Group Centre	Soviet forces
Troops	1,200,000	2,400,000
AFVs	900	5200
Artillery and Mortars	9500	36,400
Aircraft	1350	5300

June–July 1944

The Soviet summer offensive of 1944 was the most decisive single campaign of World War II. Launched three years to the day after the German invasion, and three weeks after the Western Allies landed in Normandy, it involved the largest military force in history: more than 2.4 million men smashed into the German front lines. More than one million men attacked Army Group Centre alone.

By the end of August, Soviet forces were in the Baltic states, across the Polish border and about to cross into Rumania. Army Group Centre had been virtually annihilated. Of the 97 German divisions and 13 separate brigades that had been in place in Army Group Centre, or which had been rushed into action as reinforcements throughout the two-month operation, 17 divisions and three brigades were destroyed completely. Another 50 divisions lost 60–70 per cent of their manpower.

OPERATION BAGRATION

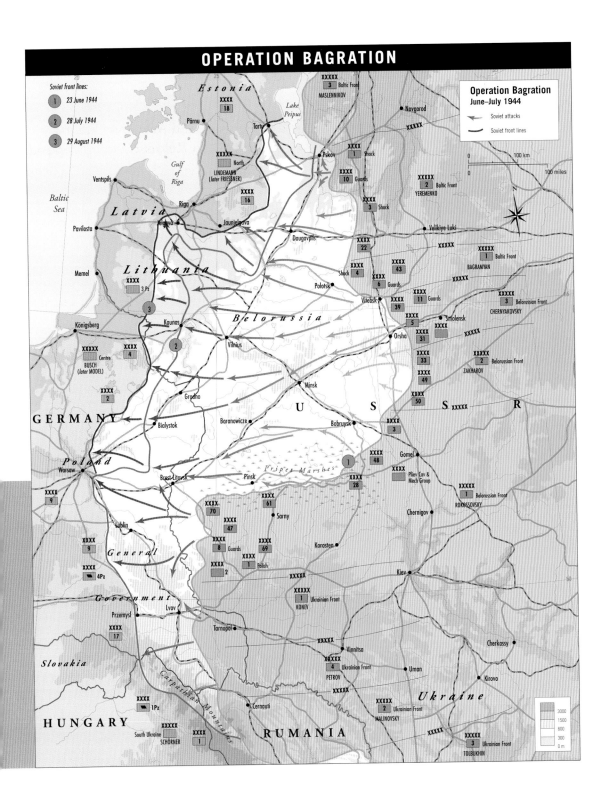

Soviet front lines:
1 23 June 1944
2 28 July 1944
3 29 August 1944

Operation Bagration
June–July 1944

Soviet attacks
Soviet front lines

0   100 km
0   100 miles

SOVIET GROUND FORCES (JULY 1944)	
Unit Type	**Number**
HEADQUARTERS	
Fronts	18
Armies	73
Rifle Corps	167
Cavalry Corps	8
Tank Corps	24
Mechanized Corps	13
INFANTRY	
Rifle Divisions (inc Mountain & Motorized)	502
Rifle Brigades	35
Ski Brigades	4
Tank Destroyer Brigades	–
Separate Rifle Regiments	10
Fortified Regions	47
CAVALRY	
Cavalry Divisions	26
ARMOUR	
Tank Divisions	2
Motorized Divisions	–
Armoured Car Brigades	–
Tank Brigades	150
Assault Gun Brigades	–
Mechanized Brigades	44
Motor Rifle Brigades	25
Motorcycle Brigades	–
Separate Tank Regiments	110
Separate Assault Gun Regiments	207
Motorcycle Regiments	11
Separate Tank Battalions	6
Separate Aerosan Battalions	–
Special Motorized Battalions	10
Armoured Train Battalions	61
Separate Armoured Car & Motorcycle Btns	47

SOVIET GROUND FORCES (JULY 1944)	
Unit Type	**Number**
AIRBORNE	
Airborne Divisions	14
Airborne Brigades	1
ARTILLERY	
Artillery Divisions	26
Rocket Divisions	7
Anti-Aircraft Divisions	80
Separate Artillery Brigades	73
Separate Anti-Aircraft Brigades	–
Separate Mortar Brigades	13
Separate Rocket Brigades	12
Anti-Tank Brigades	56
Separate Artillery Regiments	135
Separate Mortar Regiments	163
Separate Anti-Tank Regiments	147
Separate Rocket Regiments	107
Separate Anti-Aircraft Regiments	225
Separate Artillery Battalions	25
Separate Anti-Aircraft Battalions	104
Separate Rocket Battalions	48
Separate Anti-Tank Battalions	28
Separate Mortar Battalions	1
PVO STRANYI	
PVO Stranyi Corps HQ	12
PVO Stranyi Division HQ	12
PVO Stranyi Brigade Region HQ	11
Standard Anti-Aircraft Divisions	17
Standard Anti-Aircraft Machine Gun Divisions	2
Standard Anti-Aircraft Brigades	11
Searchlight Divisions	4
Anti-Aircraft Regiments	126
Anti-Aircraft Machine Gun Regiments	25
Searchlight Regiments	4
Anti-Aircraft Battalions	212
Anti-Aircraft Machine Gun Battalions	20
Searchlight Battalions	16

against the lines serving Third Panzer Army, which was to bear the brunt of the first major attack by the Red Army on the following day. As a result, all double-track lines were blocked for a period of 24 hours, while the operation of single-track lines was interrupted for over 48 hours. The virtual collapse of Army Group Centre's entire rail transportation system had disastrous effects upon its efforts to counter the massive Soviet offensive.

Training and reinforcements

Training was an essential part of Soviet preparations for the offensive – the vast majority of rifle divisions were far below their official strength of almost 9400 men. Many were down to 4000, with some reduced to skeleton formations of 2500 men. Every effort was made to bring them up to an average of 6000 troops, which meant that tens of thousands of new conscripts had to be absorbed very quickly. Their training tended to be basic and

brutal – at one point, Zhukov was furious at what he considered to be the slow rate of progress and ordered that live ammunition should be used in all future

OPERATION BAGRATION: CASUALTIES		
Losses	German	Soviet
Tanks	2000	2957
Other Vehicles	57,000	–
Artillery Pieces	–	2447
Aircraft	–	822
Dead	300,000	60,000
Wounded	250,000	110,000
Captured	120,000	–
Missing	–	8000
Overall Troop Casualties	670,000	178,000

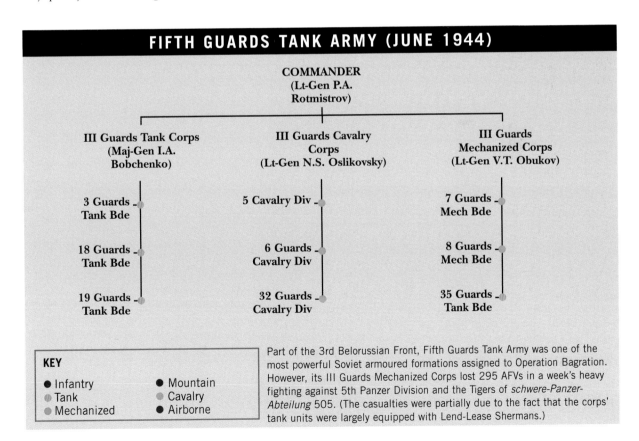

FIFTH GUARDS TANK ARMY (JUNE 1944)

COMMANDER
(Lt-Gen P.A. Rotmistrov)

III Guards Tank Corps
(Maj-Gen I.A. Bobchenko)

- 3 Guards Tank Bde
- 18 Guards Tank Bde
- 19 Guards Tank Bde

III Guards Cavalry Corps
(Lt-Gen N.S. Oslikovsky)

- 5 Cavalry Div
- 6 Guards Cavalry Div
- 32 Guards Cavalry Div

III Guards Mechanized Corps
(Lt-Gen V.T. Obukov)

- 7 Guards Mech Bde
- 8 Guards Mech Bde
- 35 Guards Tank Bde

KEY
- ● Infantry
- ● Tank
- ● Mechanized
- ● Mountain
- ● Cavalry
- ● Airborne

Part of the 3rd Belorussian Front, Fifth Guards Tank Army was one of the most powerful Soviet armoured formations assigned to Operation Bagration. However, its III Guards Mechanized Corps lost 295 AFVs in a week's heavy fighting against 5th Panzer Division and the Tigers of *schwere-Panzer-Abteilung* 505. (The casualties were partially due to the fact that the corps' tank units were largely equipped with Lend-Lease Shermans.)

exercises. In the event, all these measures were highly successful and the offensive achieved complete surprise when it opened on 22 June, the third anniversary of the start of Operation Barbarossa.

Critical superiority

The balance of forces was very much in favour of the Red Army. By this stage of the war, the Soviet Air Force had gained air superiority and flew 153,000 combat sorties in support of the offensive. Almost 1000 aircraft of Soviet Long Range Aviation based in southern Russia supplemented these operations with bombing raids on targets such as German HQs and *Luftwaffe* airfields. In contrast, the *Luftwaffe* was a shadow of its former self – *Luftflotte* 6, supporting Army Group Centre, had only 40 operational fighters and was suffering from a critical

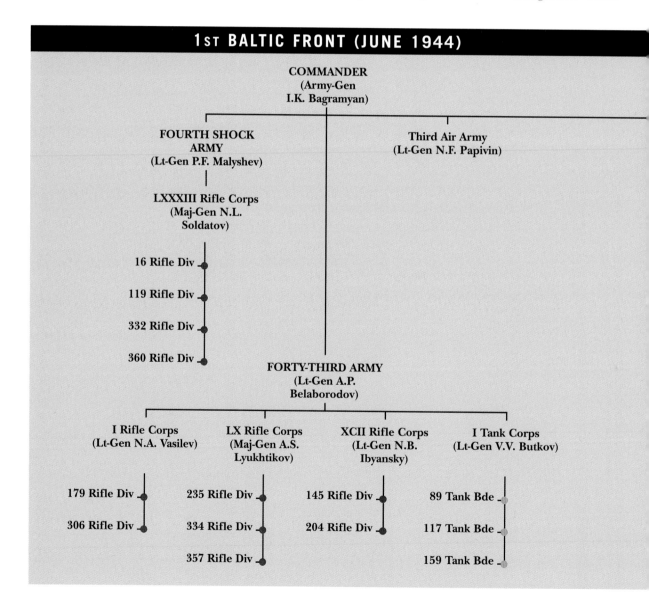

1ST BALTIC FRONT (JUNE 1944)

COMMANDER
(Army-Gen I.K. Bagramyan)

FOURTH SHOCK ARMY
(Lt-Gen P.F. Malyshev)

Third Air Army
(Lt-Gen N.F. Papivin)

LXXXIII Rifle Corps
(Maj-Gen N.L. Soldatov)

16 Rifle Div
119 Rifle Div
332 Rifle Div
360 Rifle Div

FORTY-THIRD ARMY
(Lt-Gen A.P. Belaborodov)

I Rifle Corps
(Lt-Gen N.A. Vasilev)

LX Rifle Corps
(Maj-Gen A.S. Lyukhtikov)

XCII Rifle Corps
(Lt-Gen N.B. Ibyansky)

I Tank Corps
(Lt-Gen V.V. Butkov)

179 Rifle Div
306 Rifle Div

235 Rifle Div
334 Rifle Div
357 Rifle Div

145 Rifle Div
204 Rifle Div

89 Tank Bde
117 Tank Bde
159 Tank Bde

shortage of fuel. Its 312 bombers and 106 ground-attack aircraft were equally crippled by the fuel shortage, and in any event could not operate without fighter cover.

In crucial sectors of the front, the Soviets had local numerical superiority of up to 10 to one and quickly broke through the German defences. The breakthroughs were frequently made by special assault groups, each comprising:

- A company of 10 PT-34 engineer tanks fitted with mine-clearing rollers.
- A heavy tank regiment with 21 JS-2s.
- A heavy assault gun regiment of 21 ISU-152s.
- An assault engineer battalion.

Each of these assault groups was followed up by rifle regiments, ideally supported by a company of 10 OT-34

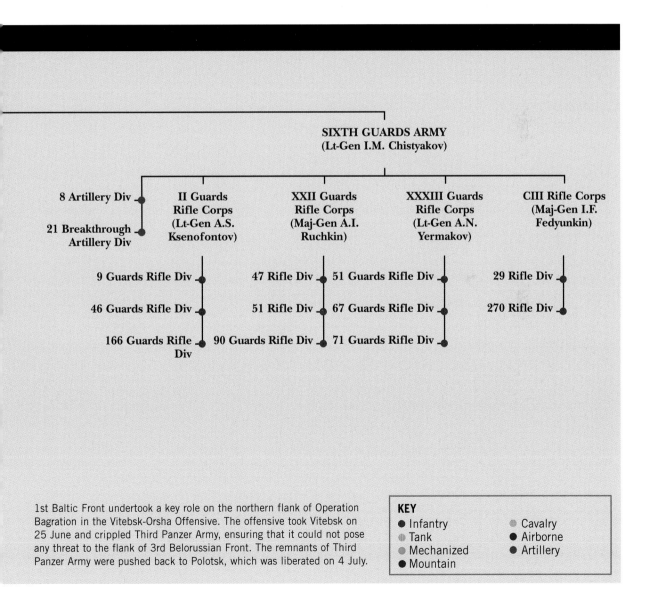

1st Baltic Front undertook a key role on the northern flank of Operation Bagration in the Vitebsk-Orsha Offensive. The offensive took Vitebsk on 25 June and crippled Third Panzer Army, ensuring that it could not pose any threat to the flank of 3rd Belorussian Front. The remnants of Third Panzer Army were pushed back to Polotsk, which was liberated on 4 July.

KEY
- Infantry
- Tank
- Mechanized
- Mountain
- Cavalry
- Airborne
- Artillery

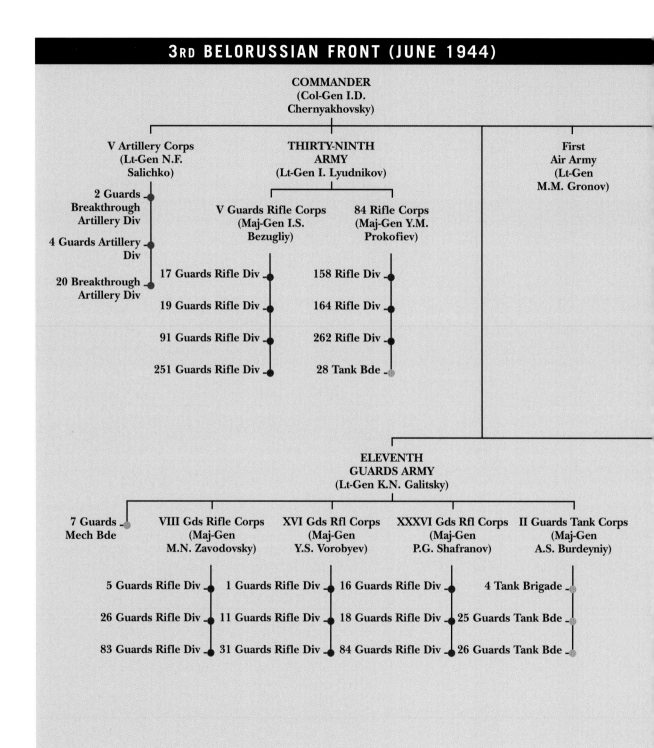

3RD BELORUSSIAN FRONT (JUNE 1944)

COMMANDER
(Col-Gen I.D. Chernyakhovsky)

V Artillery Corps
(Lt-Gen N.F. Salichko)

THIRTY-NINTH ARMY
(Lt-Gen I. Lyudnikov)

First Air Army
(Lt-Gen M.M. Gronov)

2 Guards Breakthrough Artillery Div

4 Guards Artillery Div

20 Breakthrough Artillery Div

V Guards Rifle Corps
(Maj-Gen I.S. Bezugliy)

84 Rifle Corps
(Maj-Gen Y.M. Prokofiev)

17 Guards Rifle Div

19 Guards Rifle Div

91 Guards Rifle Div

251 Guards Rifle Div

158 Rifle Div

164 Rifle Div

262 Rifle Div

28 Tank Bde

ELEVENTH GUARDS ARMY
(Lt-Gen K.N. Galitsky)

7 Guards Mech Bde

VIII Gds Rifle Corps
(Maj-Gen M.N. Zavodovsky)

XVI Gds Rfl Corps
(Maj-Gen Y.S. Vorobyev)

XXXVI Gds Rfl Corps
(Maj-Gen P.G. Shafranov)

II Guards Tank Corps
(Maj-Gen A.S. Burdeyniy)

5 Guards Rifle Div

26 Guards Rifle Div

83 Guards Rifle Div

1 Guards Rifle Div

11 Guards Rifle Div

31 Guards Rifle Div

16 Guards Rifle Div

18 Guards Rifle Div

84 Guards Rifle Div

4 Tank Brigade

25 Guards Tank Bde

26 Guards Tank Bde

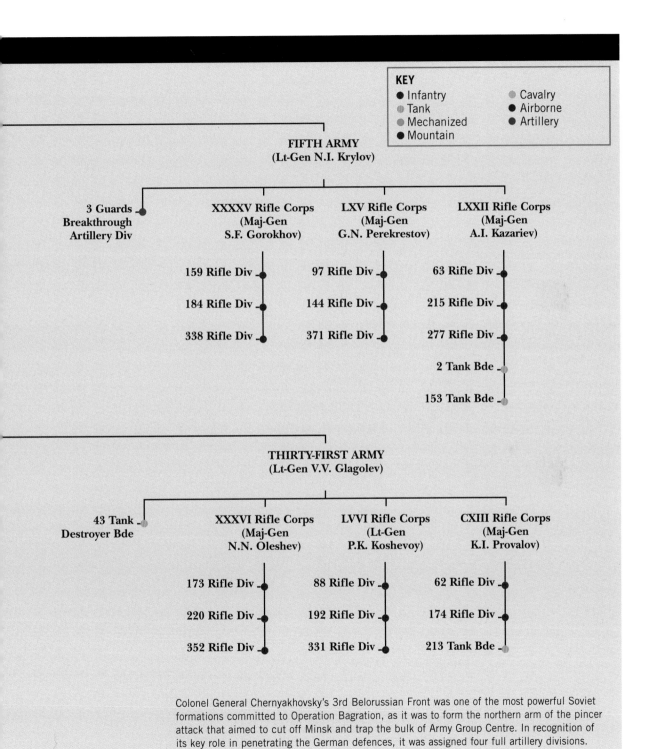

KEY
- ● Infantry
- ● Tank
- ● Mechanized
- ● Mountain
- ● Cavalry
- ● Airborne
- ● Artillery

FIFTH ARMY
(Lt-Gen N.I. Krylov)

3 Guards
Breakthrough
Artillery Div

XXXXV Rifle Corps
(Maj-Gen
S.F. Gorokhov)

159 Rifle Div
184 Rifle Div
338 Rifle Div

LXV Rifle Corps
(Maj-Gen
G.N. Perekrestov)

97 Rifle Div
144 Rifle Div
371 Rifle Div

LXXII Rifle Corps
(Maj-Gen
A.I. Kazariev)

63 Rifle Div
215 Rifle Div
277 Rifle Div
2 Tank Bde
153 Tank Bde

THIRTY-FIRST ARMY
(Lt-Gen V.V. Glagolev)

43 Tank
Destroyer Bde

XXXVI Rifle Corps
(Maj-Gen
N.N. Oleshev)

173 Rifle Div
220 Rifle Div
352 Rifle Div

LVVI Rifle Corps
(Lt-Gen
P.K. Koshevoy)

88 Rifle Div
192 Rifle Div
331 Rifle Div

CXIII Rifle Corps
(Maj-Gen
K.I. Provalov)

62 Rifle Div
174 Rifle Div
213 Tank Bde

Colonel General Chernyakhovsky's 3rd Belorussian Front was one of the most powerful Soviet formations committed to Operation Bagration, as it was to form the northern arm of the pincer attack that aimed to cut off Minsk and trap the bulk of Army Group Centre. In recognition of its key role in penetrating the German defences, it was assigned four full artillery divisions.

flamethrower tanks and a regiment of 21 SU-76 light assault guns.

Stage one

Within days, the three tank armies assigned to the operation were able to exploit the breakthroughs and advance deep into the German rear areas, whilst a cavalry-mechanized group moved through the Pripet Marshes to cut off the German Ninth Army's line of retreat. On 25 June, Vitebsk was surrounded by a second cavalry-mechanized group, and the Soviets had cut off Mogilev, Bobruysk and Minsk by 3 July. In each case, large German forces were trapped, the haul increased by Hitler's refusal to authorize timely retreats. By this time, Army Group Centre had lost 25 of its 63 divisions, and the Soviet offensive was still far from over.

The second stage of Operation Bagration began on 5 July. The German pocket around Minsk was destroyed between the 5th and the 11th, before the advance resumed, taking Vilnius on 13 July. Throughout this period, the tank armies and the cavalry-mechanized groups formed the spearhead of the advance, frequently outrunning their artillery support. For the first time, the Red Air Force proved capable of providing effective close air support to these formations and resupplying them. During the operation, it delivered 1182 tonnes (1163 tons) of fuel, 1240 tonnes (1220 tons) of ammunition and around 1016 tonnes (1000 tons) of equipment and spare parts to forward units.

Soviet progress was so rapid that the German front line disintegrated – so many pockets were formed that there was no chance of any organized relief efforts. In

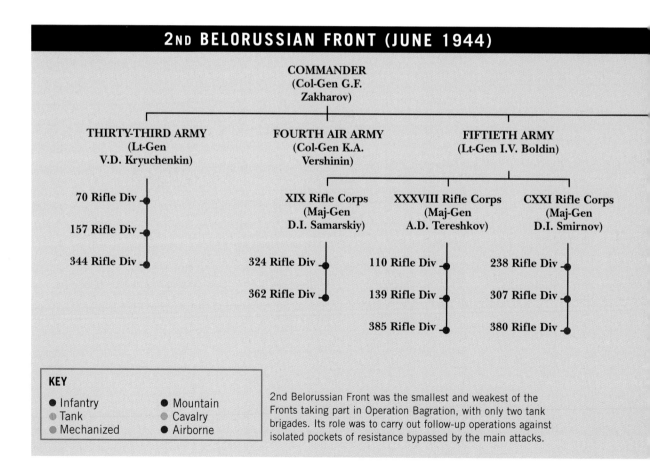

2ND BELORUSSIAN FRONT (JUNE 1944)

COMMANDER
(Col-Gen G.F. Zakharov)

THIRTY-THIRD ARMY
(Lt-Gen V.D. Kryuchenkin)

FOURTH AIR ARMY
(Col-Gen K.A. Vershinin)

FIFTIETH ARMY
(Lt-Gen I.V. Boldin)

70 Rifle Div
157 Rifle Div
344 Rifle Div

XIX Rifle Corps
(Maj-Gen D.I. Samarskiy)

XXXVIII Rifle Corps
(Maj-Gen A.D. Tereshkov)

CXXI Rifle Corps
(Maj-Gen D.I. Smirnov)

324 Rifle Div
362 Rifle Div

110 Rifle Div
139 Rifle Div
385 Rifle Div

238 Rifle Div
307 Rifle Div
380 Rifle Div

KEY
● Infantry
● Tank
● Mechanized
● Mountain
● Cavalry
● Airborne

2nd Belorussian Front was the smallest and weakest of the Fronts taking part in Operation Bagration, with only two tank brigades. Its role was to carry out follow-up operations against isolated pockets of resistance bypassed by the main attacks.

fact, there were insufficient reserves to re-establish any proper front line and the isolated units were left to their own devices. A minority managed to break out to the west, but most were destroyed by the Red Army or partisan bands. (In a move that demonstrated its new-found tactical flexibility, the Red Army created special detachments, based on infantry companies and battalions, each supported by a few tanks and mortars, to hunt down such units. These detachments and the partisans were so successful that it seems likely that only 900 German troops escaped.) Inevitably, supply problems and exhaustion took their toll as the advance continued, but by the time that the offensive wound down in the third week of August, Soviet forces had crossed into East Prussia, were on the point of reaching the Baltic and had arrived at the gates of Warsaw.

Army Group Centre had indeed been practically annihilated, with 2000 AFVs and 57,000 other vehicles destroyed or captured. German casualties may well have been as high as 300,000 dead and 250,000 wounded, plus about 120,000 taken into captivity. The *Wehrmacht* could not afford casualties on this scale – experienced NCOs were vital in restoring the effectiveness of units that had to absorb large numbers of replacement personnel, and their loss gradually reduced the tactical superiority which German units had previously taken for granted. Red Army losses were also high, with 60,000 killed, 110,000 wounded and about 8000 missing in action. In terms of equipment, the Soviets lost 2957 tanks, 2447 guns and 822 aircraft, but their war production and Lend-Lease supplies meant that the losses could readily be replaced.

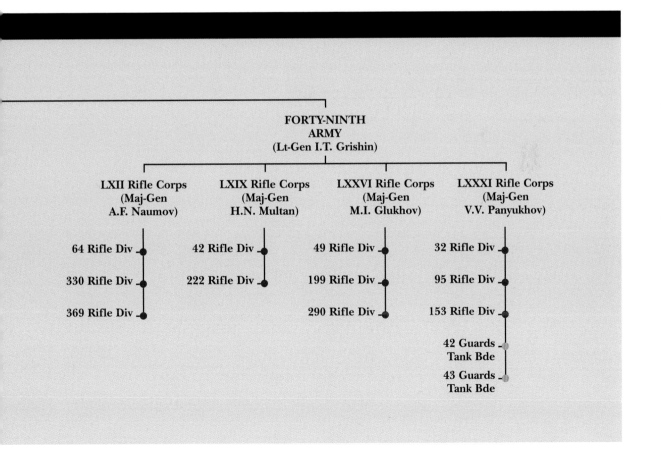

1ST BELORUSSIAN FRONT (JUNE 1944) (1)

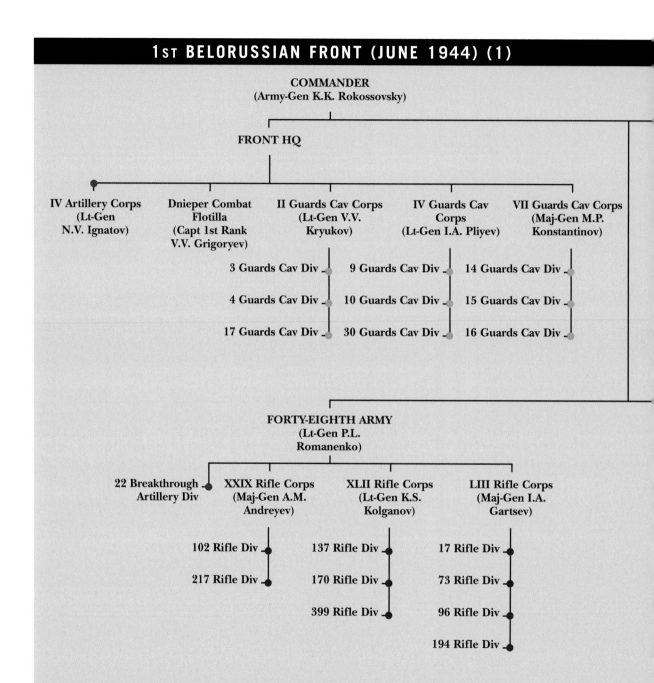

COMMANDER
(Army-Gen K.K. Rokossovsky)

FRONT HQ

IV Artillery Corps (Lt-Gen N.V. Ignatov)	Dnieper Combat Flotilla (Capt 1st Rank V.V. Grigoryev)	II Guards Cav Corps (Lt-Gen V.V. Kryukov)	IV Guards Cav Corps (Lt-Gen I.A. Pliyev)	VII Guards Cav Corps (Maj-Gen M.P. Konstantinov)
		3 Guards Cav Div	9 Guards Cav Div	14 Guards Cav Div
		4 Guards Cav Div	10 Guards Cav Div	15 Guards Cav Div
		17 Guards Cav Div	30 Guards Cav Div	16 Guards Cav Div

FORTY-EIGHTH ARMY
(Lt-Gen P.L. Romanenko)

22 Breakthrough Artillery Div	XXIX Rifle Corps (Maj-Gen A.M. Andreyev)	XLII Rifle Corps (Lt-Gen K.S. Kolganov)	LIII Rifle Corps (Maj-Gen I.A. Gartsev)
	102 Rifle Div	137 Rifle Div	17 Rifle Div
	217 Rifle Div	170 Rifle Div	73 Rifle Div
		399 Rifle Div	96 Rifle Div
			194 Rifle Div

1st Belorussian Front was intended to form the southern arm of the pincer attack on Minsk. Sixty-Fifth Army was reinforced by 26th Artillery Division to help it break through the German defences around Bobruysk and was also assigned I Guards Tank Corps and I Mechanized Corps to act as exploitation forces when the defences were breached. Three Guards cavalry corps were under direct command of the Front HQ for the deep-penetration role in the extensive forests and marshes in its sector.

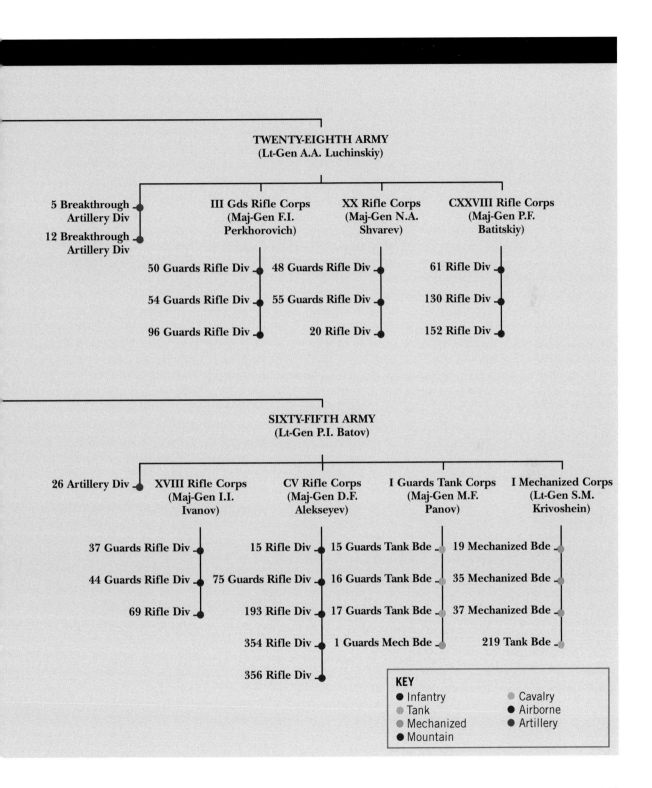

TWENTY-EIGHTH ARMY
(Lt-Gen A.A. Luchinskiy)

5 Breakthrough Artillery Div

12 Breakthrough Artillery Div

III Gds Rifle Corps
(Maj-Gen F.I. Perkhorovich)

XX Rifle Corps
(Maj-Gen N.A. Shvarev)

CXXVIII Rifle Corps
(Maj-Gen P.F. Batitskiy)

50 Guards Rifle Div

54 Guards Rifle Div

96 Guards Rifle Div

48 Guards Rifle Div

55 Guards Rifle Div

20 Rifle Div

61 Rifle Div

130 Rifle Div

152 Rifle Div

SIXTY-FIFTH ARMY
(Lt-Gen P.I. Batov)

26 Artillery Div

XVIII Rifle Corps
(Maj-Gen I.I. Ivanov)

CV Rifle Corps
(Maj-Gen D.F. Alekseyev)

I Guards Tank Corps
(Maj-Gen M.F. Panov)

I Mechanized Corps
(Lt-Gen S.M. Krivoshein)

37 Guards Rifle Div

44 Guards Rifle Div

69 Rifle Div

15 Rifle Div

75 Guards Rifle Div

193 Rifle Div

354 Rifle Div

356 Rifle Div

15 Guards Tank Bde

16 Guards Tank Bde

17 Guards Tank Bde

1 Guards Mech Bde

19 Mechanized Bde

35 Mechanized Bde

37 Mechanized Bde

219 Tank Bde

KEY
- ● Infantry
- ● Tank
- ● Mechanized
- ● Mountain
- ● Cavalry
- ● Airborne
- ● Artillery

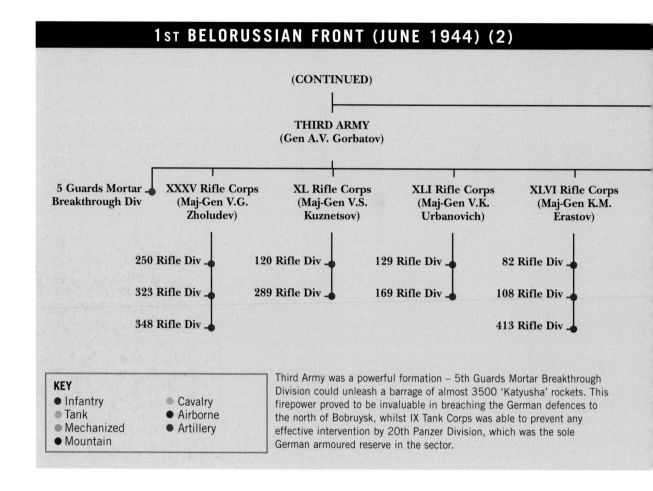

1ST BELORUSSIAN FRONT (JUNE 1944) (2)

(CONTINUED)

THIRD ARMY
(Gen A.V. Gorbatov)

5 Guards Mortar Breakthrough Div	XXXV Rifle Corps (Maj-Gen V.G. Zholudev)	XL Rifle Corps (Maj-Gen V.S. Kuznetsov)	XLI Rifle Corps (Maj-Gen V.K. Urbanovich)	XLVI Rifle Corps (Maj-Gen K.M. Erastov)
	250 Rifle Div	120 Rifle Div	129 Rifle Div	82 Rifle Div
	323 Rifle Div	289 Rifle Div	169 Rifle Div	108 Rifle Div
	348 Rifle Div			413 Rifle Div

KEY
- Infantry
- Tank
- Mechanized
- Mountain
- Cavalry
- Airborne
- Artillery

Third Army was a powerful formation – 5th Guards Mortar Breakthrough Division could unleash a barrage of almost 3500 'Katyusha' rockets. This firepower proved to be invaluable in breaching the German defences to the north of Bobruysk, whilst IX Tank Corps was able to prevent any effective intervention by 20th Panzer Division, which was the sole German armoured reserve in the sector.

Lvov-Sandomir Offensive

By the beginning of June 1944, the redesignated Army Group North Ukraine had been pushed back beyond the River Dnieper and maintained a tenuous hold on the northwestern Ukraine. Stalin ordered a new offensive to take Lvov and finally clear Axis forces from the Ukraine.

This offensive towards Lvov was intended to ensure the success of Operation Bagration by preventing the Germans from reinforcing Army Group Centre. The operation was assigned to Konev's 1st Ukrainian Front, which could deploy over 1.2 million troops, 2050 tanks, about 16,000 guns and mortars and over 3250 aircraft of the Second Air Army. They were opposed by *Generaloberst* Josef Harpe's Army Group North Ukraine, totalling roughly 370,000 men with 420 AFVs. This was the area where the Germans had expected the main

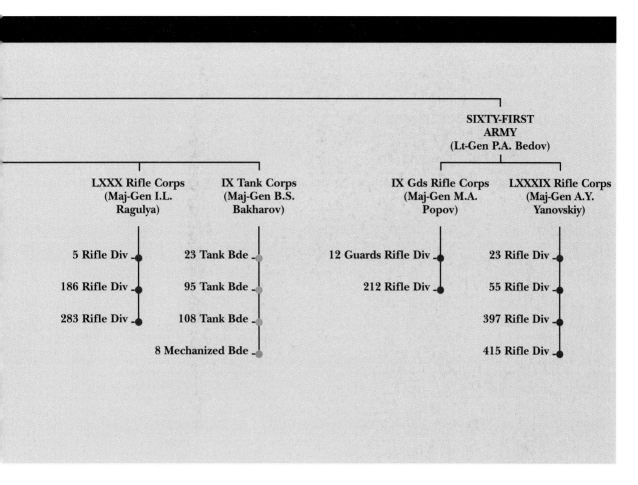

Soviet summer offensive, and they had prepared major field defences protected by 160,000 anti-personnel and 200,000 anti-tank mines.

1st Ukrainian Front

1st Ukrainian Front's offensive was launched on two axes. Three armies were to attack towards Rava-Ruska, whilst a further four advanced on Lvov. The attacks were to be made on a front of only 26km (16 miles), allowing concentrations of 240 guns and mortars per kilometre in the sectors chosen for the initial assaults. The attack towards Rava-Ruska began on 13 July 1944 and by nightfall, Thirteenth Army had advanced 20km (12.5 miles). On the following day, the advance on Lvov began, which left the German XIII Corps in a dangerously exposed salient around Brody.

The southern arm of the Soviet offensive achieved a decisive breakthrough on a front of only 3–4km (1.9–2.5 miles) – the Koltiv Corridor – between XIII Corps and XLVIII Panzer Corps. Fierce German counterattacks on the corridor were beaten off and on 16 July, Konev took the risk of committing Third Guards Tank Army to an attack through the corridor, which was still under heavy bombardment from German artillery. By 18 July, 45,000 men of XIII Corps were trapped around Brody, and a 200km (125-mile) breach had been created in the German front.

Lublin-Brest offensive

At this point, the left wing of Rokossovsky's 1st Belorussian Front, which had not been committed to Operation Bagration, launched the Lublin-Brest

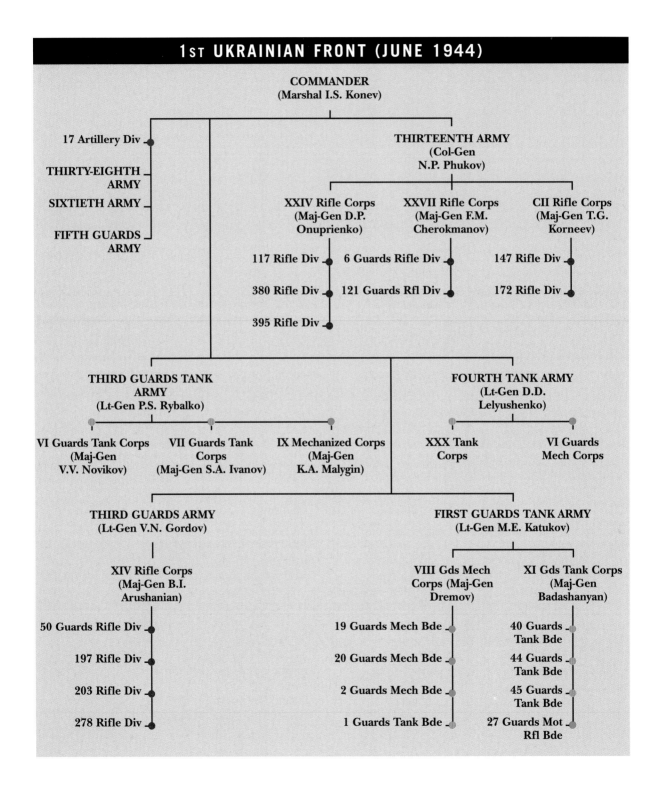

1ST UKRAINIAN FRONT (JUNE 1944)

COMMANDER
(Marshal I.S. Konev)

17 Artillery Div

THIRTY-EIGHTH
ARMY

SIXTIETH ARMY

FIFTH GUARDS
ARMY

THIRTEENTH ARMY
(Col-Gen
N.P. Phukov)

XXIV Rifle Corps
(Maj-Gen D.P.
Onuprienko)

XXVII Rifle Corps
(Maj-Gen F.M.
Cherokmanov)

CII Rifle Corps
(Maj-Gen T.G.
Korneev)

117 Rifle Div   6 Guards Rifle Div   147 Rifle Div

380 Rifle Div   121 Guards Rfl Div   172 Rifle Div

395 Rifle Div

THIRD GUARDS TANK
ARMY
(Lt-Gen P.S. Rybalko)

FOURTH TANK ARMY
(Lt-Gen D.D.
Lelyushenko)

VI Guards Tank Corps
(Maj-Gen
V.V. Novikov)

VII Guards Tank
Corps
(Maj-Gen S.A. Ivanov)

IX Mechanized Corps
(Maj-Gen
K.A. Malygin)

XXX Tank
Corps

VI Guards
Mech Corps

THIRD GUARDS ARMY
(Lt-Gen V.N. Gordov)

FIRST GUARDS TANK ARMY
(Lt-Gen M.E. Katukov)

XIV Rifle Corps
(Maj-Gen B.I.
Arushanian)

VIII Gds Mech
Corps (Maj-Gen
Dremov)

XI Gds Tank Corps
(Maj-Gen
Badashanyan)

50 Guards Rifle Div   19 Guards Mech Bde   40 Guards
Tank Bde

197 Rifle Div   20 Guards Mech Bde   44 Guards
Tank Bde

203 Rifle Div   2 Guards Mech Bde   45 Guards
Tank Bde

278 Rifle Div   1 Guards Tank Bde   27 Guards Mot
Rfl Bde

Offensive from its assembly areas around Kovel. His Eighth Guards Army and Sixty-Ninth Army broke through the defences of LVI Panzer Corps within 48 hours, allowing Second Tank Army to drive on Lublin, which was taken on 24 July. (On 1 August, the city was designated as the headquarters of the Polish Committee of National Liberation, a puppet Communist Polish provisional government.) Following the capture of Lublin, Second Tank Army was turned north towards Warsaw to help cut off the retreat of Army Group Centre, capturing Brest-Litovsk on 28 July.

Brody pocket
These successes allowed Konev to concentrate on the destruction of the Brody pocket, containing XIII Corps; the pocket was eliminated on 22 July. Lvov was captured four days later, marking the completion of the reconquest of the Ukraine. The second stage of the offensive opened on 29 July with the objective of seizing

BREAKTHROUGH ARTILLERY DIVISION (SEPT 1944)		
Unit	Rgts/Btns	Weapons (Each Rgt/Btn)
Observation Btn	–	–
Light Brigade	2 Rgts	24 x 76mm Gun
Howitzer Brigade	3 Rgts	28 x 122mm How
Heavy Howitzer Bde	4 Btns	8 x 152mm How/Gun-How
BM Howitzer Brigade	4 Btns	6 x 203mm How
Rocket Launcher Bde	3 Btns	12 x M31-12
Mortar Brigade	3 Rgts	36 x 120mm Mortar
Heavy Mortar Brigade	4 Btns	8 x 160mm Mortar

a bridgehead across the Vistula and taking Sandomir in southern Poland. The bridgehead was quickly taken but was subjected to fierce attacks, and Sandomir was not taken until 18 August.

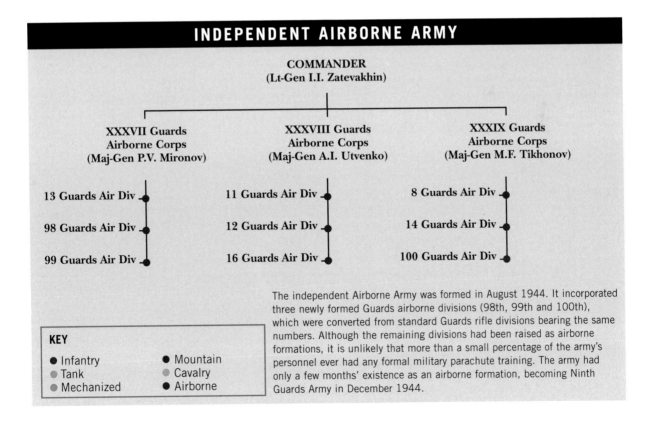

The independent Airborne Army was formed in August 1944. It incorporated three newly formed Guards airborne divisions (98th, 99th and 100th), which were converted from standard Guards rifle divisions bearing the same numbers. Although the remaining divisions had been raised as airborne formations, it is unlikely that more than a small percentage of the army's personnel ever had any formal military parachute training. The army had only a few months' existence as an airborne formation, becoming Ninth Guards Army in December 1944.

Jassy-Kishinev Operation

This offensive was a Red Army victory that had important political results – Rumania changed sides and began its transformation into a Soviet satellite state, whilst Bulgaria rapidly followed suit.

By March 1944, Soviet forces had advanced to the pre-war borders of Rumania. *Stavka* then ordered a further offensive to knock Rumania out of the war and begin the process of clearing Axis forces from the Balkans. The offensive began in late April with a series of limited attacks against German and Rumanian positions – the classic Red Army 'reconnaissance by battle'. This primarily involved company- and battalion-strength infantry raids to probe for weaknesses in the enemy defences.

Operation begins

The main operation began on 2 May at the Rumanian town of Targu Frumos, where 2nd Ukrainian Front's Second Tank Army and Twenty-Seventh Army attacked the positions of General Friedrich Kirchner's LVII Panzer Corps. The *Grossdeutschland* Panzer Division and 24th Panzer Division took the main brunt of the attacks, which included units of the still relatively new JS-2 heavy tank. General Hasso von Manteuffel, *Grossdeutschland*'s commander, later recalled:

'It was at Targu Frumos that I first met the Stalin tanks. It was a shock to find that, although my Tigers began to hit them at a range of 3000 metres [3280 yards], our shells bounced off, and did not penetrate them until we had closed to half that distance. But I was able to counter the Russians' superiority by manoeuvre and mobility, in making the best use of ground cover.' He also noted that the JS-2s had several 'disadvantages: slow, not manoeuvrable enough; as well, in my opinion, their crews were not sufficiently familiar with the tank.'

In three days of battle, the Germans fought the Red Army to a standstill, inflicting heavy casualties and claiming the destruction of 350 Soviet AFVs. Despite the swarms of Red Air Force fighters, the heavily outnumbered *Luftwaffe* and Rumanian ground-attack units played an important role in halting the onslaught

– it seems likely that between them, they destroyed a further 50 Soviet tanks.

Jassy-Kishinev

Despite its success at Targu Frumos, Army Group South Ukraine was having difficulty in holding the line of the River Dniester. Ominously, the Red Army held two bridgeheads across the river – ideal assembly points for its next offensive.

Stavka was indeed planning a double envelopment of the German and Rumanian armies by 2nd and 3rd Ukrainian Fronts. The former was to break through north of Jassy and then seize the crossings over the River Prut to cut off the German Sixth Army. Sixth Tank Army was then to seize the bridges across the River Siret and the fortified Focsani Gap between the Siret and the Danube. Tolbukhin's 3rd Ukrainian Front planned to break out from its bridgehead at Tiraspol before

8 August–15 December 1944

Rumania's defection from the Axis cut off Germany's last major source of crude oil – for a few more months, the *Reich* could rely on the small Hungarian oilfields around Lake Balaton to supplement its own synthetic fuel production. However, Allied air attacks on the synthetic fuel factories and the transport system progressively crippled the German war effort.

The Rumanian and Bulgarian armies were quickly pressed into service alongside the Soviet forces advancing through the Balkans. Although their morale, training and equipment were generally poor, they did provide valuable additional manpower. This manpower was desperately needed to support Red Army formations that had sustained heavy casualties in their earlier offensives to reconquer the Ukraine.

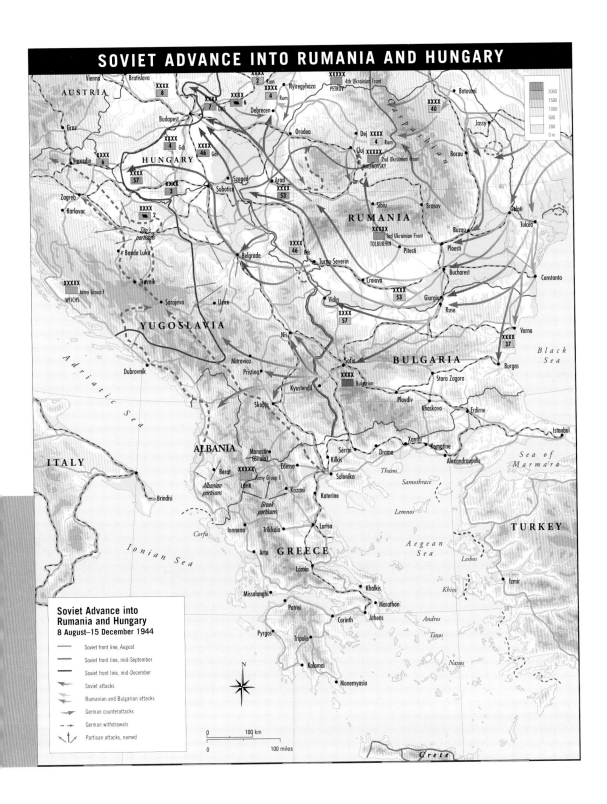

SOVIET ADVANCE INTO RUMANIA AND HUNGARY

Soviet Advance into Rumania and Hungary
8 August–15 December 1944

Soviet front line, August
Soviet front line, mid-September
Soviet front line, mid-December
Soviet attacks
Rumanian and Bulgarian attacks
German counterattacks
German withdrawals
Partisan attacks, named

0   100 km
0   100 miles

2ND UKRAINIAN FRONT (AUGUST 1944) (1)

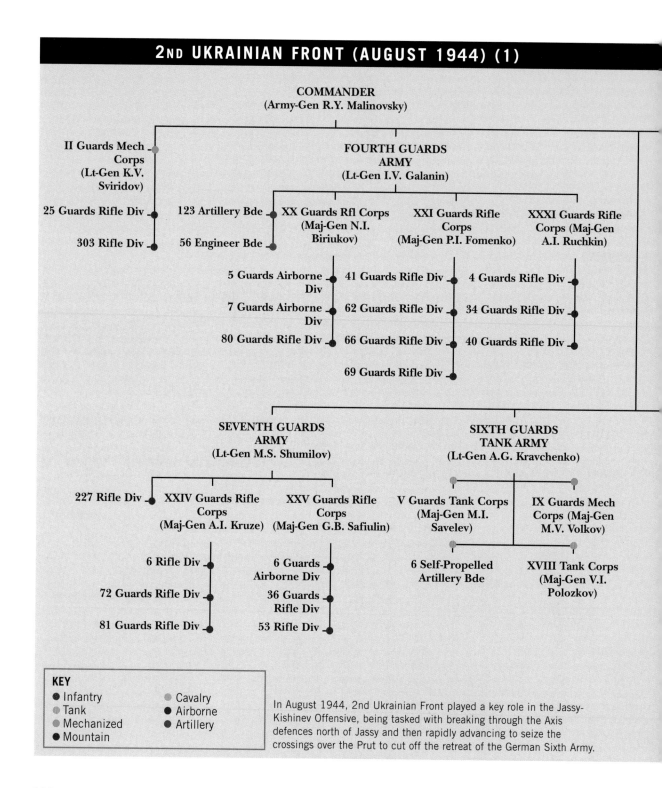

COMMANDER
(Army-Gen R.Y. Malinovsky)

II Guards Mech Corps
(Lt-Gen K.V. Sviridov)

25 Guards Rifle Div

303 Rifle Div

FOURTH GUARDS ARMY
(Lt-Gen I.V. Galanin)

123 Artillery Bde

56 Engineer Bde

XX Guards Rfl Corps
(Maj-Gen N.I. Biriukov)

XXI Guards Rifle Corps
(Maj-Gen P.I. Fomenko)

XXXI Guards Rifle Corps (Maj-Gen A.I. Ruchkin)

5 Guards Airborne Div

7 Guards Airborne Div

80 Guards Rifle Div

41 Guards Rifle Div

62 Guards Rifle Div

66 Guards Rifle Div

69 Guards Rifle Div

4 Guards Rifle Div

34 Guards Rifle Div

40 Guards Rifle Div

SEVENTH GUARDS ARMY
(Lt-Gen M.S. Shumilov)

227 Rifle Div

XXIV Guards Rifle Corps
(Maj-Gen A.I. Kruze)

XXV Guards Rifle Corps
(Maj-Gen G.B. Safiulin)

6 Rifle Div

72 Guards Rifle Div

81 Guards Rifle Div

6 Guards Airborne Div

36 Guards Rifle Div

53 Rifle Div

SIXTH GUARDS TANK ARMY
(Lt-Gen A.G. Kravchenko)

V Guards Tank Corps
(Maj-Gen M.I. Savelev)

IX Guards Mech Corps (Maj-Gen M.V. Volkov)

6 Self-Propelled Artillery Bde

XVIII Tank Corps
(Maj-Gen V.I. Polozkov)

KEY
- ● Infantry
- ● Tank
- ● Mechanized
- ● Mountain
- ● Cavalry
- ● Airborne
- ● Artillery

In August 1944, 2nd Ukrainian Front played a key role in the Jassy-Kishinev Offensive, being tasked with breaking through the Axis defences north of Jassy and then rapidly advancing to seize the crossings over the Prut to cut off the retreat of the German Sixth Army.

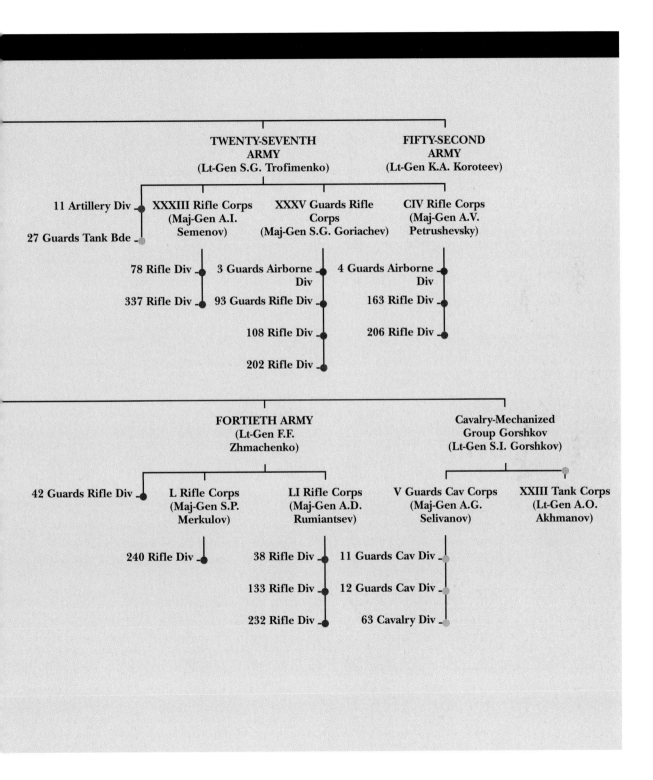

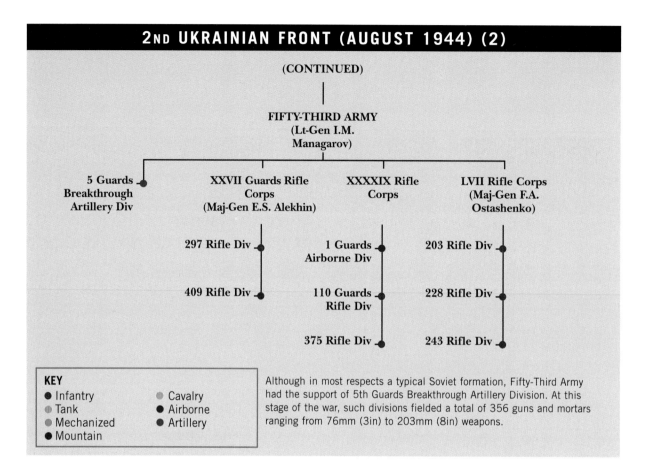

2ND UKRAINIAN FRONT (AUGUST 1944) (2)

(CONTINUED)

FIFTY-THIRD ARMY
(Lt-Gen I.M.
Managarov)

| 5 Guards Breakthrough Artillery Div | XXVII Guards Rifle Corps (Maj-Gen E.S. Alekhin) | XXXXIX Rifle Corps | LVII Rifle Corps (Maj-Gen F.A. Ostashenko) |

297 Rifle Div   1 Guards Airborne Div   203 Rifle Div

409 Rifle Div   110 Guards Rifle Div   228 Rifle Div

375 Rifle Div   243 Rifle Div

KEY
- Infantry
- Tank
- Mechanized
- Mountain
- Cavalry
- Airborne
- Artillery

Although in most respects a typical Soviet formation, Fifty-Third Army had the support of 5th Guards Breakthrough Artillery Division. At this stage of the war, such divisions fielded a total of 356 guns and mortars ranging from 76mm (3in) to 203mm (8in) weapons.

heading north to meet 2nd Ukrainian Front to trap the German and Rumanian forces. After the pocket was sealed, Sixth Tank Army and IV Guards Mechanized Corps were to take Bucharest and the Ploesti oilfields.

Overwhelming force

The Soviet forces were formidable – the two Fronts had over 1,340,000 men and at least 1800 AFVs. They faced roughly 500,000 Germans and 405,000 Rumanians, supported by only 170 tanks and assault guns. The Red Army now had a huge qualitative superiority over the Rumanian forces, whose AFVs and anti-tank weapons were totally incapable of countering T-34/85s and JS-2s.

The attacks by 2nd and 3rd Ukrainian Fronts were made on narrow frontages, typically 3–4km (1.9–2.5 miles), and supported by the fire of almost 250 guns per kilometre. This overwhelming local

superiority ensured rapid breakthroughs were achieved, leading to a double envelopment of the German Sixth Army and elements of the Eighth Army. By 22 August, the German-Rumanian front line had collapsed and IV Guards Mechanized Corps was sent in to exploit the breakthrough.

Rumania switches sides

Rumanian morale had been badly shaken by the heavy losses sustained in the evacuation from the Crimea in May 1944. (These totalled over 23,000 of the 63,000 or so Rumanian troops serving under the command of the German Seventeenth Army.) Resentment against the pro-Axis government came to a head on 23 August, when Marshal Antonescu's regime was toppled in a coup d'etat instigated by King Michael, and the country changed sides. German forces guarding the vital Ploesti oilfields were attacked by Rumanian troops and forced to withdraw into Hungary, together with those units that had managed to avoid encirclement by 2nd and 3rd Ukrainian Fronts. The equivalent of 18 German divisions had been destroyed and Germany's last major

source of crude oil was lost. Fuel shortages caused by the Allied bombing campaign had already badly affected the *Luftwaffe*'s operations, and the loss of Rumanian oil would soon also cripple the *Wehrmacht*'s efforts to repulse future Soviet offensives.

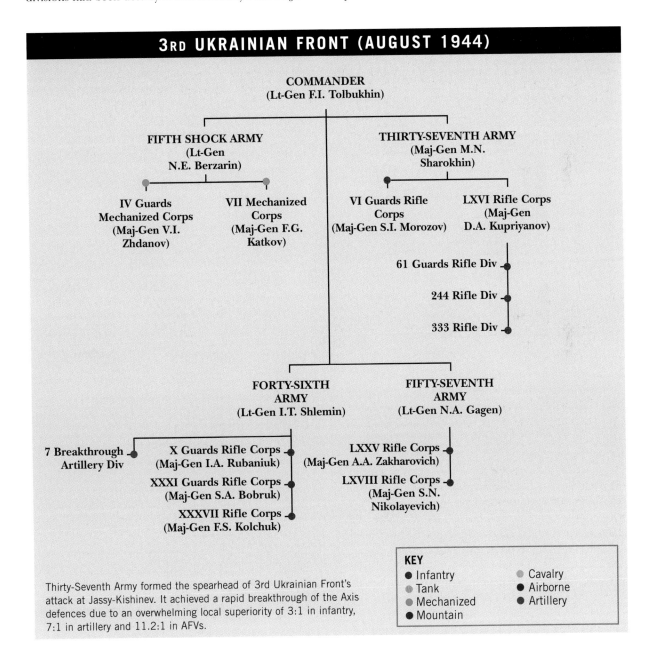

3RD UKRAINIAN FRONT (AUGUST 1944)

COMMANDER
(Lt-Gen F.I. Tolbukhin)

FIFTH SHOCK ARMY
(Lt-Gen N.E. Berzarin)

IV Guards Mechanized Corps (Maj-Gen V.I. Zhdanov)

VII Mechanized Corps (Maj-Gen F.G. Katkov)

THIRTY-SEVENTH ARMY
(Maj-Gen M.N. Sharokhin)

VI Guards Rifle Corps (Maj-Gen S.I. Morozov)

LXVI Rifle Corps (Maj-Gen D.A. Kupriyanov)

61 Guards Rifle Div

244 Rifle Div

333 Rifle Div

FORTY-SIXTH ARMY
(Lt-Gen I.T. Shlemin)

FIFTY-SEVENTH ARMY
(Lt-Gen N.A. Gagen)

7 Breakthrough Artillery Div

X Guards Rifle Corps (Maj-Gen I.A. Rubaniuk)

XXXI Guards Rifle Corps (Maj-Gen S.A. Bobruk)

XXXVII Rifle Corps (Maj-Gen F.S. Kolchuk)

LXXV Rifle Corps (Maj-Gen A.A. Zakharovich)

LXVIII Rifle Corps (Maj-Gen S.N. Nikolayevich)

KEY
- Infantry
- Tank
- Mechanized
- Mountain
- Cavalry
- Airborne
- Artillery

Thirty-Seventh Army formed the spearhead of 3rd Ukrainian Front's attack at Jassy-Kishinev. It achieved a rapid breakthrough of the Axis defences due to an overwhelming local superiority of 3:1 in infantry, 7:1 in artillery and 11.2:1 in AFVs.

Baltic Offensive

After almost 900 days, in February 1944 the siege of Leningrad by German forces was finally raised, and the Soviets began an advance which by the early autumn would take them into East Prussia.

In February 1944, the *Wehrmacht* was forced to retreat from the approaches to Leningrad to the Panther-Wotan Line on the borders of Estonia. In June and July, Operation Bagration decimated Army Group Centre and pushed it back into Poland. This created the opportunity for a Red Army offensive (the Shyaulyay Offensive Operation), which reached the Baltic on 31 July, severing the land connection between the German Army Group North and Army Group Centre.

Although Operation Doppelkopf, a German counter-offensive launched in August, temporarily reopened land links between the army groups, the 'corridor' was never more than 30km (19 miles) wide and was always vulnerable to any new Soviet offensive. Indeed, renewed operations began with an attack towards Riga by 1st and 3rd Baltic Fronts on 14 September, which rapidly broke through the German defences, beating off a counterattack by XXXIX Panzer Corps.

Memel offensive

On 5 October, 1st Baltic Front launched the Memel Offensive Operation, which destroyed Third Panzer Army and finally cut the land link between Army Groups North and Centre, isolating *Generaloberst* Ferdinand Schoerner's forces in Riga and Courland. Initially, it seemed as though Memel would soon fall, but the German XXVIII Corps was able to hold a perimeter around the port until 27 January 1945. This was largely due to naval gunfire support from heavy units of the *Kriegsmarine*, including the pocket battleship *Lützow* and the heavy cruiser *Prinz Eugen*. Their gunfire was a major factor in breaking up Soviet attacks – in a single day, *Lützow* fired 304 rounds from her main 28cm (11in) guns and a further 292 rounds from her 15cm (5.9in) secondary armament.

Hitler did not accept Schoerner's proposal to use forces freed by evacuating Riga in an attack towards

Memel to attempt to re-establish the land connection, but his position was rapidly becoming untenable. Soviet forces were still advancing and Riga was taken by 3rd Baltic Front on 13 October, forcing Army Group North to retreat into the Courland peninsula. Hitler ignored repeated advice from his generals to evacuate the 200,000 German troops bottled up in the newly formed Courland pocket, as he was convinced that the area was vital to protect the *Kriegsmarine*'s Baltic bases where the new Type XXI U-Boats were working up.

Courland pocket

The German forces in the peninsula (retitled Army Group Courland on 15 January 1945) represented a threat to the Soviet northern flank and tied down substantial elements of 1st and 2nd Baltic Fronts in prolonged 'siege operations'. The blockade of the

January–October 1944

By February 1944, the Siege of Leningrad was over, and for the first time in 900 days the people of the city could walk their streets without fear of *Wehrmacht* shells or *Luftwaffe* bombs. Now the Red Army stood poised in the wilderness of forests and lakes that ran along the Estonian border. Army Group North strove to keep the Soviets out of the Baltic, but they were undone as a side product of Operation Bagration in July 1944. Having taken Minsk, the Red Army pushed on into Lithuania, and by the end of August the Soviets were on the East Prussian border, trapping most of Army Group North in the Courland peninsula west of Riga.

On the Arctic Front, the Red Army slowly regained the territory it had lost in 1940, forcing the Finns to sign an armistice in September 1944. The German Twentieth Mountain Army was forced to retreat back into Norway.

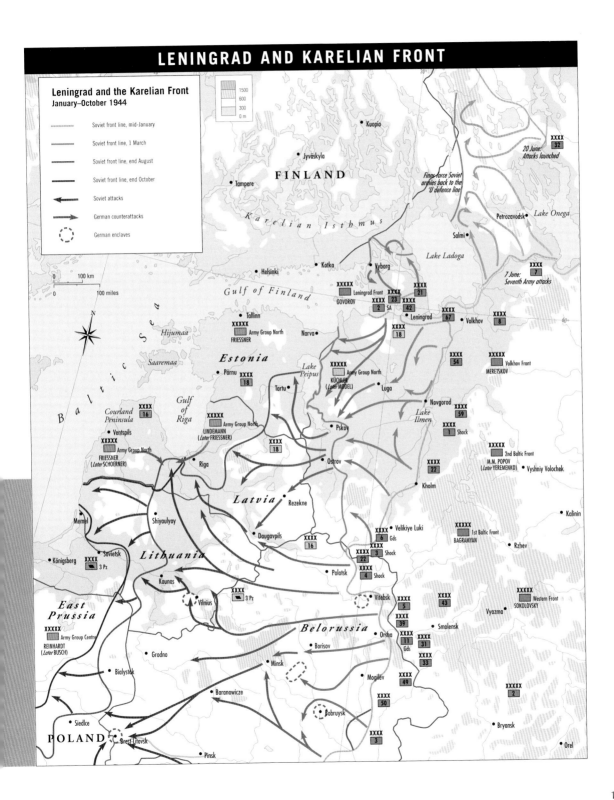

LENINGRAD AND KARELIAN FRONT

Leningrad and the Karelian Front
January–October 1944

- Soviet front line, mid-January
- Soviet front line, 1 March
- Soviet front line, end August
- Soviet front line, end October
- Soviet attacks
- German counterattacks
- German enclaves

1500
600
300
0 m

0   100 km
0   100 miles

FINLAND

Kuopio

Jyväskylä

Tampere

Karelian Isthmus

XXXX
32
20 June:
Attacks launched

Finns force Soviet
armies back to the
U defence line

Petrozavodsk   Lake Onega

Salmi

Lake Ladoga

XXXX
7
7 June:
Seventh Army attacks

Helsinki   Kotka   Vyborg

Gulf of Finland

XXXXX
Leningrad Front
GOVOROV

XXXX
23

XXXX
21

XXXX
2   SA

XXXX
42

XXXX
67

Leningrad   Volkhov

XXXX
8

Tallinn

XXXXX
Army Group North
FRIESSNER

Narva

XXXX
18

XXXX
54

XXXXX
Volkhov Front
MERETSKOV

Estonia

Hijumaa

Baltic Sea

Saaremaa

Pärnu

XXXX
18

Tartu

*Lake
Peipus*

XXXXX
Army Group North
KÜCHLER
(*Later* MODEL)

Luga

Novgorod

XXXX
59

*Lake
Ilmen*

XXXX
1   Shock

Courland
Peninsula

XXXX
16

Gulf
of
Riga

XXXXX
Army Group North
LINDEMANN
(*Later* FRIESSNER)

Ventspils

XXXXX
Army Group North
FRIESSNER
(*Later* SCHOERNER)

Riga

XXXX
18

Pskov

Ostrov

XXXX
22

Kholm

XXXXX
2nd Baltic Front
M.M. POPOV
(*Later* YEREMENKO)   Vyshniy Volochek

Latvia   Rezekne

Kalinin

Memel

Shiyaulyay

Daugavpils

XXXX
16

XXXX
6   Gds

Velikiye Luki

XXXXX
1st Baltic Front
BAGRAMYAN

Rzhev

Königsberg   Sovietsk

XXXX
3 Pz

Lithuania

Kaunas

Polotsk

XXXX
22

XXXX
3   Shock

XXXX
4   Shock

Vitebsk

XXXX
5

XXXX
43

XXXXX
Western Front
SOKOLOVSKY

Vilnius

XXXX
3 Pz

Vyazma

XXXX
39

*East
Prussia*

XXXXX
Army Group Centre
REINHARDT
(*Later* BUSCH)

Grodno

Belorussia   Orsha

XXXX
11
Gds

XXXX
31

Smolensk

Borisov

XXXX
33

Minsk

Mogilev

XXXX
49

XXXXX
2

Baranowicze

Bialystok

Bobruysk

Bryansk

Siedlce

POLAND   Brest-Litovsk

XXXX
50

XXXX
3

Pinsk

Orel

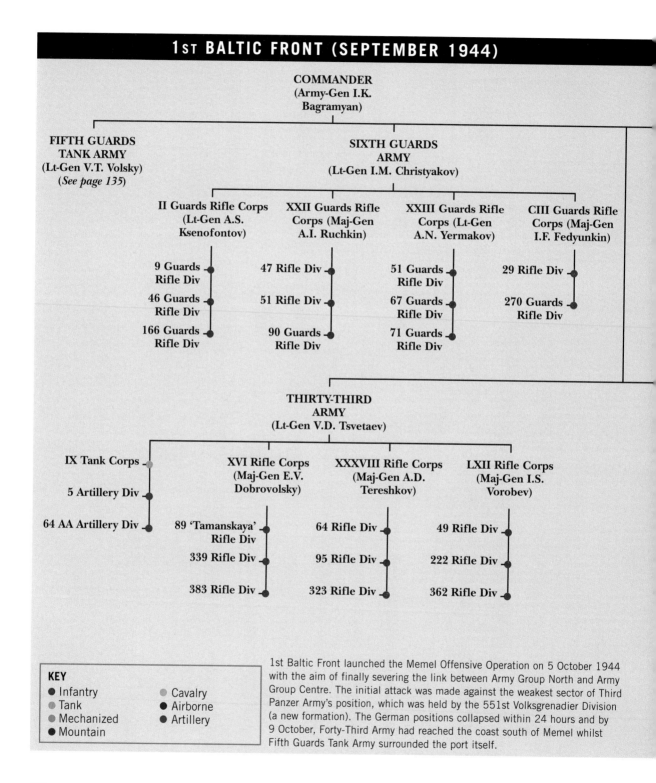

1ST BALTIC FRONT (SEPTEMBER 1944)

COMMANDER
(Army-Gen I.K. Bagramyan)

FIFTH GUARDS TANK ARMY
(Lt-Gen V.T. Volsky)
(*See page 135*)

SIXTH GUARDS ARMY
(Lt-Gen I.M. Christyakov)

II Guards Rifle Corps (Lt-Gen A.S. Ksenofontov)

XXII Guards Rifle Corps (Maj-Gen A.I. Ruchkin)

XXIII Guards Rifle Corps (Lt-Gen A.N. Yermakov)

CIII Guards Rifle Corps (Maj-Gen I.F. Fedyunkin)

9 Guards Rifle Div

46 Guards Rifle Div

166 Guards Rifle Div

47 Rifle Div

51 Rifle Div

90 Guards Rifle Div

51 Guards Rifle Div

67 Guards Rifle Div

71 Guards Rifle Div

29 Rifle Div

270 Guards Rifle Div

THIRTY-THIRD ARMY
(Lt-Gen V.D. Tsvetaev)

IX Tank Corps

5 Artillery Div

64 AA Artillery Div

XVI Rifle Corps (Maj-Gen E.V. Dobrovolsky)

XXXVIII Rifle Corps (Maj-Gen A.D. Tereshkov)

LXII Rifle Corps (Maj-Gen I.S. Vorobev)

89 'Tamanskaya' Rifle Div

339 Rifle Div

383 Rifle Div

64 Rifle Div

95 Rifle Div

323 Rifle Div

49 Rifle Div

222 Rifle Div

362 Rifle Div

KEY
- Infantry
- Tank
- Mechanized
- Mountain
- Cavalry
- Airborne
- Artillery

1st Baltic Front launched the Memel Offensive Operation on 5 October 1944 with the aim of finally severing the link between Army Group North and Army Group Centre. The initial attack was made against the weakest sector of Third Panzer Army's position, which was held by the 551st Volksgrenadier Division (a new formation). The German positions collapsed within 24 hours and by 9 October, Forty-Third Army had reached the coast south of Memel whilst Fifth Guards Tank Army surrounded the port itself.

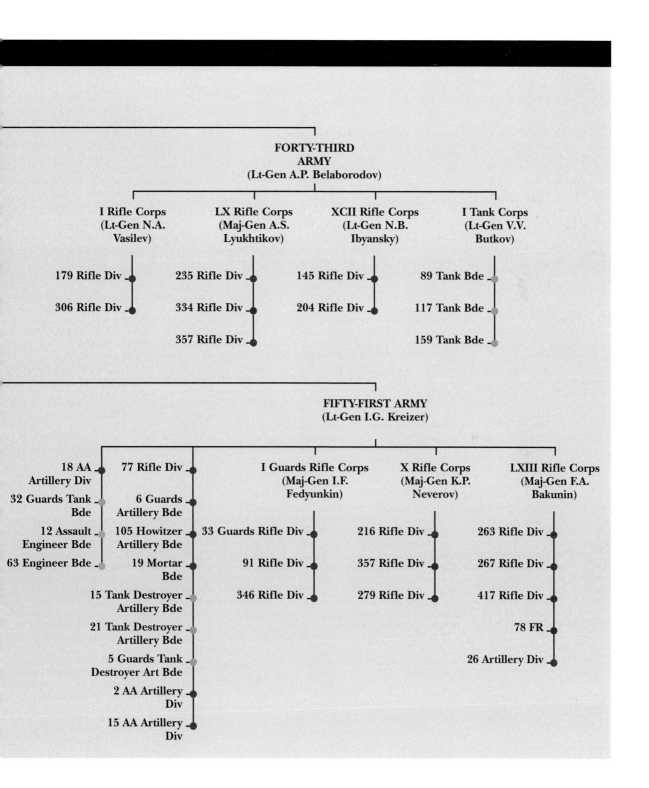

FORTY-THIRD
ARMY
(Lt-Gen A.P. Belaborodov)

I Rifle Corps
(Lt-Gen N.A.
Vasilev)

LX Rifle Corps
(Maj-Gen A.S.
Lyukhtikov)

XCII Rifle Corps
(Lt-Gen N.B.
Ibyansky)

I Tank Corps
(Lt-Gen V.V.
Butkov)

179 Rifle Div

306 Rifle Div

235 Rifle Div

334 Rifle Div

357 Rifle Div

145 Rifle Div

204 Rifle Div

89 Tank Bde

117 Tank Bde

159 Tank Bde

FIFTY-FIRST ARMY
(Lt-Gen I.G. Kreizer)

18 AA
Artillery Div

32 Guards Tank
Bde

12 Assault
Engineer Bde

63 Engineer Bde

77 Rifle Div

6 Guards
Artillery Bde

105 Howitzer
Artillery Bde

19 Mortar
Bde

15 Tank Destroyer
Artillery Bde

21 Tank Destroyer
Artillery Bde

5 Guards Tank
Destroyer Art Bde

2 AA Artillery
Div

15 AA Artillery
Div

I Guards Rifle Corps
(Maj-Gen I.F.
Fedyunkin)

33 Guards Rifle Div

91 Rifle Div

346 Rifle Div

X Rifle Corps
(Maj-Gen K.P.
Neverov)

216 Rifle Div

357 Rifle Div

279 Rifle Div

LXIII Rifle Corps
(Maj-Gen F.A.
Bakunin)

263 Rifle Div

267 Rifle Div

417 Rifle Div

78 FR

26 Artillery Div

pocket was interspersed with major Soviet offensives, including one by an estimated 52 divisions in late 1944. All of these attacks were beaten off with heavy losses – the Germans claimed to have inflicted 390,000 casualties by mid-March 1945. Army Group Courland held out until May 1945, surrendering only on direct orders from the new German head of state, Admiral Karl Dönitz.

Into East Prussia

The success of the Memel Offensive Operation prompted *Stavka* to attempt a new offensive into East Prussia by Chernyakhovsky's 3rd Belorussian Front. The plan was for Fifth and Eleventh Guards Armies to break through the German defences, after which II Guards Tank Corps and Twenty-Eighth Army would advance on Königsberg, with Thirty-First and Thirty-Ninth Armies providing flank protection. *Stavka* was becoming overconfident and failed to appreciate that the defenders had been heavily reinforced and would be aided by substantial fortifications.

On 16 October, Fifth and Eleventh Guards Armies began their attacks, making an 11km (7-mile)

ADVANCE INTO THE BALTIC (SEPTEMBER 1944)

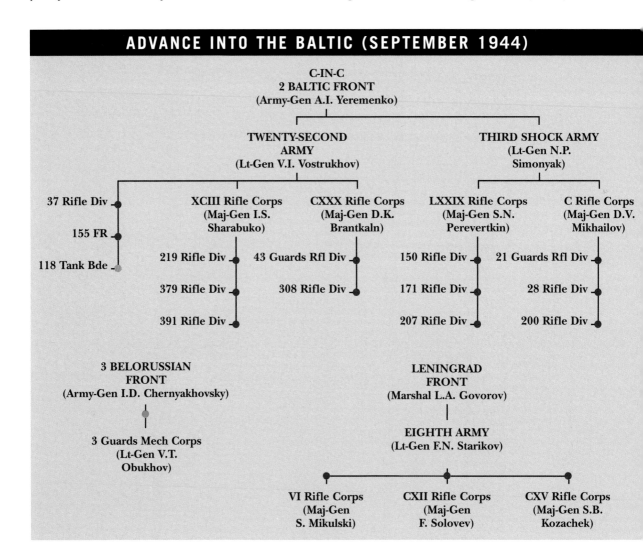

C-IN-C
2 BALTIC FRONT
(Army-Gen A.I. Yeremenko)

TWENTY-SECOND ARMY (Lt-Gen V.I. Vostrukhov)

THIRD SHOCK ARMY (Lt-Gen N.P. Simonyak)

37 Rifle Div

155 FR

118 Tank Bde

XCIII Rifle Corps (Maj-Gen I.S. Sharabuko)
- 219 Rifle Div
- 379 Rifle Div
- 391 Rifle Div

CXXX Rifle Corps (Maj-Gen D.K. Brantkaln)
- 43 Guards Rfl Div
- 308 Rifle Div

LXXIX Rifle Corps (Maj-Gen S.N. Perevertkin)
- 150 Rifle Div
- 171 Rifle Div
- 207 Rifle Div

C Rifle Corps (Maj-Gen D.V. Mikhailov)
- 21 Guards Rfl Div
- 28 Rifle Div
- 200 Rifle Div

3 BELORUSSIAN FRONT (Army-Gen I.D. Chernyakhovsky)

3 Guards Mech Corps (Lt-Gen V.T. Obukhov)

LENINGRAD FRONT (Marshal L.A. Govorov)

EIGHTH ARMY (Lt-Gen F.N. Starikov)

VI Rifle Corps (Maj-Gen S. Mikulski)

CXII Rifle Corps (Maj-Gen F. Solovev)

CXV Rifle Corps (Maj-Gen S.B. Kozachek)

penetration of the outer German defences and crossing the East Prussian border within the first 24 hours. It soon became clear, though, that the German defences had been underestimated – it took four days to break through the first defensive line, and the second was so strong that II Guards Tank Corps had to be committed.

The second line was finally broken at the cost of very heavy casualties, but it took the addition of the Front's reserve, Twenty-Eighth Army, to push back the defending units, which had been reinforced by 18th Flak Division, whose guns inflicted heavy losses on the

Russian tanks. Gumbinnen was finally taken on 22 October, only to be recaptured two days later.

There was equally fierce fighting around Goldap on the southern flank of the Soviet offensive. The town was retaken by the Germans on 25 October, successfully assaulted by the Soviet Thirty-First Army in a surprise attack on 28 October and finally recaptured by 5th Panzer Division on 3 November. The Soviet offensive had been a bloody failure, sustaining an estimated 79,500 casualties, and the Red Army would not re-enter East Prussia in strength until January 1945.

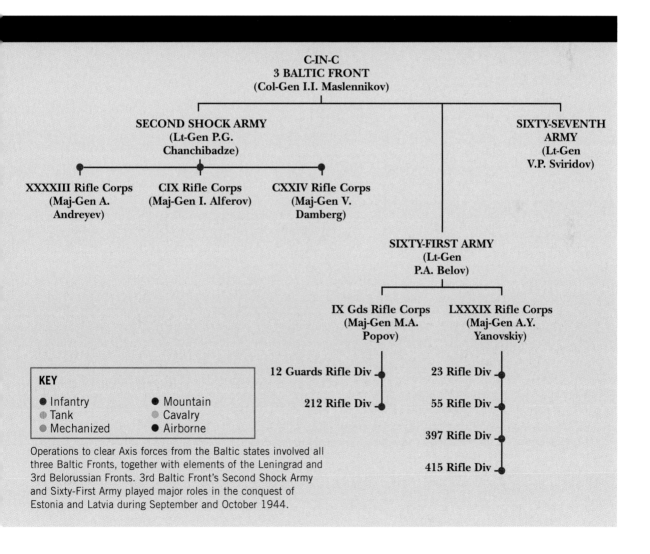

Operations to clear Axis forces from the Baltic states involved all three Baltic Fronts, together with elements of the Leningrad and 3rd Belorussian Fronts. 3rd Baltic Front's Second Shock Army and Sixty-First Army played major roles in the conquest of Estonia and Latvia during September and October 1944.

Into the Balkans

The Red Army's offensive into Yugoslavia was supported by Tito's partisans, who had become one of the world's most effective guerrilla organizations.

In September 1944, the two German army groups in the Balkans (E and F) were in danger of being cut off by the rapid advance of the Red Army and the defection of former German satellite forces. The Soviet victory at Jassy-Kishinev had forced Bulgaria and Rumania to change sides, adding them to Germany's list of enemies. *Stavka* now planned to carry the war into Yugoslavia and take the country's capital, Belgrade.

Advance on Belgrade

By the end of September, 3rd Ukrainian Front (with Second Bulgarian Army under command) had moved up to the Bulgarian–Yugoslav border in preparation for an advance on Belgrade. In Rumania, elements of 2nd Ukrainian Front were assembling in readiness for an attack to cut the rail link between Belgrade and Hungary. Partisans of the anti-fascist resistance under the command of Tito now controlled large swathes of territory in Yugoslavia, and Tito himself flew to Moscow on 19 September for a meeting with Stalin to coordinate plans for the partisans' role in the offensive. (In a bizarrely formal gesture, Tito authorized Soviet troops to enter Yugoslav territory to assist in the liberation of the country.) Before the start of ground operations, the 3rd Ukrainian Front's Seventeenth Air Army carried out a week-long series of air attacks against German units withdrawing from Greece and southern Yugoslavia.

Offensive begins

The offensive began in late September – Second Bulgarian Army's advance was contested by 7th SS Mountain Division *Prinz Eugen*, which was overwhelmed and forced to withdraw. The Bulgarian forces then moved on Kosovo in an attempt to cut Army Group E's line of retreat from Greece. The Soviet Fifty-Seventh Army led 3rd Ukrainian Front's attack towards Belgrade, with considerable support from Tito's partisans and the gunboats of the Danube Military Flotilla. However, it

quickly became apparent that there were problems in coordinating the operations of the various nationalities. In an attempt to sort out the problem, Tito flew to Rumania on 5 October to thrash out operational details with 3rd Ukrainian Front's Chief of Staff and to make arrangements with Bulgarian representatives about the participation of their forces in the campaign.

Partisan link up

By 12 October, IV Guards Mechanized Corps was moving up from Bulgaria in preparation for a

November–December 1944

The speed of 3rd Ukrainian Front's capture of Belgrade on 20 October was rivalled by the rapid advance into Hungary by Marshal Malinovsky's 2nd Ukrainian Front. On 15 October, Admiral Horthy's Hungarian government attempted to follow the Rumanians and Bulgarians in defecting from the Axis, but was ousted in a German-led coup that installed a fanatical pro-Nazi regime under Ferenc Szálasi.

In the midst of this political intrigue, a combined German/Hungarian force inflicted a sharp reverse on the invading Soviet and Rumanian armies at Debrecen (6–29 October), in which Pliyev's elite cavalry-mechanized group was effectively destroyed.

Despite this setback, Stalin ordered 2nd Ukrainian Front into a new offensive aimed directly at Budapest, which reached the city's eastern suburbs by 7 November, where it was halted by German reinforcements which included four Panzer divisions.

The exhausted Soviet forces were operating at the end of over-extended supply lines and it was not until 25–26 December that 2nd and 3rd Ukrainian Fronts were finally able to break through the German defences to surround the Hungarian capital, Budapest.

breakthrough to Belgrade when it was surprised by the appearance of large partisan forces. Despite efforts to establish formal command procedures, it seems that ad hoc combined forces evolved during the course of the campaign as the partisans recognized the benefits of operating with Soviet armour and artillery support. In

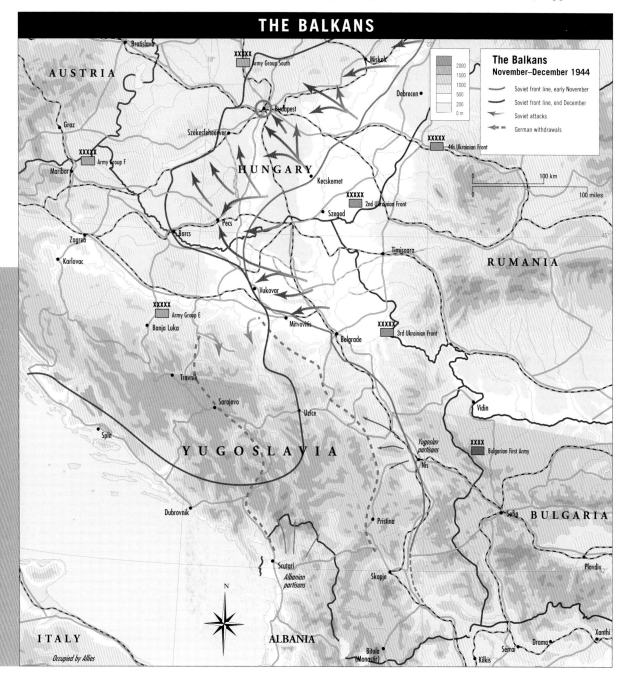

THE BALKANS

The Balkans
November–December 1944

Soviet front line, early November

Soviet front line, end December

Soviet attacks

German withdrawals

turn, the Red Army came to appreciate the value of infantry familiar with the local terrain.

Further north, 2nd Ukrainian Front's Forty-Sixth Army advanced in an attempt to outflank the German Belgrade defensive position from the north by cutting the river and rail supply lines running along the River Tisa. With close air support from Fifth Air Army, its

X Guards Rifle Corps made rapid progress to threaten the main rail routes from Belgrade.

Belgrade liberated
On 14 October, IV Guards Mechanized Corps and the Yugoslav XII Corps broke through the German defences south of Belgrade. Although the assault on the city was

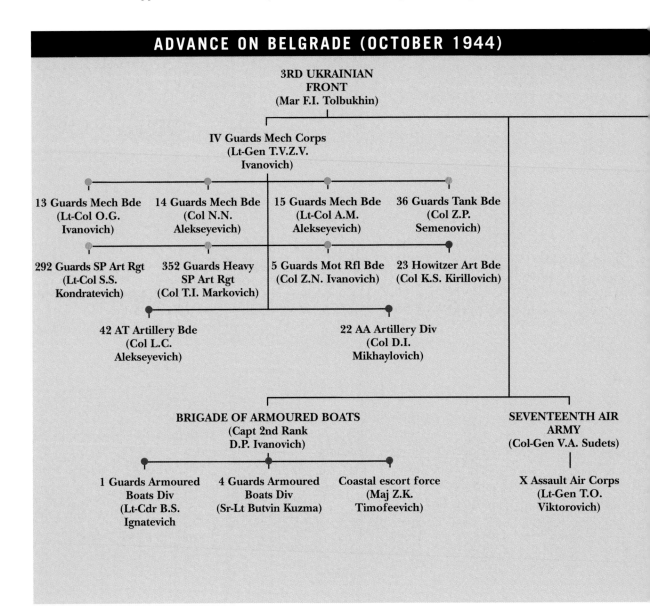

ADVANCE ON BELGRADE (OCTOBER 1944)

3RD UKRAINIAN FRONT
(Mar F.I. Tolbukhin)

IV Guards Mech Corps
(Lt-Gen T.V.Z.V. Ivanovich)

13 Guards Mech Bde
(Lt-Col O.G. Ivanovich)

14 Guards Mech Bde
(Col N.N. Alekseyevich)

15 Guards Mech Bde
(Lt-Col A.M. Alekseyevich)

36 Guards Tank Bde
(Col Z.P. Semenovich)

292 Guards SP Art Rgt
(Lt-Col S.S. Kondratevich)

352 Guards Heavy SP Art Rgt
(Col T.I. Markovich)

5 Guards Mot Rfl Bde
(Col Z.N. Ivanovich)

23 Howitzer Art Bde
(Col K.S. Kirillovich)

42 AT Artillery Bde
(Col L.C. Alekseyevich)

22 AA Artillery Div
(Col D.I. Mikhaylovich)

BRIGADE OF ARMOURED BOATS
(Capt 2nd Rank D.P. Ivanovich)

SEVENTEENTH AIR ARMY
(Col-Gen V.A. Sudets)

1 Guards Armoured Boats Div
(Lt-Cdr B.S. Ignatevich

4 Guards Armoured Boats Div
(Sr-Lt Butvin Kuzma)

Coastal escort force
(Maj Z.K. Timofeevich)

X Assault Air Corps
(Lt-Gen T.O. Viktorovich)

delayed by the need to clear German forces holding out in the surrounding area, Belgrade was finally liberated on 20 October by combined Soviet and Yugoslav forces. At this time, the Bulgarian Second Army and Yugoslav XIII Corps were still advancing from the southeast. Their operations had forced Army Group E to retreat through Montenegro and Bosnia, preventing it from

reinforcing German formations in Hungary. By late November, German forces had been cleared from virtually the whole of Yugoslavia and the Red Army was poised for its next offensives. Whilst its military victories had been spectacular, they were overshadowed by their political results – a new Soviet empire, which would rival that of the Tsars, was rapidly being formed.

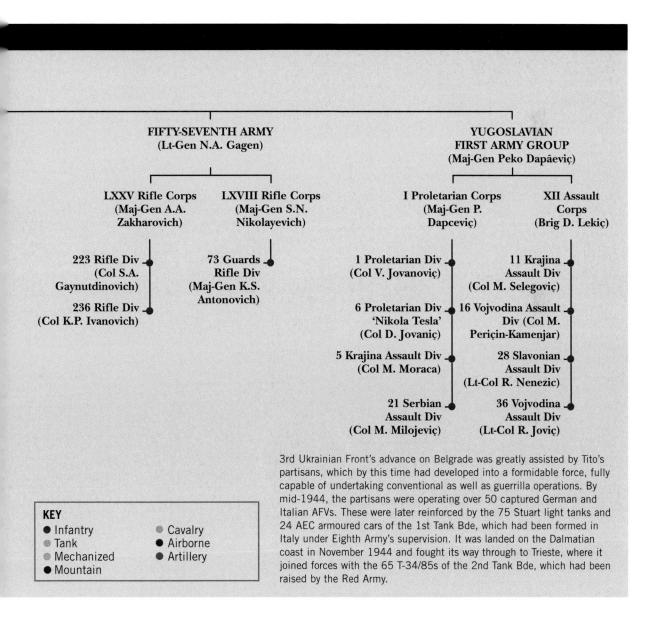

FIFTY-SEVENTH ARMY
(Lt-Gen N.A. Gagen)

LXXV Rifle Corps
(Maj-Gen A.A. Zakharovich)

LXVIII Rifle Corps
(Maj-Gen S.N. Nikolayevich)

223 Rifle Div
(Col S.A. Gaynutdinovich)

236 Rifle Div
(Col K.P. Ivanovich)

73 Guards Rifle Div
(Maj-Gen K.S. Antonovich)

YUGOSLAVIAN FIRST ARMY GROUP
(Maj-Gen Peko Dapãeviç)

I Proletarian Corps
(Maj-Gen P. Dapceviç)

XII Assault Corps
(Brig D. Lekiç)

1 Proletarian Div
(Col V. Jovanoviç)

6 Proletarian Div 'Nikola Tesla'
(Col D. Jovaniç)

5 Krajina Assault Div
(Col M. Moraca)

21 Serbian Assault Div
(Col M. Milojeviç)

11 Krajina Assault Div
(Col M. Selegovic)

16 Vojvodina Assault Div (Col M. Periçin-Kamenjar)

28 Slavonian Assault Div
(Lt-Col R. Nenezic)

36 Vojvodina Assault Div
(Lt-Col R. Joviç)

3rd Ukrainian Front's advance on Belgrade was greatly assisted by Tito's partisans, which by this time had developed into a formidable force, fully capable of undertaking conventional as well as guerrilla operations. By mid-1944, the partisans were operating over 50 captured German and Italian AFVs. These were later reinforced by the 75 Stuart light tanks and 24 AEC armoured cars of the 1st Tank Bde, which had been formed in Italy under Eighth Army's supervision. It was landed on the Dalmatian coast in November 1944 and fought its way through to Trieste, where it joined forces with the 65 T-34/85s of the 2nd Tank Bde, which had been raised by the Red Army.

KEY
- Infantry
- Tank
- Mechanized
- Mountain
- Cavalry
- Airborne
- Artillery

Victory in Europe: 1945

At the beginning of 1945, the Red Army's victory was inevitable, but it would be won at the cost of horrifying casualties in the final struggle to capture the German capital, Berlin.

On the road to Berlin – a column of JS-2 heavy tanks passes an abandoned German truck.

The Soviet writer Ilya Ehrenburg had been writing savage propaganda articles throughout the war, which struck a chord with the feelings of the *Frontoviki*, the front-line troops. As the Red Army's advance crossed the borders of the *Reich* itself, that propaganda would have fearful results and become a two-edged weapon.

Extracts from a propaganda leaflet written early in 1945 read: 'Not only divisions and armies are advancing on Berlin. All the trenches, graves and ravines with the corpses of the innocents are advancing on Berlin … The hour of revenge has struck!' The message was reinforced by each unit's political officers with their slogans: 'A soldier's rage in battle must be terrible. He does not merely seek to fight, he must also be the embodiment of the court of his people's justice.'

Spoils of war

Stalin and his commanders were indifferent to the tens of thousands of cases of rape and looting which occurred as the Red Army advanced across eastern Europe and into Germany itself. Stalin dismissed a Yugoslav partisan leader's complaints about the Red Army's conduct, commenting, 'Can't he understand it if a soldier who has crossed thousands of kilometres through blood and fire and death has fun with a woman or takes some trifle?'

This attitude began to change as it became apparent that the atrocities were provoking fanatical resistance from German forces; at the same time, the incidence of casual looting and rape was undermining military discipline. From April 1945, orders were issued that at least a small proportion of offenders were to be executed in front of their units to keep the situation under control, and it seems that a number of shootings were carried out.

A mirror to history?

In many respects, reports on the conduct of the Red Army of 1944–45 recall accounts of the British Army of the Napoleonic Wars. Even Wellington could not prevent his men's looting and rape after the siege of Badajoz, and their readiness to drink themselves insensible was fully matched by Soviet troops almost 150 years later. During the advance through Hungary, a veteran recalled finding the bodies of three of his comrades in a cellar, floating in knee-deep wine. They had smashed wine barrels with machine-gun fire and then become so drunk that they collapsed and drowned in a 'wine lake'.

Hungary and Austria

By the summer of 1944, the Hungarian regime of Admiral Horthy was an increasingly reluctant German ally as the Red Army advanced towards the Carpathians.

Hitler was determined to keep control of the oilfields around Lake Balaton, which were the *Reich's* last significant source of crude oil. German troops had occupied key points throughout Hungary since March 1944, when Hitler had first learned of Admiral Horthy's initial 'peace feelers' to the Allies. On 15 October, renewed Hungarian attempts to negotiate with the Allies provoked Operation Panzerfaust, carried out by German commando operations specialist Otto Skorzeny, which deposed Admiral Horthy and set up a puppet fascist government led by Ferenc Szálasi.

Whilst the Germans had secured their rear areas, their defences in Hungary were rapidly crumbling as Malinovsky's 2nd Ukrainian Front advanced on Budapest. The first Red Army units penetrated the city's eastern suburbs on 7 November, but were halted by the German/Hungarian garrison, which had just received major reinforcements, including four Panzer divisions.

The Siege of Budapest

During the next six weeks, the Soviet forces ranged against Budapest were joined by Tolbukhin's 3rd

Ukrainian Front, and on 18 December both Fronts launched a new offensive to encircle the city. Despite fierce counterattacks by several Panzer divisions, 3rd Ukrainian Front's XVIII Tank Corps linked up with

SOVIET GROUND FORCES (JANUARY 1945)	
Unit Type	Number
HEADQUARTERS	
Fronts	18
Armies	72
Rifle Corps	174
Cavalry Corps	8
Tank Corps	24
Mechanized Corps	14
INFANTRY	
Rifle Divisions (inc Mountain & Motorized)	517
Rifle Brigades	15
Ski Brigades	2
Tank Destroyer Brigades	–
Separate Rifle Regiments	8
Fortified Regions	47
Ski Battalions	–
CAVALRY	
Cavalry Divisions	26
Separate Cavalry Regiments	1
ARMOUR	
Tank Divisions	2
Tank Brigades	145
Assault Gun Brigades	9
Mechanized Brigades	47
Motor Rifle Brigades	24
Motorcycle Brigades	–
Separate Tank Regiments	75
Separate Assault Gun Regiments	212
Motorcycle Regiments	11
Separate Tank Battalions	–
Special Motorized Battalions	11
Armoured Train Battalions	61
Separate Armoured Car & Motorcycle Btns	46

SOVIET GROUND FORCES (JANUARY 1945)	
Unit Type	Number
AIRBORNE	
Airborne Divisions	9
Airborne Brigades	3
ARTILLERY	
Artillery Divisions	37
Rocket Divisions	7
Anti-Aircraft Divisions	80
Separate Artillery Brigades	66
Separate Anti-Aircraft Brigades	–
Separate Mortar Brigades	8
Separate Rocket Brigades	15
Anti-Tank Brigades	56
Separate Artillery Regiments	144
Separate Mortar Regiments	150
Separate Anti-Tank Regiments	111
Separate Rocket Regiments	107
Separate Anti-Aircraft Regiments	214
Separate Artillery Battalions	24
Separate Anti-Aircraft Battalions	97
Separate Rocket Battalions	44
Separate Anti-Tank Battalions	10
Separate Mortar Battalions	1
PVO STRANYI	
PVO Stranyi Corps HQ	14
PVO Stranyi Division HQ	11
Standard Anti-Aircraft Divisions	17
Standard Anti-Aircraft Machine Gun Divisions	2
Standard Anti-Aircraft Brigades	21
Searchlight Divisions	4
Anti-Aircraft Regiments	137
Anti-Aircraft Machine Gun Regiments	26
Searchlight Regiments	4
Anti-Aircraft Battalions	193
Anti-Aircraft Machine Gun Battalions	26
Searchlight Battalions	20

2nd Ukrainian Front on 26 December to seal off the city. Although the garrison of 76,000 was heavily outnumbered by the opposing 300,000-strong Soviet Fronts, the cover provided by the 'urban terrain' went a long way towards levelling the odds. (The city was divided by the Danube – Buda lay on the hills of the river's west bank and Pest covered the relatively flat ground to the east of the river.)

Into the city

The Soviet offensive began in the eastern suburbs, advancing into Pest itself along the broad main streets. The outnumbered German and Hungarian defenders fought delaying actions, slowly withdrawing to more defensible positions in the city centre. Soviet armoured units quickly discovered that Panzerfausts represented the greatest single threat to their tanks in street fighting. This was especially true when the defenders managed to pin down their accompanying infantry, before stalking the isolated tanks to make close-range shots against their relatively thin side and rear armour.

By this stage of the battle, the attackers were taking heavy losses in street fighting and in combat within the tunnels, sewers and cellars beneath the city. The Red Army began to appreciate the disadvantages of using satellite forces when VII Rumanian Corps, part of Malinovsky's 2nd Ukrainian Front, had to be withdrawn from combat after losing over 11,000 of its 36,000 men in three weeks. (The long-standing antagonism between Hungarians and Rumanians had ensured that Hungarian troops fought ferociously wherever the corps was committed to action.)

The attackers also took significant casualties from the garrison's use of a number of simple but imaginative tactics – one of the most effective was to withdraw from a building, leaving plenty of alcohol lying around for the Russians to find when they followed up. Very few Red Army conscripts could resist such bait and a counterattack next morning was usually a 'walkover' against blind drunk or badly hung-over opponents.

Stalin was rapidly losing patience with the Red Army's slow progress and Malinovsky ordered the formation of a special combat group, including heavy weapons and assault engineers equipped with flamethrowers to spearhead assaults. Rifle divisions were assigned attack sectors up to 700m (766 yards) wide, with regiments advancing on fronts of no more than 300m (328 yards). Large numbers of guns, including 122mm (4.8in), 152mm (6in) and 203mm (8in) howitzers, were brought up to support attacks with direct fire. Experience showed that mortars were amongst the deadliest weapons in urban combat, as they could fire over city buildings to drop their bombs almost vertically into trenches. In many cases, the effectiveness of their HE bombs was increased by the stone splinters that were blown from buildings and the cobbled streets.

German counterattacks

Whilst Malinovsky was struggling to crush resistance in the city, three attempts by IV SS Panzer Corps to raise the siege (Operations Konrad I, II and III) came tantalizingly close to success before being blocked by hastily reinforced Soviet units. On 18 January, the corps launched a further attack after redeploying to the south,

OPERATIONAL AFVs IN HUNGARY (JANUARY 1945)								
Unit	T-34	IS-2	SU-76	SU-85	SU-100	ISU-122	ISU-152	M4A2 Sherman
XVIII Tank Corps	120	19	–	11	–	–	–	–
I Gds Mechanized Corps	–	–	–	–	62	–	–	184
II Gds Mechanized Corps	35	8	–	11	–	–	–	–
VII Mechanized Corps	–	65	12	14	10	–	–	–
I Gds Fortified Region	7	–	4	–	–	–	–	–
V Gds Cavalry Corps	2	–	13	–	–	–	–	–
XXIII Tank Corps	–	174	–	–	–	–	19	–

BATTLE OF BUDAPEST AND VIENNA

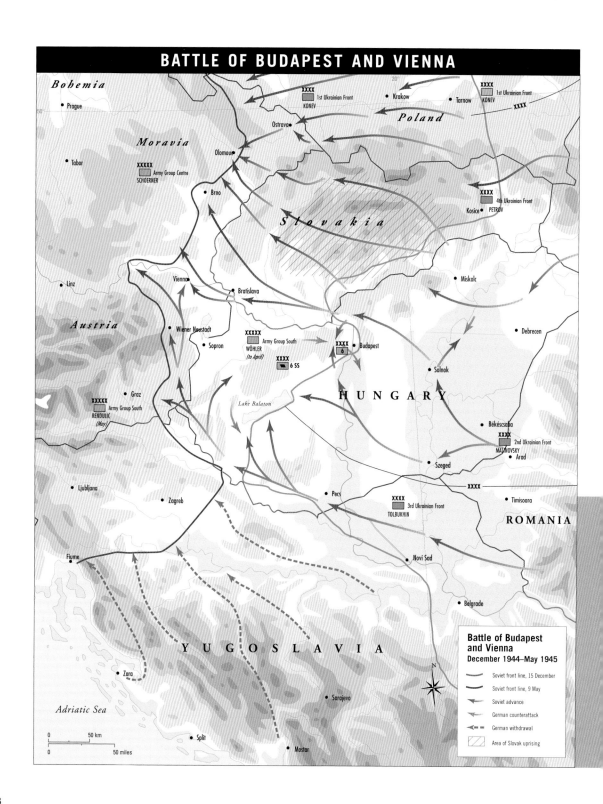

Bohemia

• Prague

Poland

XXXX
1st Ukrainian Front
KONEV

• Krakow

• Tarnow

XXXX
1st Ukrainian Front
KONEV

XXXX

Ostrava•

Moravia

Olomouc•

• Tabor

XXXXX
Army Group Centre
SCHOERNER

• Brno

Slovakia

XXXX
4th Ukrainian Front
PETROV

Kosice•

• Linz

Vienna•

○ Bratislava

• Miskolc

Austria

• Wiener Neustadt

• Debrecen

• Sopron

XXXXX
Army Group South
WÖHLER
(to April)

XXXX
6
• Budapest

XXXX
6 SS

• Solnok

H U N G A R Y

• Graz

Lake Balaton

XXXXX
Army Group South
RENDULIC
(May)

• Békéscsaba

XXXX
2nd Ukrainian Front
MALINOVSKY

• Arad

• Szeged

XXXX

• Ljubljana

• Zagreb

• Pecs

XXXX
3rd Ukrainian Front
TOLBUKHIN

• Timisoara

R O M A N I A

Fiume•

• Novi Sad

• Belgrade

Y U G O S L A V I A

**Battle of Budapest
and Vienna
December 1944–May 1945**

N

• Zara

Adriatic Sea

	Soviet front line, 15 December
	Soviet front line, 9 May
	Soviet advance
	German counterattack
	German withdrawal
	Area of Slovak uprising

0   50 km

0   50 miles

• Split

• Sarajevo

• Mostar

penetrating 32km (20 miles) in the first 24 hours, beating off a counterattack by VII Mechanized Corps.

The next day further counterattacks by XVIII Tank Corps and CXXXIII Rifle Corps were broken up, largely by the fire of *Totenkopf*'s anti-tank battalion, equipped with the new Jagdpanzer IV tank destroyers. Within three days, the leading German units had advanced 100km (62.5 miles) and had reached the Danube, cutting into the rear of 3rd Ukrainian Front's Fifty-Seventh Army. By 24 January, the force had advanced to within 24km (15 miles) of Budapest and inflicted heavy losses on I Guards Mechanized Corps and V Guards

Cavalry Corps. It was only the arrival of the last Soviet reserve formation, XXIII Tank Corps, that halted the advance. By 28 January, IV SS Panzer Corps was forced to withdraw, leaving Budapest to the Red Army.

Amazingly, though, some parts of the city held out until 13 February, largely due to air-dropped supplies, supplemented by larger shipments brought in at night by small river craft. Losses on both sides were heavy – an estimated 100,000 Soviet casualties to set against over 75,000 Germans and Hungarians killed or captured. Only 785 survivors managed to safely cross the 40km (25 miles) to the German lines.

The Vistula-Oder Offensive

The Vistula-Oder operation was first planned as the centrepiece of a series of offensives beginning in late January 1945, which were intended to take Berlin in no more than 45 days.

However, a scaled-down version of the original plan was implemented ahead of schedule in response to US and British requests for action to ease the pressure of the Ardennes Offensive. Primary responsibility for the

December 1944 – May 1945

The Red Army's advance to Budapest and Vienna was no easy matter. Much difficult terrain had to be crossed, often against fierce resistance. It was found that heavy armour was barely able to negotiate much of this ground, where lighter vehicles were far more effective. These included the SU-57 tank destroyer (a Lend-Lease M3 halftrack mounting a US version of the British 6pdr anti-tank gun) and fire-support jeeps fitted with eight-round 82mm (3.2in) 'Katyusha' salvo rocket-launchers.

The terrain posed problems for both sides – the last major German counterattack of the war was made across soft ground bordering Lake Balaton in March 1945. The 61-tonne (60-ton) Tiger IIs sank up to their turrets as soon as they attempted any off-road movement, prompting one junior commander to refuse an order to attack with the comment that he had tanks, not submarines.

offensive, which was now intended to secure the line of the River Oder, was assigned to two Fronts: Zhukov's 1st Belorussian Front, holding the sector around Warsaw plus the Magnuszew and Pulawy bridgeheads across the Vistula; Konev's 1st Ukrainian Front, operating from the Sandomir bridgehead. Zhukov and Konev fielded a total of 163 divisions for the operation, comprising 2,203,000 troops, 4529 tanks, 2513 assault guns, 13,763 guns, 14,812 mortars, 4936 anti-tank guns, 2198 'Katyusha' salvo rocket-launchers and 5000 aircraft.

The logistic preparations for the offensive were staggering – 2.5 million shells and mortar bombs were stockpiled in the Magnuszew bridgehead, with a further 1.3 million held in the Pulawy sector. (In comparison, the Don Front had fired less than 1 million shells at Stalingrad.) The two Fronts also held 137 million litres (30 million gallons) of fuel for the planned advance of up to 500km (312 miles).

The opposing Army Group A, initially under the command of *Generaloberst* Josef Harpe, could assemble at best 400,000 troops, 4100 guns and 1150 AFVs, whilst its freedom of manoeuvre was limited both by dire fuel shortages and by Hitler's obsession with holding every scrap of territory. When Konev's attack opened on 12 January, it rapidly broke through the understrength Fourth Panzer Army, which was stunned by the ferocity of the preliminary Soviet bombardment. A German battalion commander recalled that he '…began the operation with an under-strength battalion … after the

smoke of the Soviet preparation cleared … I had only a platoon of combat effective soldiers left'.

Zhukov's 1st Belorussian Front attacked on 14 January and achieved an equally rapid breakthrough of the German defences in its sector. Within a matter of hours, its leading elements were well on the way to Lodz. On 17 January, First Polish Army took Warsaw, whilst Konev's forces made equally impressive advances, occupying the industrial centres of Upper Silesia by the end of the month.

Fortress Poznan

Various cities in the path of the Soviet advance had been designated as *Festungen* (Fortresses) by Hitler, with the intention that their garrisons should hold out 'to the last man' in order to disrupt the Red Army's supply lines and communications. In many cases, these fortresses were protected by little more than poorly constructed anti-tank ditches and trenches manned by poorly trained and ill-equipped *Volkssturm* militia, but a few were far more formidable and played a significant role in slowing the Soviet advance. Of these, the most important was Posen (now Poznan), commanding the main route from Warsaw to Berlin, which was ringed with nine elaborate nineteenth-century forts and garrisoned by at least 40,000 troops supported by

THIRD GUARDS TANK ARMY, PERSONNEL (JAN 1945)	
Unit	Strength
VI Guards Tank Corps	12,010
VII Guards Tank Corps	12,010
IX Mechanized Corps	16,442
50 Motorcycle Regiment	–
1381 Anti-Aircraft Regiment	396
1394 Anti-Aircraft Regiment	396
91 Rocket Launcher Regiment	695
16 Assault Gun Brigade	1112
199 Light Artillery Brigade	–
57 Guards Heavy Tank Regiment	374
90 Engineer Tank Regiment	–
19 Engineer Mine Brigade	–
Army Troops	–

THIRD GUARDS TANK ARMY, AFV STRENGTH (JAN 1945)								
Unit	BM-13	T-34/76	T-34/85	IS-2	SU-57	SU-76	SU-85	ISU-122
VI Guards Tank Corps	8	–	207	–	–	21	21	21
VII Guards Tank Corps	8	–	207	–	–	21	21	21
IX Mechanized Corps	8	–	182	–	–	21	21	21
50 Motorcycle Regiment	–	–	10	–	–	–	–	–
1381 Anti-Aircraft Rgt	–	–	–	–	–	–	–	–
1394 Anti-Aircraft Rgt	–	–	–	–	–	–	–	–
91 Rocket Launcher Rgt	24	–	–	–	–	–	–	–
16 Assault Gun Brigade	–	–	–	–	65	–	–	–
199 Light Artillery Bde	–	–	–	–	–	–	–	–
57 Guards Heavy Tank Rgt	–	–	1	21	–	–	–	–
90 Engineer Tank Rgt	–	18	4	–	–	–	–	–
19 Engineer Mine Bde	–	–	–	–	–	–	–	–
Army Troops	–	–	20	–	–	1	1	1

8000 *Volkssturm*. On 25 January, the 105,000 men of General Chuikov's Eighth Guards Army began the siege of the city. The nineteenth-century fortifications proved to be surprisingly resistant to modern weapons, and the city was not taken until 22 February, when Soviet armour was finally able to force its way into the citadel.

On 31 January, the 1st Belorussian Front secured bridgeheads over the frozen River Oder only 60km

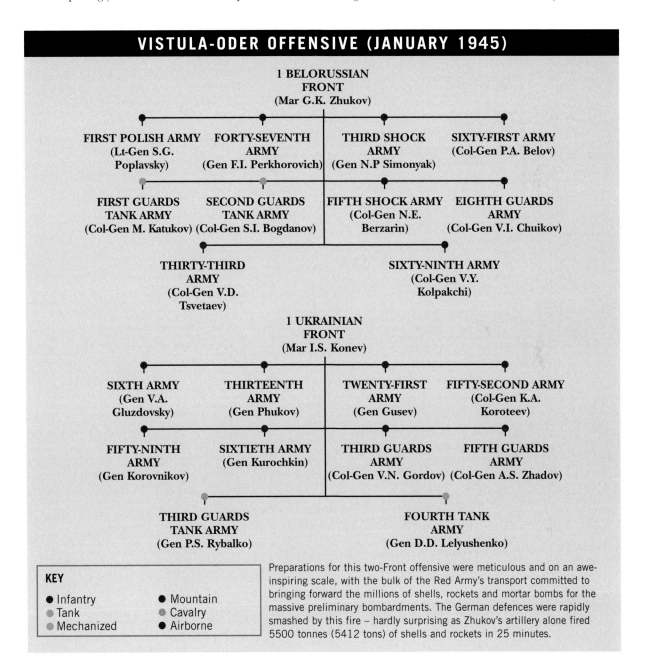

VISTULA-ODER OFFENSIVE (JANUARY 1945)

1 BELORUSSIAN FRONT
(Mar G.K. Zhukov)

FIRST POLISH ARMY
(Lt-Gen S.G. Poplavsky)

FORTY-SEVENTH ARMY
(Gen F.I. Perkhorovich)

THIRD SHOCK ARMY
(Gen N.P Simonyak)

SIXTY-FIRST ARMY
(Col-Gen P.A. Belov)

FIRST GUARDS TANK ARMY
(Col-Gen M. Katukov)

SECOND GUARDS TANK ARMY
(Col-Gen S.I. Bogdanov)

FIFTH SHOCK ARMY
(Col-Gen N.E. Berzarin)

EIGHTH GUARDS ARMY
(Col-Gen V.I. Chuikov)

THIRTY-THIRD ARMY
(Col-Gen V.D. Tsvetaev)

SIXTY-NINTH ARMY
(Col-Gen V.Y. Kolpakchi)

1 UKRAINIAN FRONT
(Mar I.S. Konev)

SIXTH ARMY
(Gen V.A. Gluzdovsky)

THIRTEENTH ARMY
(Gen Phukov)

TWENTY-FIRST ARMY
(Gen Gusev)

FIFTY-SECOND ARMY
(Col-Gen K.A. Koroteev)

FIFTY-NINTH ARMY
(Gen Korovnikov)

SIXTIETH ARMY
(Gen Kurochkin)

THIRD GUARDS ARMY
(Col-Gen V.N. Gordov)

FIFTH GUARDS ARMY
(Col-Gen A.S. Zhadov)

THIRD GUARDS TANK ARMY
(Gen P.S. Rybalko)

FOURTH TANK ARMY
(Gen D.D. Lelyushenko)

KEY

- Infantry
- Tank
- Mechanized
- Mountain
- Cavalry
- Airborne

Preparations for this two-Front offensive were meticulous and on an awe-inspiring scale, with the bulk of the Red Army's transport committed to bringing forward the millions of shells, rockets and mortar bombs for the massive preliminary bombardments. The German defences were rapidly smashed by this fire – hardly surprising as Zhukov's artillery alone fired 5500 tonnes (5412 tons) of shells and rockets in 25 minutes.

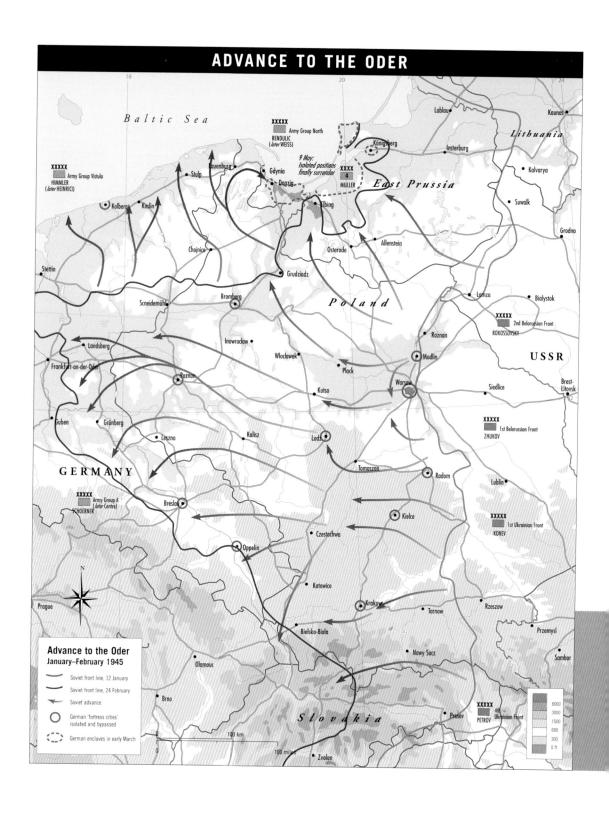

ADVANCE TO THE ODER

Baltic Sea

XXXXX
Army Group North
RENDULIC
(*later* WEISS)

9 May:
Isolated positions
finally surrender

Lablau

Kaunas

Lithuania

Königsberg

Insterburg

XXXXX
Army Group Vistula
HIMMLER
(*later* HEINRICI)

XXXXX
4
MÜLLER

East Prussia

Kalvarya

Stulp

Lauenburg

Gdynia

Suwalk

Kolberg

Koslin

Danzig

Elbing

Grodno

Stettin

Chojnice

Osterode

Allenstein

Grudziadz

Schneidemühl

Bromberg

Poland

Lomza

Bialystok

Inowroclaw

Wloclawek

Plock

Roznan

XXXXX
2nd Belorussian Front
ROKOSSOVSKY

Landsberg

Modlin

USSR

Frankfurt-an-der-Oder

Poznan

Kutso

Warsaw

Siedlce

Brest-Litovsk

Guben

Grünberg

Leszno

Kalisz

Lodz

XXXXX
1st Belorussian Front
ZHUKOV

GERMANY

XXXXX
Army Group A
(*later* Centre)
SCHOERNER

Breslau

Tomaszon

Radom

Lublin

Kielce

XXXXX
1st Ukrainian Front
KONEV

Oppelin

Czestochwa

Katowice

Krakow

Tarnow

Rzeszow

Przemysl

Prague

Bielsko-Biala

Nowy Sacz

Sambor

Olomouc

Advance to the Oder
January–February 1945

Soviet front line, 12 January

Soviet front line, 24 February

Soviet advance

German 'fortress cities'
isolated and bypassed

German enclaves in early March

Brno

Slovakia

Presov

XXXXX
4th
Ukrainian Front
PETROV

6000
3000
1500
600
300
0 ft

100 km

100 miles

Zvolen

(37 miles) from Berlin. Although both Zhukov and Konev advocated continuing the offensive all the way to the German capital, Stalin closed down the operation on 2 February. In retrospect, it was the correct decision – both Fronts had advanced roughly 500km (312 miles) in little more than three weeks and their supply lines were dangerously overstretched, a problem made more acute by the stubborn resistance of the Posen garrison.

The Lake Balaton Offensive

Codenamed Operation *Frühlingserwachen* (Spring Awakening), the Lake Balaton operation was the last significant German offensive of the war. It was ordered by Hitler in a typically unrealistic attempt not only to secure the Hungarian oilfields but to retake Budapest and destroy 3rd Ukrainian Front.

Good operational security (and an understandable Soviet belief that the Germans were incapable of launching any major offensive) ensured that complete surprise was achieved. Spearheaded by *SS-Oberstgruppenführer* Sepp Dietrich's Sixth Panzer Army, the attack went in on 6 March and made good progress. An early thaw had turned the entire region into a muddy morass and the appalling ground conditions posed as many problems as the Soviet forces. In some sectors, Tiger IIs sank up to their turrets in the thick mud and at least 15 had to be abandoned. Delays imposed by these conditions gave time for Tolbukhin to call in reinforcements from Ninth Guards Army and launch a counterattack on 16 March, which pushed the German forces back to their start lines within 24 hours. By the end of the month, the remnants of Sixth Panzer Army had retreated into Austria in an attempt to protect

Vienna. Sepp Dietrich remarked with only slight exaggeration that 'Sixth Panzer Army is well named — we have just six tanks left!'

TANK CORPS, PERSONNEL (APRIL 1945)	
Unit	**Strength**
Corps Headquarters	32
Signal Battalion	253
Motorcycle Battalion	451
3 x Tank Brigades, each	1362
Motorized Rifle Brigade	3222
Heavy Assault Gun Rgt (SU-152)	374
Assault Gun Regiment (SU-85/100)	318
Light Assault Gun Regiment	225
Light Artillery Regiment	625
Rocket Launcher Battalion	203
Mortar Regiment	596
Anti-Aircraft Regiment	397
Pioneer Battalion	455
Trains Elements	298

TANK CORPS, EQUIPMENT (APRIL 1945)	
	Strength
PERSONNEL	
Total Troops	11,788
ARMOUR	
T-34s	207
SU-76s	21
SU-85s	21
SU-152s/ISU-152s	21
GUNS & MORTARS	
82mm (3.2in) Mortars	52
120mm (4.7in) Mortars	42
45mm AT Guns	12
57mm (2,2in) AT Guns	16
37mm (1.5in) AA Guns	16
76mm (3in) Guns	36
M-13 Rocket Launchers	8

January–February 1945

The Vistula-Oder Offensive was a remarkable achievement by the 1st Belorussian and 1st Ukrainian Fronts, which advanced some 500km (312 miles) in 23 days. This striking military success was made possible only by extraordinary efforts by the supply services – special motor transport units of 600 trucks each were formed to keep the rapidly moving tank armies supplied with fuel and ammunition, but at times the advance was reliant on the stocks of captured German fuel dumps.

VIENNA OFFENSIVE: 3RD UKRAINIAN FRONT (APRIL 1945)

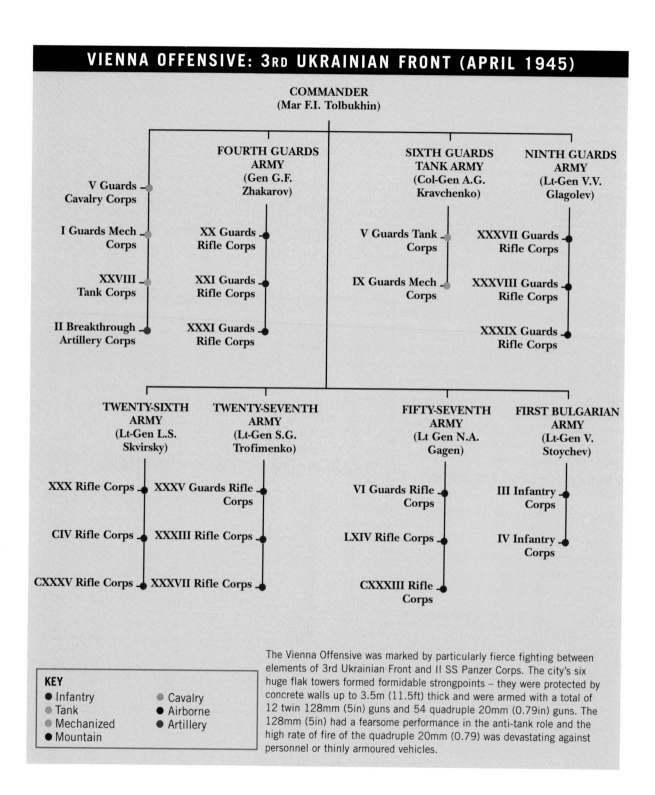

COMMANDER
(Mar F.I. Tolbukhin)

FOURTH GUARDS ARMY
(Gen G.F. Zhakarov)

SIXTH GUARDS TANK ARMY
(Col-Gen A.G. Kravchenko)

NINTH GUARDS ARMY
(Lt-Gen V.V. Glagolev)

V Guards Cavalry Corps

I Guards Mech Corps

XXVIII Tank Corps

II Breakthrough Artillery Corps

XX Guards Rifle Corps

XXI Guards Rifle Corps

XXXI Guards Rifle Corps

V Guards Tank Corps

IX Guards Mech Corps

XXXVII Guards Rifle Corps

XXXVIII Guards Rifle Corps

XXXIX Guards Rifle Corps

TWENTY-SIXTH ARMY
(Lt-Gen L.S. Skvirsky)

TWENTY-SEVENTH ARMY
(Lt-Gen S.G. Trofimenko)

FIFTY-SEVENTH ARMY
(Lt Gen N.A. Gagen)

FIRST BULGARIAN ARMY
(Lt-Gen V. Stoychev)

XXX Rifle Corps

CIV Rifle Corps

CXXXV Rifle Corps

XXXV Guards Rifle Corps

XXXIII Rifle Corps

XXXVII Rifle Corps

VI Guards Rifle Corps

LXIV Rifle Corps

CXXXIII Rifle Corps

III Infantry Corps

IV Infantry Corps

KEY
- Infantry
- Tank
- Mechanized
- Mountain
- Cavalry
- Airborne
- Artillery

The Vienna Offensive was marked by particularly fierce fighting between elements of 3rd Ukrainian Front and II SS Panzer Corps. The city's six huge flak towers formed formidable strongpoints – they were protected by concrete walls up to 3.5m (11.5ft) thick and were armed with a total of 12 twin 128mm (5in) guns and 54 quadruple 20mm (0.79in) guns. The 128mm (5in) had a fearsome performance in the anti-tank role and the high rate of fire of the quadruple 20mm (0.79) was devastating against personnel or thinly armoured vehicles.

Vienna

Tolbukhin's 3rd Ukrainian Front followed up Sixth Panzer Army's retreat and quickly assembled around Vienna, which had been hastily fortified and was garrisoned by *SS-Obergruppenführer* Wilhelm Bittrich's II SS Panzer Corps, supported by an ad hoc group of flak and security units. The Soviet assault began on 2 April with attacks by Fourth and Ninth Guards Armies but made only limited progress until Sixth Guards Tank Army was committed on the 8th. The additional pressure forced Bittrich's units westwards to avoid being trapped, and the city surrendered on 13 April. Even so, II SS Panzer Corps delivered a sharp reminder of the tactical expertise of the dwindling number of veteran Panzer crews as the formation withdrew on the 12th – a single Panther of *Das Reich*, commanded by *Leutnant* Arno Giesen, knocked out 14 T-34s and JS-2s whilst holding one of the Danube bridges.

Seelow Heights and Berlin

During the second week of April 1945, a massive Soviet force was assembled in the small bridgehead on the west bank of the Oder near Küstrin.

Zhukov's 1st Belorussian Front was preparing to attack the Seelow Heights, the last natural defence line before Berlin. The Front had 908,000 men, 3155 AFVs and 16,934 guns, and had stockpiled over seven million rounds of artillery ammunition. On its northern flank, Rokossovsky's 2nd Belorussian Front was to attack to the north of Berlin, whilst Konev's 1st Ukrainian Front covered its southern flank.

At the beginning of April, Stalin had played on the intense rivalry between Zhukov and Konev, authorizing whomever first broke through the German defences to take Berlin. The combined strength of the three Fronts stood at 2.5 million men, 6250 AFVs, 7500 aircraft, 41,600 guns and mortars, 3255 'Katyusha' rocket-launchers and 95,383 motor vehicles.

Zhukov's forces were opposed by *Generaloberst* Gotthard Heinrici's Army Group Vistula. Its Ninth Army, under the command of *General der Infanterie* Theodor Busse, would bear the brunt of the assault on the Seelow Heights. Busse's force fielded 14 divisions, 512 AFVs, 344 guns and 300–400 anti-aircraft guns. Further south, the front was held by Fourth Panzer Army, which faced Konev's 1st Ukrainian Front.

Although heavily outnumbered, Heinrici had done much to reduce the odds against him. Correctly anticipating that the main Soviet attacks would be made on the Seelow Heights along the line of the main east–west autobahn, he had thinned out other sectors of the front to reinforce the area. The Heights themselves were well fortified, forming part of three defence lines

MECHANIZED CORPS (APRIL 1945)	
	Strength
PERSONNEL	
Total troops	16,438
ARMOURED VEHICLES	
Light Tanks	–
Medium Tanks	183
Heavy Tanks	–
Light Assault Guns	21
Medium Assault Guns	21
Heavy Assault Guns	21
GUNS & MORTARS	
82mm (3.2in) Mortars	100
120mm (4.7in) Mortars	54
45mm (1.8in) AT Guns	36
57mm (2.2in) AT Guns	8
37mm (1.5in) AA Guns	16
76mm (3in) Guns	36
BM-13 Rocket Launchers	8

up to 25km (15.6 miles) deep. The Oder's flood plain, already saturated by the spring thaw, was turned into a swamp by water released from a reservoir upstream, and minefields were laid to protect key points.

Offensive begins

At 0500 on 16 April, the offensive began with a massive bombardment by thousands of guns and 'Katyushas' of 1st Belorussian Front before the main assault went in.

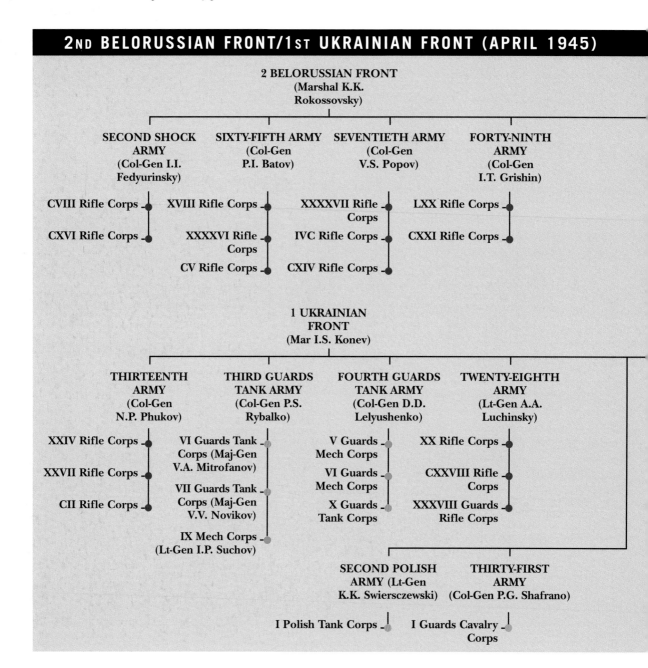

2ND BELORUSSIAN FRONT/1ST UKRAINIAN FRONT (APRIL 1945)

2 BELORUSSIAN FRONT
(Marshal K.K. Rokossovsky)

SECOND SHOCK ARMY
(Col-Gen I.I. Fedyurinsky)

SIXTY-FIFTH ARMY
(Col-Gen P.I. Batov)

SEVENTIETH ARMY
(Col-Gen V.S. Popov)

FORTY-NINTH ARMY
(Col-Gen I.T. Grishin)

CVIII Rifle Corps

CXVI Rifle Corps

XVIII Rifle Corps

XXXXVI Rifle Corps

CV Rifle Corps

XXXXVII Rifle Corps

IVC Rifle Corps

CXIV Rifle Corps

LXX Rifle Corps

CXXI Rifle Corps

1 UKRAINIAN FRONT
(Mar I.S. Konev)

THIRTEENTH ARMY
(Col-Gen N.P. Phukov)

THIRD GUARDS TANK ARMY
(Col-Gen P.S. Rybalko)

FOURTH GUARDS TANK ARMY
(Col-Gen D.D. Lelyushenko)

TWENTY-EIGHTH ARMY
(Lt-Gen A.A. Luchinsky)

XXIV Rifle Corps

XXVII Rifle Corps

CII Rifle Corps

VI Guards Tank Corps (Maj-Gen V.A. Mitrofanov)

VII Guards Tank Corps (Maj-Gen V.V. Novikov)

IX Mech Corps (Lt-Gen I.P. Suchov)

V Guards Mech Corps

VI Guards Mech Corps

X Guards Tank Corps

XX Rifle Corps

CXXVIII Rifle Corps

XXXVIII Guards Rifle Corps

SECOND POLISH ARMY (Lt-Gen K.K. Swierszczewski)

THIRTY-FIRST ARMY (Col-Gen P.G. Shafrano)

I Polish Tank Corps

I Guards Cavalry Corps

Almost immediately, things started to go wrong – the debris and smoke from the massive bombardment meant that the glare of the 140-plus searchlights intended to blind the Germans was reflected and blinded the attackers. (It also turned them into easy targets, silhouetted against the light.) Worse still, the bombardment had largely been wasted on empty defences – a Russian prisoner had revealed the timing

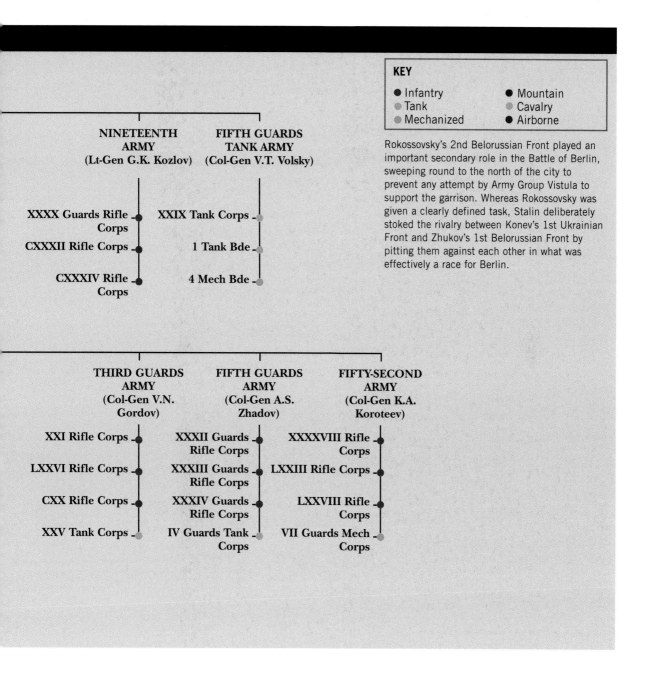

KEY

- Infantry
- Tank
- Mechanized
- Mountain
- Cavalry
- Airborne

Rokossovsky's 2nd Belorussian Front played an important secondary role in the Battle of Berlin, sweeping round to the north of the city to prevent any attempt by Army Group Vistula to support the garrison. Whereas Rokossovsky was given a clearly defined task, Stalin deliberately stoked the rivalry between Konev's 1st Ukrainian Front and Zhukov's 1st Belorussian Front by pitting them against each other in what was effectively a race for Berlin.

NINETEENTH ARMY
(Lt-Gen G.K. Kozlov)

FIFTH GUARDS TANK ARMY
(Col-Gen V.T. Volsky)

XXXX Guards Rifle Corps

CXXXII Rifle Corps

CXXXIV Rifle Corps

XXIX Tank Corps

1 Tank Bde

4 Mech Bde

THIRD GUARDS ARMY
(Col-Gen V.N. Gordov)

FIFTH GUARDS ARMY
(Col-Gen A.S. Zhadov)

FIFTY-SECOND ARMY
(Col-Gen K.A. Koroteev)

XXI Rifle Corps

LXXVI Rifle Corps

CXX Rifle Corps

XXV Tank Corps

XXXII Guards Rifle Corps

XXXIII Guards Rifle Corps

XXXIV Guards Rifle Corps

IV Guards Tank Corps

XXXXVIII Rifle Corps

LXXIII Rifle Corps

LXXVIII Rifle Corps

VII Guards Mech Corps

1ST BELORUSSIAN FRONT (APRIL 1945) (1)

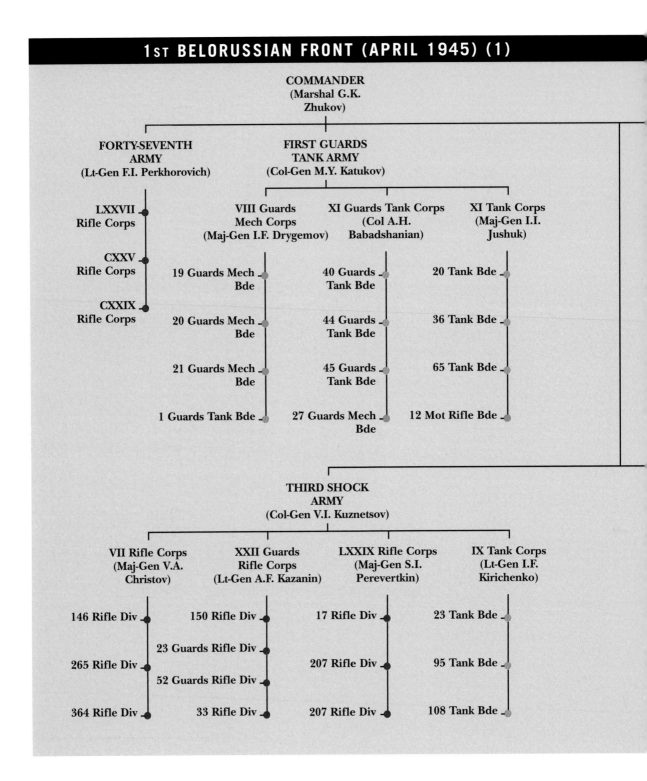

COMMANDER
(Marshal G.K. Zhukov)

FORTY-SEVENTH ARMY
(Lt-Gen F.I. Perkhorovich)

FIRST GUARDS TANK ARMY
(Col-Gen M.Y. Katukov)

LXXVII Rifle Corps

CXXV Rifle Corps

CXXIX Rifle Corps

VIII Guards Mech Corps
(Maj-Gen I.F. Drygemov)

XI Guards Tank Corps
(Col A.H. Babadshanian)

XI Tank Corps
(Maj-Gen I.I. Jushuk)

19 Guards Mech Bde

20 Guards Mech Bde

21 Guards Mech Bde

1 Guards Tank Bde

40 Guards Tank Bde

44 Guards Tank Bde

45 Guards Tank Bde

27 Guards Mech Bde

20 Tank Bde

36 Tank Bde

65 Tank Bde

12 Mot Rifle Bde

THIRD SHOCK ARMY
(Col-Gen V.I. Kuznetsov)

VII Rifle Corps
(Maj-Gen V.A. Christov)

XXII Guards Rifle Corps
(Lt-Gen A.F. Kazanin)

LXXIX Rifle Corps
(Maj-Gen S.I. Perevertkin)

IX Tank Corps
(Lt-Gen I.F. Kirichenko)

146 Rifle Div

265 Rifle Div

364 Rifle Div

150 Rifle Div

23 Guards Rifle Div

52 Guards Rifle Div

33 Rifle Div

17 Rifle Div

207 Rifle Div

207 Rifle Div

23 Tank Bde

95 Tank Bde

108 Tank Bde

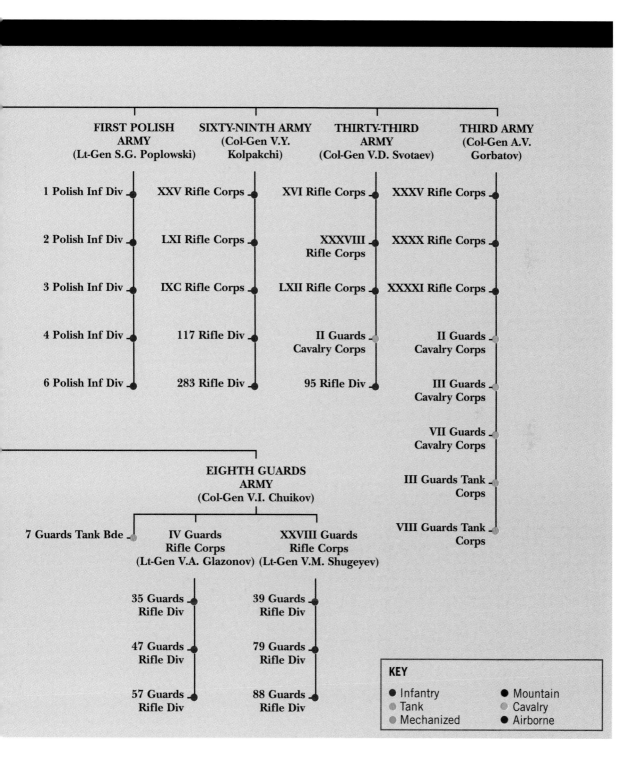

FIRST POLISH ARMY
(Lt-Gen S.G. Poplowski)

1 Polish Inf Div

2 Polish Inf Div

3 Polish Inf Div

4 Polish Inf Div

6 Polish Inf Div

SIXTY-NINTH ARMY
(Col-Gen V.Y. Kolpakchi)

XXV Rifle Corps

LXI Rifle Corps

IXC Rifle Corps

117 Rifle Div

283 Rifle Div

THIRTY-THIRD ARMY
(Col-Gen V.D. Svotaev)

XVI Rifle Corps

XXXVIII Rifle Corps

LXII Rifle Corps

II Guards Cavalry Corps

95 Rifle Div

THIRD ARMY
(Col-Gen A.V. Gorbatov)

XXXV Rifle Corps

XXXX Rifle Corps

XXXXI Rifle Corps

II Guards Cavalry Corps

III Guards Cavalry Corps

VII Guards Cavalry Corps

III Guards Tank Corps

VIII Guards Tank Corps

EIGHTH GUARDS ARMY
(Col-Gen V.I. Chuikov)

7 Guards Tank Bde

IV Guards Rifle Corps
(Lt-Gen V.A. Glazonov)

35 Guards Rifle Div

47 Guards Rifle Div

57 Guards Rifle Div

XXVIII Guards Rifle Corps
(Lt-Gen V.M. Shugeyev)

39 Guards Rifle Div

79 Guards Rifle Div

88 Guards Rifle Div

KEY

- Infantry
- Tank
- Mechanized
- Mountain
- Cavalry
- Airborne

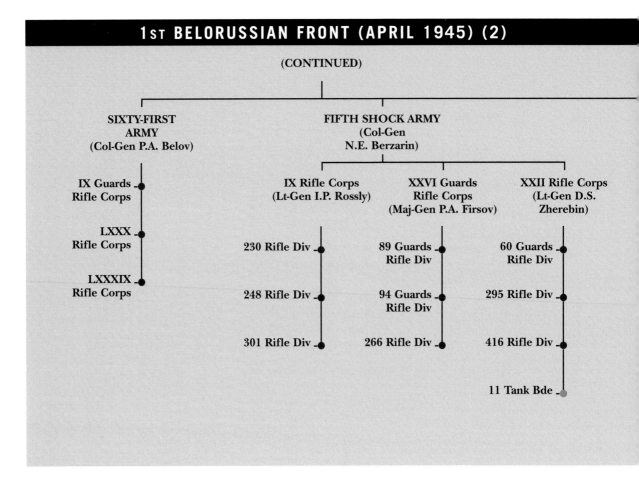

1ST BELORUSSIAN FRONT (APRIL 1945) (2)

(CONTINUED)

SIXTY-FIRST ARMY
(Col-Gen P.A. Belov)

- IX Guards Rifle Corps
- LXXX Rifle Corps
- LXXXIX Rifle Corps

FIFTH SHOCK ARMY
(Col-Gen N.E. Berzarin)

IX Rifle Corps
(Lt-Gen I.P. Rossly)
- 230 Rifle Div
- 248 Rifle Div
- 301 Rifle Div

XXVI Guards Rifle Corps
(Maj-Gen P.A. Firsov)
- 89 Guards Rifle Div
- 94 Guards Rifle Div
- 266 Rifle Div

XXII Rifle Corps
(Lt-Gen D.S. Zherebin)
- 60 Guards Rifle Div
- 295 Rifle Div
- 416 Rifle Div
- 11 Tank Bde

of the attack and Heinrici had pulled his forces back to their second defensive line. Taking advantage of the slow and confused Soviet advance, the Germans reoccupied their forward defences and brought down a murderous fire on the attackers. By the next day, 1st Belorussian Front had advanced no more than 8km (5 miles) and was still bogged down in the German defences.

An enraged Zhukov overruled the protests of his army commanders and committed the 1337 AFVs of his two tank armies to the attack, but the huge number of vehicles deployed on a narrow front caused a massive traffic jam, providing more targets for the German artillery and anti-tank fire.

In contrast to the bloody confusion at the Seelow Heights, Konev's attack, launched at almost the same

time, was far more subtle. No searchlights were used, as Konev intended to cross the Neisse under cover of complete darkness. Instead, he ordered a 145-minute artillery bombardment to cover the entire crossing operation and employed extensive smokescreens along a 390km (244-mile) front to hinder enemy observation when darkness lifted. The attack made excellent progress – by 17 April, 1st Ukrainian Front's forward units had broken through the main German defences and had crossed the River Spree.

Konev seized the opportunity and obtained Stalin's permission to make for Berlin. With Third Tank Army and Fourth Guards Tank Army in the lead, his forces charged along the autobahn towards the city. On 21 April, they captured the bunker complex at Zossen, which had housed the HQ of *Oberkommando des Heeres*

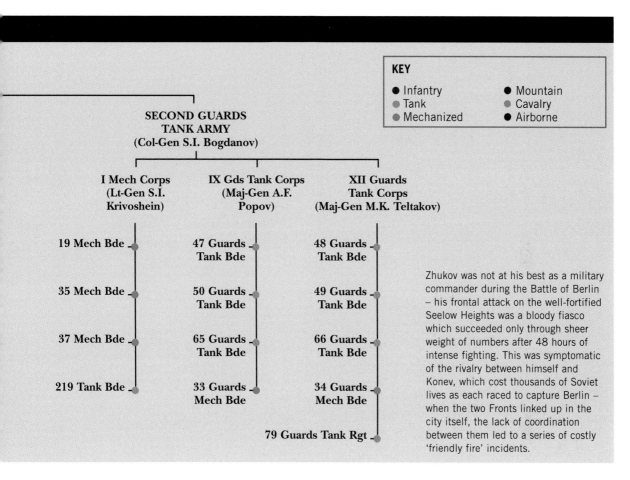

KEY

- Infantry
- Tank
- Mechanized
- Mountain
- Cavalry
- Airborne

SECOND GUARDS TANK ARMY
(Col-Gen S.I. Bogdanov)

I Mech Corps (Lt-Gen S.I. Krivoshein)	IX Gds Tank Corps (Maj-Gen A.F. Popov)	XII Guards Tank Corps (Maj-Gen M.K. Teltakov)
19 Mech Bde	47 Guards Tank Bde	48 Guards Tank Bde
35 Mech Bde	50 Guards Tank Bde	49 Guards Tank Bde
37 Mech Bde	65 Guards Tank Bde	66 Guards Tank Bde
219 Tank Bde	33 Guards Mech Bde	34 Guards Mech Bde
	79 Guards Tank Rgt	

Zhukov was not at his best as a military commander during the Battle of Berlin – his frontal attack on the well-fortified Seelow Heights was a bloody fiasco which succeeded only through sheer weight of numbers after 48 hours of intense fighting. This was symptomatic of the rivalry between himself and Konev, which cost thousands of Soviet lives as each raced to capture Berlin – when the two Fronts linked up in the city itself, the lack of coordination between them led to a series of costly 'friendly fire' incidents.

(OKH) responsible for directing all German operations on the Eastern Front.

On 19 April, Zhukov's forces finally broke through the last defences on the Seelow Heights and were also on their way to Berlin. The cost had been appalling – more than 700 Soviet AFVs had been destroyed in the battle for the Heights and the Red Army had sustained at least 30,000 casualties (three times the German total).

Berlin

On 26 April, Zhukov and Konev's forces completed the encirclement of Berlin – the city had been under artillery bombardment since 20 April and attacks on the suburbs had begun on the 24th. (The initial attack was made by First Guards Tank Army under cover of a barrage from 3000 guns and heavy mortars – 650 guns

per kilometre/1093 yards of front!) Stalin had finally decided that both Fronts should combine to assault the city but that Zhukov would have the honour of taking the *Reichstag*, which Soviet propaganda portrayed as the symbol of Hitler's *Reich*.

The defenders of Berlin were a 'mixed bag', ranging from hard-bitten veterans to hastily raised, virtually untrained *Volkssturm* militia, totalling possibly 60,000 men and 50–60 AFVs, supported by police and fanatical Hitler Youth units. The Soviet forces assembling for the attack on the city comprised five armies and four tank armies – 464,000 men, 12,700 guns and mortars, at least 2000 'Katyushas' and 1500 AFVs.

Between 24 and 28 April, both Fronts slowly ground their way through the Berlin suburbs against fierce resistance – Third Shock Army took three days to

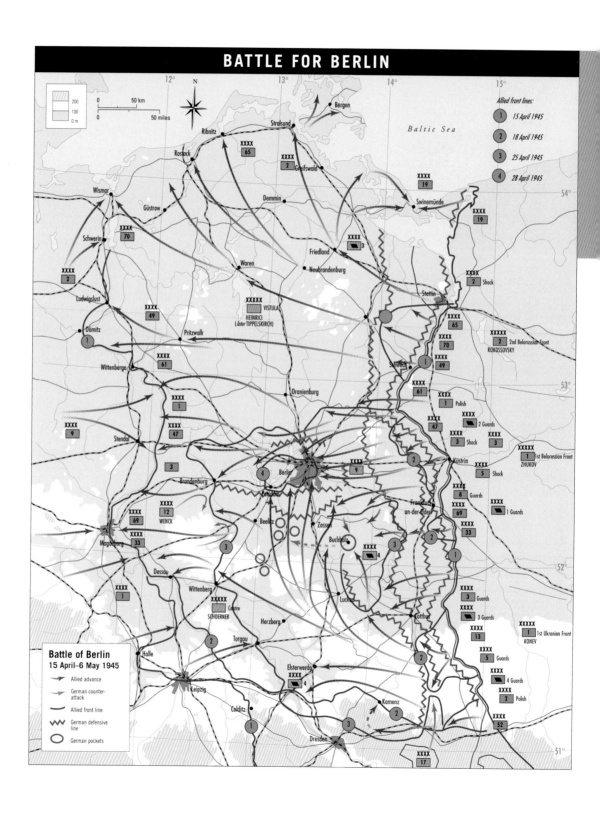

BATTLE FOR BERLIN

Allied front lines:
1. 15 April 1945
2. 18 April 1945
3. 25 April 1945
4. 28 April 1945

Baltic Sea

Bergen

Stralsund

Ribnitz

Rostock

XXXX 65

Greifswald

XXXX 2

Wismar

Güstrow

Demmin

XXXX 19

Swinemünde

XXXX 19

Schwerin

XXXX 70

Waren

Neubrandenburg

Friedland

XXXX 3

Stettin

XXXX 2 Shock

Ludwigslust

XXXX 2

XXXXX VISTULA HEINRICI (later TIPPELSKIRCH)

XXXX 65

XXXX 70

2nd Belorussian Front ROKOSSOVSKY

XXXXX 2

Dömitz

XXXX 49

Pritzwalk

Stettin

XXXX 49

Wittenberge

XXXX 61

Schwedt

XXXX 61

XXXX 1 Polish

Oranienburg

XXXX 47

XXXX 2 Guards

Stendal

XXXX 9

XXXX 47

XXXX 1

XXXX 3 Shock

XXXX 3

Küstrin

XXXXX 1 1st Belorussian Front ZHUKOV

XXXX 3

Berlin

XXXX 9

XXXX 2

XXXX 5 Shock

Brandenburg

Potsdam

XXXX 8 Guards

XXXX 12 WENCK

XXXX 69

Beelitz

Zossen

Frankfurt an-der-Oder

XXXX 69

XXXX 1 Guards

Magdeburg

XXXX 33

XXXX 3

Buchholz

XXXX 3

XXXX 4

XXXX 2

XXXX 1

XXXX 33

Dessau

Wittenberg

Luckau

XXXX 3 Guards

XXXX 1

XXXXX Centre SCHOERNER

Herzberg

Cottbus

XXXX 3 Guards

Torgau

XXXX 2

XXXXX 1 1st Ukranian Front KONEV

XXXX 13

Halle

Elsterwerda

XXXX 5 Guards

XXXX 4 Guards

XXXX 4

XXXX 2 Polish

Leipzig

Colditz

Kamenz

XXXX 2

XXXX 52

XXXX 1

Dresden

XXXX 3

XXXX 17

Battle of Berlin
15 April–6 May 1945

- Allied advance
- German counter-attack
- Allied front line
- German defensive line
- German pockets

15 April–6 May 1945

Although the Red Army forces assembled for the assault on Berlin had overwhelming firepower, the task was no 'walkover', as the city's garrison had the advantage of several lines of substantial field defences. The rubble caused by Allied bombing and Soviet shelling was also readily defensible and acted as a barrier to attempts to push armoured forces into the city centre. The risks of overconfidence in this situation were dramatically emphasized by the fate of a detachment of Third Guards Tank Army, which ran out of fuel in the suburbs and was wiped out by a Hitler Youth unit armed with Panzerfausts.

advance 3km (1.9 miles). All Soviet units took heavy casualties, largely due to poor coordination between tanks, infantry and artillery. General Chuikov's Eighth Guards Army initially sent unsupported tank columns straight down main streets – Panzerfausts and anti-tank guns trapped these columns by knocking out the lead and rear vehicles, before infantry anti-tank teams moved in to destroy the remaining AFVs.

As Chuikov ruefully remarked, 'A battle within a city is a battle of firepower.' Units quickly developed special assault teams comprising an infantry platoon or company, a tank platoon, a section of self-propelled guns, a section of 'Katyushas' and a detachment of assault engineers. The assault drills almost invariably involved artillery and 'Katyushas' smothering the objective with smoke and close-range direct fire before the infantry attacked. A Soviet war correspondent described how the gunners '…sometimes fired a

thousand shells on to one small square, a group of houses, or even a tiny garden'. As the Red Army reached the city centre, the larger government buildings proved to have been turned into fortresses, supported by fire from Berlin's three enormous flak towers. These were six storeys high, each with a 1000-strong garrison to man the tower's four twin 128mm (5in) and 12 quadruple 20mm (0.79in) guns. Dealing with these demanded exceptional measures – at one stage, 500 Soviet guns were firing from a 1km (1093-yard) section of Unter den Linden.

Hard going

Despite such massive firepower, Soviet losses continued to rise – at least 108 tanks were destroyed in the city centre by weapons ranging from 128mm (5in) AA guns to the ubiquitous Panzerfaust. As always, infantry casualties were the heaviest – between 19 and 30 April, one infantry company was reduced from 104 men to just 20 exhausted survivors.

By the time that the last German units surrendered on 2 May after Hitler's suicide and the capture of the battered shell of the *Reichstag*, the losses on both sides were horrendous. Soviet casualties totalled over 352,000, including more than 78,000 dead; in addition, the First and Second Polish Armies lost almost 9000 men. The 'best estimate' of Russian AFV losses is 2000 vehicles, whilst the two air armies supporting the offensive lost 527 aircraft – the majority to AA fire. The fall of Berlin effectively marked the end of the war in Europe for the Red Army, but Stalin was already planning to unleash it against an old enemy half a world away – Japan.

Red Army might

Any army is only as good as the men who fill its ranks – without them the best organization and equipment would be useless.

The millions of conscripts who served in the Red Army had more in common with those of the Napoleonic era than with their sophisticated Western counterparts, but, despite casualties which would have broken many other

armies, they withstood the massive *Wehrmacht* offensives of 1941–42. Even more remarkably, in the midst of gruelling campaigns they learned the practical battlefield skills that led to the decisive victories of 1944

COMPARATIVE MILITARY STRENGTHS (1939–45)		
Year	**Population**	**Military Strength**
SOVIET UNION		
1939	170,560,000	1,300,000
1941	202,000,000	5,500,000
1945	169,000,000	6,500,000
Total deaths	–	10,700,000
THIRD REICH		
1939	80,600,000	3,772,000
1941	not known	5,150,000
1945	64,600,000	6,130,000
Total deaths	–	5,533,000
UK		
1939	47,700,000	525,000
1945	48,700,000	2,920,000
Total deaths	–	382,700
US		
1939	131,000,000	174,000
1945	132,481,000	3,186,000
Total deaths	–	416,800

MILITARY PRODUCTION (1939–45)	
Country	**Quantity**
TANKS AND SELF-PROPELLED GUNS	
USSR	105,251
USA	88,410
Germany	46,857
UK	27,896
ARTILLERY	
USSR	516,648
USA	257,390
Germany	159,147
UK	124,877
MILITARY AIRCRAFT OF ALL TYPES	
USSR	324,750
USA	189,307
Germany	157,261
UK	131,549
MILITARY TRUCKS	
USSR	197,100
USA	2,382,311
Germany	345,914
UK	480,943

and 1945. The Red Army's pre-war expansion from 885,000 in 1934 put enormous strain on an already inadequate infrastructure – barracks were grossly overcrowded, whilst there were often insufficient rifles and ammunition to allow even basic infantry training. The massive influx of conscripts during the war years put an even greater strain on the training and supply systems, but despite enormous casualties, it proved possible to steadily increase manpower throughout the war.

Soviet statistics are almost always approximations that have often been doctored to suit the 'Party line', but the figures (see table above) provide some comparison with German, British and US military data.

War production

Military power is never easy to assess, as it is affected by many factors. Sheer size is one of the most obvious – Stalin summed it up in his remark that, 'Quantity has a quality of its own'. However, numbers are not the whole story, as shown by the ease with which the German panzers massacred thousands of obsolescent Soviet tanks and their poorly trained crews in 1941. It was fortunate for the Red Army that it had such an outstanding design as the T-34 in production at the time of the German invasion. It proved to be just the sort of low-cost, low maintenance AFV which the relatively unsophisticated Soviet factories could turn out in huge numbers. This was in marked contrast to German attempts to gain decisive qualitative superiority by producing sophisticated, costly designs such as the Panther. All major Russian types were incrementally upgraded, producing such 'classic' designs as the T-34/85.

In addition to home-based production, well over 12,000 AFVs were supplied by the United States,

SOVIET GROUND FORCES (MAY 1945)	
Unit Type	Number
HEADQUARTERS	
Fronts	16
Armies	72
Rifle Corps	174
Cavalry Corps	8
Tank Corps	24
Mechanized Corps	14
INFANTRY	
Rifle Divisions (inc Mountain & Motorized)	517
Rifle Brigades	17
Separate Rifle Regiments	5
Fortified Regions	47
CAVALRY	
Cavalry Divisions	26
ARMOUR	
Tank Divisions	2
Tank Brigades	147
Assault Gun Brigades	12
Mechanized Brigades	47
Motor Rifle Brigades	25
Separate Tank Regiments	78
Separate Assault Gun Regiments	235
Motorcycle Regiments	11
Special Motorized Battalions	11
Armoured Train Battalions	59
Separate Armoured Car & Motorcycle Btns	43

SOVIET GROUND FORCES (MAY 1945)	
Unit Type	Number
AIRBORNE	
Airborne Divisions	9
Airborne Brigades	3
ARTILLERY	
Artillery Divisions	37
Rocket Divisions	7
Anti-Aircraft Divisions	80
Separate Artillery Brigades	69
Separate Anti-Aircraft Brigades	–
Separate Mortar Brigades	8
Separate Rocket Brigades	11
Anti-Tank Brigades	66
Separate Artillery Regiments	136
Separate Mortar Regiments	142
Separate Anti-Tank Regiments	98
Separate Rocket Regiments	107
Separate Anti-Aircraft Regiments	210
Separate Artillery Battalions	24
Separate Anti-Aircraft Battalions	97
Separate Rocket Battalions	46
Separate Anti-Tank Battalions	9
Separate Mortar Battalions	1
PVO STRANYI	
PVO Stranyi Corps HQ	15
PVO Stranyi Division HQ	18
PVO Stranyi Brigade HQ	3
Standard Anti-Aircraft Divisions	18
Standard Anti-Aircraft Machine Gun Divisions	1
Standard Anti-Aircraft Brigades	21
Searchlight Divisions	4
Anti-Aircraft Regiments	131
Anti-Aircraft Machine Gun Regiments	27
Searchlight Regiments	7
Anti-Aircraft Battalions	204
Anti-Aircraft Machine Gun Battalions	24
Searchlight Battalions	23

Canada and the United Kingdom under Lend-Lease, together with approximately 470,000 other vehicles, including almost 78,000 jeeps and nearly 352,000 medium trucks. It was only the huge numbers of Lend-Lease trucks which gave the Red Army the mobility to undertake the major offensives of 1944–45 – without them, more Soviet factories would have had to be diverted to producing existing 'home-grown' designs at the expense of badly needed AFVs.

Glossary of Key Abbreviations

AA	Anti-Aircraft	Mort	Mortar	**Red Army ranks**	
AAMG	Anti-Aircraft Machine Gun	Mot	Motorized	Army-Gen	General of the Army (Red Army rank, approximating to Field Marshal)
AC	Armoured Car	MRD	Motor Rifle Division	Brig	Brigadier
AFV	Armoured Fighting Vehicle	NCO	Non-Commissioned Officer	Col-Gen	Colonel-General (Red Army rank, approximating to General)
APCR	Armour-Piercing, Composite Rigid	NKVD	*Narodnyy Kommissariat Vnutrennikh Del* (People's Commissariat for Internal Affairs)	Komandarm	Army Commander (pre-1940 Red Army rank in two classes: 1st Rank, approximating to Field Marshal; 2nd Rank, approximating to General)
Arm Car	Armoured Car				
AT	Anti-Tank	OKH	*Oberkommando des Heeres* (German Army High Command)		
ATR	Anti-Tank Rifle			Kombrig	Brigade Commander (pre-1940 Red Army rank, approximating to Brigadier)
Bde	Brigade	Pol Off	Political Officer		
Btn	Battalion	Ptn	Platoon		
BM	'Katyusha' style rocket launchers	PURKKA	*Politicheskoe Upravlenie Krasnoi Armii* (Political Administration of the Red Army)	Komdiv	Divisional Commander (pre-1940 Red Army rank, approximating to Major-General)
Coy	Company				
Div	Division				
FR	Fortified Region	PVO Stranyi	*Protivo Vozdushnaya Oborona* (Soviet air defence)	Komkor	Corps Commander (pre-1940 Red Army rank, approximating to Lieutenant-General)
GKO	*Gosudarstvennyj Komitet Oborony* (State Defence Committee)				
		R&D	Research and Development		
Gun-How	Gun-Howitzer	Recon	Reconnaissance	Lt-Cdr	Lieutenant-Commander
GZI WP	*Glówny Zarzàd Informacji Wojska Polskiego* (Main Directorate of Information of the Polish Army)	Rgt	Regiment	Lt-Gen	Lieutenant-General
		Rfl Rgt	Rifle Regiment	Maj	Major
		RKKA	*Raboche Krest'yanskaya Krasnaya Armiya* (Workers'-Peasants' Red Army)	Maj-Gen	Major-General
HE	High Explosive			Mar	Marshal (of the Soviet Union)
HMG	Heavy Machine Gun			Sr-Lt	Senior-Lieutenant
How	Howitzer	Sctn	Section	WO	Warrant Officer
HQ	Headquarters	Semi–AP	Semi-Armour-Piercing		
KMG	*Konno-Mekhanizirovannaya Gruppa* (Cavalry Mechanized Group)	Sep	Separate	**Germany Army ranks**	
		SMERSH	*Smert' Shpionam* – lit. 'Death to Spies' (Soviet military counterintelligence)	*General der Artillerie, der Infanterie, der Panzertruppe* – German Army ranks, approximating to Lieutenant-General	
LMG	Light Machine Gun				
LWP	*Ludowe Woisko Polskie* (Polish People's Army)	SPG	Self-Propelled Gun		
		Sqd	Squad	*General der Waffen SS* – Waffen SS rank, approximating to Lieutenant-General	
Mcl	Motorcycle	Sqn	Squadron		
MD	Military District	Stavka	Soviet High Command	*Generaloberst* – Colonel-General; German Army rank, approximating to General	
Mech	Mechanized	STB	Separate Tank Battalion		
Med	Medium	TBde	Tank Brigade	*SS-Oberstgruppenführer* – SS rank, approximating to General	
MG	Machine Gun	TD	Tank Division		
MMG	Medium Machine Gun	TO&E	Table of Organization and Equipment		
Mntd	Mounted	VVS	*Voenno Vozdushnye Sily* (Soviet Air Force)		

Acknowledgements

Books

Bellamy, Chris. **Absolute War, Soviet Russia in the Second World War.** Macmillan, 2007.

Bonn, Keith E. **Slaughterhouse: The Handbook of the Eastern Front.** Aberjona Press, 2005.

Merridale, Catherine. **Ivan's War, The Red Army 1939–1945.** Faber and Faber Ltd., 2006.

Perret, Bryan. **Iron Fist, Classic Armoured Warfare Case Studies.** Brockhampton Press, 1999.

Porter, David. **'Armour in Battle' articles in Miniature Wargames Magazine.** Issues 186 (Nov 1998) and 201 (Feb 2000).

Porter, David. **The Essential Vehicle Identification Guide: Soviet Tank Units 1939–1945.** Amber Books, 2009.

Winchester, Charles D. **Hitler's War on Russia.** Osprey Publishing, 2007.

Zaloga, Steven J. & Grandsen, James. **Soviet Tanks and Combat Vehicles of World War Two.** Arms and Armour Press, 1984.

Zaloga, Steven J. & Grandsen, James. **The Eastern Front, Armour, Camouflage and Markings, 1941 to 1945.** Arms and Armour Press, 1989.

Zaloga, Steven J. & Ness, Leland S. **Red Army Handbook 1939–1945.** Sutton Publishing Ltd., 1998.

Web sites

http://www.o5m6.de/ – Oliver Missing's excellent website 'Engines of the Red Army in WW2', which contains superb illustrations of an ever-increasing range of Soviet and Lend-Lease AFVs.

http://rkkaww2.armchairgeneral.com/index.htm – 'RKKA in World War II'. Another extremely useful website covering the equipment and operations of the Red Army during the World War II.

http://www.winterwar.com/mainpage.htm – 'The Battles of the Winter War'. This website provides fascinating details of all aspects of Finland's 'Winter War' against the Red Army.

http://niehorster.orbat.com/ – 'World War II Armed Forces: Orders of Battle and Organizations'.

Index of Units

Index of Commanders

General Index

Index